Say Good Bye To
HOLLYWOOD

Anthony 'A-Class' Quinones

 www.trafford.com

North America & international
toll-free: 1 888 232 4444 (USA & Canada)
fax: 812 355 4082

This book is dedicated to Kenny Thugged Out Medina. My brother, best friend and craziest kid the world's ever seen . . . we miss you Kenny

Acknowledgments

So many people I have to thank for making this project materialize before my eyes . . . Firstly **God** . . . My **Family** for supporting me and putting up with my B.S. Especially my mom! Everyone from **Spanish Harlem** who shows me love and keep it real always. **Mr. Parada** from Horizon Academy, who told me Write! Write! Write! **Malik** *Milk* **Madera** for fueling the idea of writing my book back in 2009 . . . My lawyer **Mr. Richard Greenberg** for his assistance throughout the years. **Jeffery** *Fru'quan* **Goodson** for helping me print out hundreds of pages a week back in Wallkill. The great **Piri Thomas**, **Down These Mean Streets** was my first book I read in prison, and hands down a classic. **Mr. Derrick Moultrie**, for giving me the best advice ever in my life. **Ms. Deborah** *Sexy* **Cardona** for introducing me to the book world and motivating me to have my story heard. To **Maya, Littlez, Ruby, Clari, Melly, Sonia** etc . . . I love all of you ladies, your all beautiful women and I thank god for placing me in your lives at some point. The squad **Dave**, **R-Dee**, **Chris**, **Malcolm**, **Puertorican Kenny**, **Steve**, **Rudy**, **Rabbit**, **Jacob** and the **L.B. Family**, Salute! My Nephews **Orion**, **Jason, Justin** and my niece **Brianna,** the future is in your hands but this book is too explicit for you so don't think about it lol **Trafford**

Publishing of course for seeing the potential of this project and giving me this golden opportunity. And finally, to **Mr. Hollywood Hulk Hogan** for inspiring to re-create myself, at a time in my life where I was lost and alone, who knew professional wrestling could impact one's life so dramatically.

Hollywood, a name which comes form the Holly Bush, the holly (Holy) wood of the Druid Magicians. Hollywood is called a place of magic. Exactly what it is, its playing with our minds, manipulating illusions . . .

David Icke—The Biggest Secret 1999

The Famz: Pedro Diaz, Victor Rivera, Maria Rivera,
Margarita Quinones, Anthony Quinones, Millie Baez
1996

Introduction

It was too much of a beautiful day to be stuck with any headaches thought *Ant* while walking out the back door of the 1738 building on Lexington Avenue. He forced a smile across his face heading towards his group of friends up the block of 109th street. Upstairs at his home base just moments ago, his oldest sister *Millie* exploded in anger towards his unacceptable behavior as of late. She commanded to be allowed to take her younger brother along with her out to California and away from the streets of New York before he ended up in jail.

It was all in light of Ant's recent brush in with the law. The scrawny fourteen year old had been caught red handed tagging up **ANT LIVE 4 97!** On the 110th street train station wall, as he and his two best friends awaited the arrival of the downtown 6 train. Just earlier in the summer he was arrested along with 10 other people for breaking and entering, then vandalizing the Community Center on 110th street.

He only received a year's probation where in this case he could had easily been let off with only a warning, but to humiliate and teach him a lesson; Officer Riley decided to personally escort Ant-live upstairs to notify his parents. His best friends Kenny and Chris followed behind trying to convince the officer to let Ant go and not bring him upstairs, but the tall Caucasian officer only found humor in their pleas.

Millie on the other hand was furious! Whereas Ant's mother Margarita who was also angry, was more embarrassed and didn't react like her oldest daughter had. Margarita actually felt powerless about Ant's behavior. She realized that his behavior was out of control, but she loved her son and didn't want to see anyone take him away from her.

So with that Ant-Live sat on top of the white Old's Mobile along side of his boys pondering the situation. *Damn! Why the fuck is Millie sweatin me so hard?! Fuck yo . . . Cali??* He thought to himself, sucking his teeth in disapproval. Then he gave it a second thought. *Go out to Cali?? Maybe I should go . . . These nigga's out here ain't helpin me do shit . . . Should I bounce?* He had only told one person about the situation and that was *Chris*.

Chris and Ant had become best friends in the 4 years of them meeting. They walked around Spanish Harlem together politicking, sharing each others ideas and dreams. Unfortunately for Ant, Chris had no advice on the Cali issue leaving him on his own to figure it out.

Crossing the street towards Ant and the bunch was his off and on girlfriend *Maya*, a Dominican cutie who lived one flight below him in 1738. The young caramel beauty always made it her business to be noticed, heard and kept up to speed with whatever gossip and news was happening on the block.

She hugged and kissed Ant then greeted everyone else. *Damn Maya . . . you gotta' nice lil' fatty on you!* He thought as Maya turned back towards him catching his stare. She playfully smacked him and perched her arms on his knees, then noticed the subtle troubled look on his face.

"What up my nigga'? What's wrong??" Ant gazed into Maya's dark brown eyes and weighed the options of sharing his dilemma with her.

"Nuffin . . . my sister's upstairs buggin' tryin' to get me to move out to Cali wit' her cuz' I got knocked taggin' up in the train station." He chuckled and went on. "She was tight!! But I doubt that my momz gonna' let her take me anywhere . . . but now tho' I'm actually thinkin' about it."

"And when she wants you to go with her?" Maya asked, curious about it but more skeptical if anything. If anybody knew Ant could be full of shit it was she!

"Like next week I think." He answered softly cracking a mild smile across his face, tracing his index finger along her eyebrows. "You gonna miss me if I leave?" Ant asked rubbing his chin as Maya watched him closely. *This nigga's full of shit!!* She thought to herself.

"Yea Im'a miss you stupid . . . you better not leave." Ant watched her chime into the conversation among the rest of the group scanning her from head to toe. He loved her long dark hair, full lips and yes, even her wide forehead that they all teased her about! She was wearing a long white T-shirt, black spandex shorts that hugged her thighs, and a pair of fairly new black Reebok Classics.

He couldn't deny how beautiful she was and how it was just a few years ago when he first met her while looking out of his kitchen window. It was her younger brother *Pipo* who introduced them at the window. Before then Ant had never seen Maya around but then he was still new in 1738 and hadn't established himself on the block yet. Nevertheless the two of them quickly developed a friendship that would extend beyond their windows, eventually leading into a childhood attraction.

Now here he was too bothered by the fiasco upstairs to even think about disappearing with Maya somewhere inside of the building. Instead he was staring at the Metro North Overpass tunnel, aloof from the rest of the group. Maya didn't know if he was serious or not, but she knew who did.

"Chriiis!!! Come here please!!" She hollered. Chris walked over to where she was standing. "Chris is he playin' or he's serious?" It didn't take Chris long to figure out what she was referring to.

"What? That his sister wants him to move out to Cali?? It's true." He nodded his head at Maya who shot a look at both of them. "He's serious ya' heard . . ." He added before turning back to the others. Ant read the look on her face and assumed she was convinced now. He pulled her closer to him to feel on her fatty.

"So . . . think they'll miss me when I'm gone?" He tightened his grip around her waist and felt his fingertips on her ass.

"HELL YEAH NIGGA'! "She yelled out, wrapping her arms around his neck then pulled away to smack his hands off her ass. Her shout caught the attention of the others and she finally asked them if they were aware of Ant possibly leaving. The group all looked at him puzzled, shocked by the news and asked if it was true.

Ant confirmed it for them all, feeling uncomfortable by the awkward moment. Maya tucked her hair behind her ears and grinned at him.

"Ya' nigga's betta' convince him to stay cuz' he's thinkin' bout going!" The fellas all shouted "NAH ANT!!" and rushed him to give him a huge group hug. Maya luckily moved out the way just in time before she got swallowed up in the group hug as well.

World Champion Hollywood Hulk Hogan 1997

CHAPTER 1
Say Hello To Hollywood

Ant's mind wouldn't be made up until a few days before Millie's flight was scheduled. It happened while Chris, Kenny, Dave and him were watching their favorite Monday night wrestling program *Monday Night Nitro!* His favorite wrestler the legendary *Hulk Hogan* had become the new Heavyweight Champion Of The World.

Hogan had recently become a villain on the program and helped create a new crew on the wrestling program called *The N.W.O. New World Order.* Hogan also acquired the name *Hollywood Hogan* transforming his image and persona along with the entire wrestling world abroad. Watching Hogan's transformation inspired Ant to make his own transformation in his life.

This nigga's the truth . . . I need to do some shit like this. He thought to himself. *Hollywood?? Okay I got you Hollywood!*

Ant realized that he didn't want to go to California anymore, even though it was a chance to live out his dreams. A chance to experience the west coast life home of his favorite rapper **Tupac Shakur**, visit the real Hollywood, maybe even land a movie, T.V. or commercial role. The thought of it all intrigued him but his insecurities would never allow him to leave New York let alone Spanish Harlem. He loved 109th and established a reputation since moving there.

Amazingly he believed that he was the future of Dewitt Clinton Houses. With Maya's words echoing in his mind and those inner fears stabbing at his conscience he couldn't fathom leaving with his sister Millie, but he wasn't saying good bye to Hollywood just yet! Ant convinced himself that 109th needed him. That Maya along with the rest of Clinton loved him and would suffer without him. Either or he needed Hollywood . . . no he wanted Hollywood! So just like Hulk Hogan he decided to become Hollywood and bring Hollywood to Clinton.

It gave birth to a whole new persona and ego in him that immediately affected the rest of his 109th squad called **Hakala**.

Hakala was a name that he concocted in school. The name somehow stuck and it formed an alliance between his school mates and him until it eventually blossomed on 109th. Until then Hakala were just a bunch of kids who tagged along with the rest of the teens in Clinton. They rode bikes, roller bladed, played tag, man hunt, cops n robbers . . . fun activities for normal kids. However there was a change conjuring inside them all, a reflection of the change taking place all around their environment.

Ant had graduated from junior High School, gangs were spilling into New York, Hip Hop was under a West Coast and East Coast war and kids were rapidly growing into young adults way too fast! The days of innocent fun for these teenagers were coming to an end. Those days of playing tag and building club houses were becoming a thing of the past. It was now all about the gratification of the young male's testosterone; sex! Sex! SEX!

In becoming Hollywood his once peaceful Hakala squad was now imitating the acts of the N.W.O. as seen on T.V. and he loved it! They brawled with each other in school then began warring with kids on 109th as well. They spray painted Hakala everywhere, chased and jumped kids up and down East Harlem and even as far down to 86th street! They saw it as harmless fun but day in and day out, this renewed Hakala squad turned Clinton Houses into a mild war zone!

For Ant it was reminiscent of the Clinton Houses from the 80's and 90's when Clinton was the stomping ground for groups like the *Latin Kings*, *Netas* and even the *Zulu Nation*. He grew up idolizing these groups in awe as they came and went one by one. Their images destroyed by their internal conflicts mostly due to drug use and the negative media exposure targeting them.

Since then no group dominated the grounds of Clinton, but that was getting ready to change. New groups like the infamous *F.E.B /Fuck Everybody* crew from Madison Avenue joined in the war games being played on 109th. Not only did they help Ant and the others run down their opposition but they went as far as hanging them by their underwear from the 8 to 10 foot black gates surrounding the parks, super wedgies! Other groups included the *Bloods, Crips, Lehman Clan* and *Jeff Mob* aka *Rat Pack*.

While Ant aka Hollywood now known as *Woodz* and his Hakala/N.W.O. squad continued to stir up trouble on 109th street there was another group quietly migrating and settling on 110th street on Park Avenue. This group was much older and subtle compared to the others. They were engaged in the Dope game and brought a new attitude to the quiet and unclaimed avenue. They called themselves the *L.B.C.*

Reminiscent of the legendary *L.B.C Long Beach Crew* out in the West Coast and also recent emerging *Lost Boy L.B. Family* out in South Jamaica Queens, this new L.B.C. faction was about one thing money, hoes and clothes! L.B.C stood for *Lick Balls Correctly*, a degrading description of their attitude towards the females they catered to. The L.B.C. protocol didn't discriminate either it didn't matter if the female was a dime, duck, hood rat, model, pretty, ugly, fat, skinny, or short. If she had no problem exploiting her body to either one or multiple partners at a time then she was labeled an L.B.

The crew originated on 103rd Street between Lexington and Park Avenue consisting of Puertoricans and Morenos. This group of cocky go getters immediately set shop up in Clinton and also Lehman. They observed and studied their new surroundings spreading the word of their arrival, while also keeping an eye out for the already established groups. There was one group in particular that caught their attention and that was no other than the Hakala squad.

From the moment Ant transformed into Woodz everything in his life seem to change simultaneously. His Hakala squad was creating a buzz or rather disturbance in the community. Out in Cali his oldest sister Millie had gotten re married, and his other older sister Maria who was a working college girl was planning to finally move out to get her own place. Finally his oldest brother Tito / Big Tee was moving back in after a failed attempt of living on his own. Big Tee would now have Maria's old room and it was music to Woodz ears because he was tired of sharing a room with his brother.

Woodz graduated from his Junior High School *New York Prep* on Second Avenue 112th Street and was now working another summer at *Highway Christian Academy* as a summer day camp counselor. So despite his screw ups it seemed as if the young hard headed Aries was slowly maturing into a responsible man. Since deciding to stay in NY three years ago Woodz had established himself as somewhat of a playboy on 109th street.

The subtle leader of Hakala was in and out of relationships with just about every girl in Clinton projects! After Maya there was *Littlez* also from 1738. After her was *Ruby*, a beautiful hazel eye Puertorican girl who was considered the baddest looking girl in the neighborhood along with her cousin *Caroline*. Woodz didn't know how he scored with Ruby when he was in his rollerblading phase, but he did making a lot of people in Clinton mad!

Claribel, who was the younger sister of Thugged Out and also his childhood sweetheart. Finally *Tasha,* a beautiful pale skin Puertorican girl who lived in 1760. Girls from **New York Prep**, Spanish, black . . . the list goes on! However Woodz was now looking towards the future, reaching new places and meeting new faces. One new face exploded on the scene around the end of the summer of 1997 and her name was *Sonia*. She was allegedly Maya's cousin from the Bronx. Woodz met Sonia over the phone while he was talking to Maya who was his girl at the time. The two of them broke night on the phone while Maya was sleeping over her place and fell asleep.

They finally met and compared to Maya who was quiet, spunky and flirty, Sonia was more daring, out spoken, feisty and flirtatious just how Woodz liked them! She smoked cigarettes, drank, was in and out of school and had the biggest breast that Woodz ever saw on a girl in Clinton. Kenny was infatuated with her and Chris was the first out the trio to hook up with her but it didn't even last a month.

Eventually Woodz gave the mouthy Sonia a shot but it only lasted a few weeks. He didn't know if it was because of his carelessness or his shady Maya filling her cousin's ear with bullshit. Nevertheless, he was certain that their story was far from over. Woodz was thinking about High School and what it would be like. He also had thoughts of signing up for a summer Housing job next . . . it was his coming of age.

Unknown to him Chris and Kenny were mingling with the new L.B.C. click on Park Avenue having their own vision of transformation. They jolted up to Woodz home base on a beautiful late summer afternoon finding Woodz playing his *Die Hard Trilogy* game on his Sony PlayStation. The two of them barged into his room anxious to share their news.

"My nigga' it's a wrap!" Kenny proclaimed loudly planting his behind on the bed next to Woodz who was fully focused on the game and not at all concerned about what they were up to.

"What happen?" He asked still focused on the game.

"Nigga' fuck the game! Listen nigga'!" Kenny shut the game off to get Woodz full attention and he got it!

"Yo! What the fuck mothafucka'!? Ah man! I didn't even save the shit nigga'! What is it?!" He angrily set the controller down and turned to Kenny who flashed his famous cheesy braces smile.

"Dogz! We takin' ova' again! No more Hakala and no more N.W.O. shit." Kenny paused for a second seeing that Woodz was still pissed about the game being shut off.

"No more Hakala? Fuck is wrong wit' you nigga' . . . you bugging."

"My nigga' we L.B. Masters now!!" Woodz stared at his best friend's face clueless about what Kenny was rambling about.

"L.B. what?? Chris what da' fuck is this crazy nigga talkin' about?" Chris smiled.

"Dogz it's time for nigga's to change the game again. We've been hollerin' at them L.B. nigga's in my building, Pops and them . . . you know them right?" Woodz knew who Chris was referring to but he didn't know them personally.

"Yea I know Pops and them, what about em'?" Chris continued.

"Dogz them nigga's is cool and they want nigga's to join up with them." Woodz quickly cut in.

"Join up with them? Like what? I don't . . ." This time Kenny chimed in and fully animated.

"My nigga' join up Hakala and L.B.C. nigga' but this different instead of L.B.C. we L.B. Masters!!" Woodz looked at his comrades puzzled, trying to figure out what Kenny meant. Kenny continued. "Instead of L.B.C. we L.B. Masters!"

"L.B. Masters lika' . . . set of L.B.C. and shit?" Woodz asked. Chris with his always cool manor tried to clarify it for him.

"Not lika' set my nigga' but like the next wave of L.B.C. we gonna' take L.B. to da' next level." Kenny started bouncing up and down wildly on Woodz bed.

"The next level nigga! Masters nigga'!! Lick my balls correct bitch!!!" The three of them laughed hysterically at his buffoonery. Woodz was still doubtful however.

"But L.B.C. is that West Coast shit and now nigga's in Queens got that Lost Boys shit too . . . I don't know . . . and nigga's is cool with it?" He asked Chris.

"Yea dogz nigga's already know Dave, oh this nigga's Dave's cousin is L.B. His cousin Edo you know Edo nigga." Woodz shrugged his shoulders. "They wanna' meet you now." Chris added surprising Woodz also.

"They wanna meet me why me?" He asked naively. He stood up to grab his keys hanging off one of his dresser drawers. Chris sucked his teeth and gave him a smug look.

"You Hollywood nigga' you know that. They already met Thugged Out." Woodz jerked his head at Chris.

"Thugged Out? Who da' fuck is that!?"

"Thugged Out nigga'!" Kenny answered. "Thugged Out in dis' piece and we got the new handshake already, shit is butter right Capone?" Woodz smirked.

"Capone? Handshake?? Ya' nigga's is crazy. C'mon we out . . . let's troop up the ave I wanna see what up wit' dis' L.B. Shit."

CHAPTER 2

The Fun House

The East Side Billiards was lively this brisk November evening. The drinks were flowing, jukebox was booming and the sound of pool balls being cracked on the tables filled the air. The Billiard's section was mainly for the older mature crowd whereas on the other side of the floor there was an arcade/gaming section intended to entertain the younger crowd.

A variety of games lined the wall like *Street Fighter vs. Marvel Comics, Grand Turismo, The Crazy Cab game, Tekken II*, an inner active *Jurassic Park* booth and *Neon Hockey Table*. All the latest and hottest games were available to keep the kids at bay. The Pool Room was one of the more popular spots on the Upper East Side complimenting the movie theaters on Lexington and Third Avenue.

It was home for the around the way teenagers and adults who stopped in after school, during school, work and before or after the movies. Now the Pool Room was also home to another group of teens who resided further Uptown on the East Side specifically on 110th Street. They called themselves the *L.B. Masters*.

The year was nearing 1998, three years almost since Ant-Live transformed into Hollywood/Woodz. Since then his oldest sister Millie had gotten remarried in California. He'd begun his first year of High School at Park East High School right across the street from the building his family lived in prior to moving to Clinton. It was difficult at first finding him a school due to New York Prep losing his school records, but with the help of his sister Maria and after being bounced from Brandeis High School and Career Academy, Park East had accepted him.

Woodz was satisfied with Park East. There were a lot of people there that he knew already. It was a hop, skip and a jump away from home and more importantly he saw some of the prettiest girls there as soon as he walked in! In all Woodz was focused and had remained diligent about continuing his transformation and rise. His Hakala squad had evolved into L.B.M. Maya and him were messing around again, and more importantly he believed in himself and the squad believed in him also.

His right hand man was *Chris* aka *Capone*. A mixed Puertorican and Panamanian kid who lived on Park Avenue with his mother and older sister. He was the more cautious and serious one out of the trio. Completing the trio was always animated *Kenny* aka **Thugged Out**, a pale blonde headed Dominican kid and the nut case of the crew.

He hardly went to school, always in the mist in trouble and lived across the street on 110th with his mother and two younger sisters. The rest of the squad consisted of guys who either met Woodz at school or who lived in Clinton. There was *Ralph* aka **R-Dee** another Dominican kid from Jefferson and his brother *Rudy*. *Steve* aka **Pretty Boy** along with his brother *Isaiah*, they lived in Jefferson also, *David* aka **Ace** from Park Avenue. Who was a taller version of Woodz. Finally there was *Melvin* aka **Rabbit** who lived a few doors down from Woodz. Rabbit was short, stocky and had a more leery and shy character compared to the others.

Their L.B.M. protocol mirrored that of L.B.C. Who could get the most girls, props and basically who had the most swagger! It was a battle between adolescent egos. A group of kids mimicking what they heard in music and saw on T.V. They expressed what they felt from the environment around them in their own unique way. However for Woodz L.B.M had become his new family and not just a crew or squad anymore. A family to help shelter him from his real family upstairs who he seemed to always be in odds with.

Woodz saw his squad growing larger and defying the odds all around them. They all meshed together and possessed the same energy to travel, play ball, always dressed fly and loved the streets. Woodz though seem to possess an aura that none of the others could match nor understood. A swagger that no one could explain! Anthony Diaz was 120 pounds soak and wet, a hot headed little bastard! Full of charisma and ego, he could be the life of any party in a second then in a flash become the quietest of the bunch. The girls on the block loved him where as many of the guys young and older despised and envied him.

Woodz projected a whole new image and picked up new habits from the moment L.B.M was born. He'd begun experimenting with cigarettes and weed and drinking 40's. He wasn't getting into any serious trouble but the new habits were taking their effect on his overall character. He adopted the notion that he had a reputation to uphold and was determined to shine and be accepted by the older crowd around him.

Tonight however he had his mind on more important things. Her name was *Lauri*, a beautiful dark skinned Cuban girl with long dark hair that touched her lower back. He and the fellas awaited the arrival her sister *Tina* and *Annie*, the younger sister of their newest L.B. candidate *Joey* aka ***J.O.***

Joey used to live on Park Avenue but now lived with Annie and their father a few blocks away from the Billiards. It seemed like years ago when Joey was a part of the bike and rollerblading craze that was Clinton. He wasn't a bad rider either, but was treated as a geeky kind of kid and taunted by everyone. Tonight however he was looking to be accepted into the L.B.M squad that he'd been hearing about. He already knew most of the guys so he figured that his chances were great. He had a fling going on with Tina but wasn't satisfied with just her. Joey yearned to upgrade his swag and acquire L.B. status.

L.B.M had become an extension of the L.B.C crew on Park Avenue that had taken over 110th Street almost a year ago. Thugged Out and Capone introduced Woodz to two chubby Puertoricans name *Papo* and *Hutty Hut*. Woodz was skeptical at first but once he got to know his new older peers he quickly realized that he already embodied elements of L.B.C in Hakala, so the collaboration was perfect! He was quickly embraced and distinguished as the leader of the group. A position that he was naive to at times, he liked to think that everyone in the group was his own leader.

He saw no problem with their unification with L.B.C thus making Hakala a set of L.B.M the grittier side to the squad which ranks was quickly filled with the less flamboyant bunch of 109th. These L.B. Masters quickly spread the word of their arrival. They tagged L.B.M on building walls, storefronts and yelled it out proudly just about everywhere they went. Surprisingly their influence was felt on the block immediately. Other guys from Lexington and Park Avenue were screaming L.B. now and hoped to share in the spoils of the squad. They wanted the girls . . . the wild slutty girls that L.B.M attracted to the block which they weren't. Even the younger crowd coming up on the block gravitated towards the squad while they themselves were establishing their own identity.

The icing on the cake was Thugged Out spraying L.B.M under Woodz window in large black letters, perfectly visible for all of 109th and Lexington Avenue to see. But not even a day after Woodz had to blog it out due to complaints from Housing and residents of Clinton but the message was loud and clear, L.B.M was in the building!

Woodz played it all back in his head as he sat on a bar stool facing the entire game room zooted next to the Jurassic Park game booth. He was drunk, high and hot! So he unzipped his blue Polo bubble coat that Pedro had given him revealing his gold chain with no piece resting over his white Pelle Pelle shirt. He watched as the squad jumped from game to game, patiently awaiting the arrival of Joey and the girls.

Then he spotted a familiar face entering the arcade room with a crowd. A girl who he knew from Park East, her name was *Christina*. She spotted him also and cordially approached him.

"What up shorty?" She gave him a soft hug and light kiss on the cheek, smelling the weed scent on him. She took another look at him and flashed a smile realizing how chinky eye he was. "Ooh let me find out you be smokin'? Your name is Ant or Anthony right?" Christina grinned while Woodz admired her cuteness. She was about 5'5 with long curly blonde hair, slim with a pierced nose and a few on her ears. He wondered if she was white or just a white Spanish girl.

"Yea but everybody calls me Hollywood or Woodz ya' heard . . . Christina." He replied holding her left hand, and planting a soft kiss on it. The move was one that he'd seen on T.V. and in movies a lot and wondered if it really drove the girls wild. Woodz wanted to make it his trademark and from the look that Christina gave him, the move was a winner! He stared into her eyes that seemed to sparkle from the effect of his charm. *Got her*. He thought to himself.

"How you know my name?" She asked still grinning. Woodz reached for her black North face zipper and gently pulled it down half way revealing a set of gold chains she wore. One in particular had her name plate covered with white gold that he saw around her neck at school. He admired it in his hands then laid it back with the others and smiled at her. "Okay . . . so that's how you know my name . . . you think you cute huh?" Christina quickly took a liking to the cute lil' guy she saw around school. She bit her lip and massaged the side of Woodz face with her left hand, then began swaying slowly to **Aaliyah's** *Try Again* record that played from the jukebox.

While she swayed between his legs Woodz glanced over her shoulder and saw both Thugged Out and Rabbit making L.B. signals asking who she was. Woodz smiled smugly, it was one of those moments he was becoming accustomed to. He seemed to always shine at the right time and was certain that Christina would spread the word around school about him. The feeling made him feel superb! He was already smacked from the Bacardi and the L' he, Capone, Pretty Boy, and Thugged Out indulged in before they ventured to the Billiards. Now if everything went according to plan they would be getting extra nice at Joey's place nicknamed the Fun house.

Joey had bragged about a liquor stash belonging to his father that he supposedly had access to. Now it was time for him to produce it or kiss L.B.M goodbye. Rabbit brought along his camera to take pictures of the group so he asked Woodz and Christina if they wanted their pictures taken. She left it up to Woodz who loved having his picture taken. So without a word he gave Rabbit the signal to snap the picture as he positioned Christina between his legs posing, secretly flashing the L.B. sign over her shoulder.

"Oh shit time for me to go." Christina spotted her friends exiting the Billiards. "See you at school shorty aight." She planted a wet long kiss on his lips and dashed after her friends. Woodz ran his fingers over his lips as he was swarmed by Rabbit and Thugged Out.

Rabbit was fairly new to the group. He had to undergo an initiation of two elevator rides where he was pummeled by the squad, then forced to fight

Thugged Out's little cousin Omar and one of his friends in the park. He was considered soft by most of the squad but Woodz sensed loyalty in his character. He was unaware that Rabbit was admiring him and the others greatly, after having been cautious to be around them at first. The squad had become his new family as well, where like Woodz he was feuding with his family at home regularly.

Woodz glanced up in the direction of the entrance where Christina had just disappeared through and spotted Annie, Lauri, Tina and Joey walking in finally. The girls rushed over to the crazy cab game, played a few games there then barged into the *Jurassic Park* booth where the fellas were. After ten minutes Woodz summoned Joey over to him.

"Yo' J.O. it's almost 9:00 Joe lets wrap this shit up and bounce to your crib before they wanna play every fuckin' game here. Nigga' I'm ready to L.B. ya heard!" Joey agreed and slapped Woodz a pound.

"Aight my nigga' I got you, as soon as these bitches finish playin' this shit we out ya heard Woodz, L.B. my nigga'!" Woodz smiled smugly at Joey while watching Thugged Out making moves on Annie. Both Pretty Boy and Capone had Tina in a sandwich. Pretty Boy even tried to grab a hold of Lauri's arm but she brushed him off and headed towards where Woodz was sitting. She caught his attention and flashed him a big smile. She looked like Pocahontas as he scanned her from head to toe.

"Oh now you wanna come ova' here and say hi right?" She stopped in front of him and leaned her waist on his knees. "You done playin' games luv?" Woodz asked sarcastically. He grabbed Lauri by her brown North Face coat and pulled her closer to him.

"I don't play games but I can." She replied pulling down his black and gold Astros fitted cap over his eyes.

"Yea aight." He shot back pulling her even closer to him, grabbing her by her plump rear. Lauri pushed off him, stuck out her tongue at him and returned to her friends. Woodz didn't mind the games as long as he could play by his rules!

The bunch finally trooped towards Joey's place on 84th Street. He and Annie lived in a quiet middle class neighborhood where the walls had eyes and ears everywhere. In three groups they quietly made their way towards the building. Joey led the first group, Annie the second and Woodz the third. They all made it inside the five story white building and ascended up a carpet covered staircase.

"Yo' J.O. this is a pretty aight spot . . . too bad a fuck up like you gotta' be the one to fuck it up." R-Dee cracked up at his own comment.

"Shhh! Yo' ya' gotta' chill these people here be on some bull shit . . . I don't want them to call the cops."

"Nigga'! Your pops is the fuckin' cops! Open the fuckin' door!" The whole group cracked up at R-Dee's comment this time as Joey rushed everybody into the apartment. The fun house was small but cozy. Once you entered you were a few steps away from the living room. To the left was the kitchen then about ten to fifteen feet towards the right was the bedroom, and then the bathroom at the far end.

Woodz had been their once before and chose the fun house for Joey's initiation. In a matter of weeks Joey's place became the smoke house, fun house, and spot to cut school at. The living room had two long brown sofas covered with quilts accompanied by two love seats by the windows and a wooden coffee table at the center.

Woodz grabbed a seat on the couch on the right and sank into it while Thugged Out and Capone fought for a love seat. Everyone else either sat on the sofa or in the kitchen. There was a portable C.D. and cassette radio on a magazine stand near the kitchen covered with C. D's Pretty Boy pressed play and the **Funk Master Flex The Tunnel** C.D. began playing.

"Yo' Pretty play the first song B'!" Woodz shouted. It was the **Tupac** and **Biggie** song and they all sang the lyrics. *"I got 7 Mak elevens, about 8 thirty eights, 9 nines, 10 Mak tens the shits neva' end!"* Tina lowered the volume and was immediately attacked by R-Dee who was acting as D.J. They shot words back and forth at each other until she finally gave up and walked away so he raised the volume full blast.

Woodz watched in silence amused by their squaring off as Lauri took a seat next to him on the sofa. He met R-Dee in New York Prep who he already knew to be a native of Jefferson Projects. A loose cannon affiliated with the infamous Low Life Crew along with his younger wilder brother Rudy. Woodz wound up embracing R-Dee during the summer while he was on the verge of meeting up with one of his first L.B's/Hakala hoes inside of Thugged Out's building. R-Dee strolled into the park with basketball in hand and spotted Woodz standing by the gate looking across the street.

"Ant what up my nigga'?"

"R-Dee! What brings you to my neck of the woods B'?"

"Ain't shit my nigga' . . . came to bust as you know how I do what's good?" R-Dee was already his Hakala comrade in school and was beginning to spend a lot of time in Clinton and less in Jefferson giving Woodz the impression that he was beginning to latch on to him.

Woodz kept his eyes on *Jessica* across the street walking past him on her way down 109th towards Lexington Avenue. She gave him the signal to meet inside of the building and left him with an idea. Woodz called R-Dee back over to him who had jumped in a game of 21.

"Yo' what if I told you that I'm about to go see a chic in that building to get sucked off . . . and that you might be able to get blessed along wit' me?" R-Dee placed his hands on his hips and eyeballed Woodz suspiciously, not knowing if he was serious or not.

"What bitch??" He asked in quietly looking across the street. Woodz directed his attention towards Jessica who was turning the corner on Lexington. R-Dee cracked a grin. "Fuck it nigga' let's roll." Woodz showed up to meet Jessica and told her R-Dee was his cousin and a virgin! She was leery at first but it was anything for Woodz. She blessed both of them one at a time for about two hours. R-Dee's only complaint was Jessica's buck teeth scraping his dick, other than that it was marvelous!

Woodz was surprised that R-Dee had the gift of gab to make up for his not so pretty boy features. He respected that his boy had swag to make up for it and quickly embraced him into the Hakala family. His mind returned to the fun house where Lauri and him were still on the sofa, her hand working its way down his blue Pelle Pelle jeans. In the kitchen Joey, Capone and Thugged Out were having a minor dispute over the stash and Annie was right in the middle of it.

"Joey! Don't fuck with dad's stash! You know if he finds out and starts buggin' you on your own nigga'!" Annie spoke at a high pinch, fast pace annoying voice but was adorable in Woodz eye. He watched her from under the quilt while Lauri sucked on his neck and played with his dick like a joystick. Thugged Out was supposedly claiming her as his girl but from what Woodz could tell Annie wasn't acting like his girl. On the contrary she was very flirty with the guys especially him! So he didn't feel bad about having to be the one to test the waters out himself.

It was only L.B. protocol. If someone claimed any girl as his own or wifey you had to respect it, only if she was living up to the standards because if the claim was weak and the opportunity presented itself to make a move then the girl was up for grabs . . . according to how Woodz saw it at least!

Thugged Out called Woodz to the kitchen and broke him out of his zone. Woodz yanked Lauri's hand out of his pants. He stood up, stretched, and wiped his forehead then adjusted his fitted. Lauri tailed right behind Woodz as he made his way through the dark living room with the Tunnel C.D. still blasting.

"Aight what we workin' with dogz!"

"This nigga' actin' lika' bitch Woodz!" Thugged Out yelled peeking inside the kitchen cabinets searching for the Alcohol. Annie was cursing at him to get away from the cabinets but he told her to shut the fuck up, certain that Woodz would regulate the situation.

"J.O. what up? You was poppin' shit and bragging bout' this stash and how you L.B. material and shit . . . how Tina's on your dick . . ." Tina twisted her head at Joey.

"ill! Nigga'! Ain't nobody on your dick! That lil' ass shit nigga'!" Joey shot words back at her while everyone laughed their asses off. Woodz brought his attention back to him.

"Chill chill listen my nigga' . . . what bottle or bottles does your pops not fuck with? Let's see c'mon." Joey walked over to the cabinet under the sink unveiling the stash of booze. There must have been fifty bottles at least! *Vodkas, Bacardi, Rums* . . . Jackpot! Joey gave Woodz an uncertain look while Thugged Out taunted him. Annie was on his case and he didn't want to look like a bitch. More importantly he wanted to smoke already! Woodz examined the stash quickly.

"What up with that one?" He pointed to an open dusty bottle of Russian Vodka. Joey pulled out the half-filled bottle. "Aight see . . ." Woodz knelt down beside him. "Let's fuck wit' that and if anything nigga' we'll replace it . . . I'll replace it J.O." Woodz looked at Joey and then at Annie, giving her the don't you say shit! look. She shrugged her shoulders while J.O. thought about it for a second. Then he closed the cabinet shut and blew the dust off the bottle.

"Aight fuck it my nigga' . . . lets party! My nigga's L.B.!!" The fellas yelled out L.B. and that was that. Thugged Out and J.O. grabbed some plastic cups while *Cypha,* a chubby young Dominican kid from Park Avenue known for smoking heavily, Rabbit and Pretty Boy lit up the first L' by the living room window. The music was still blaring so the party was on.

The girls drifted around the fun house sneaking sips of the Vodka that was flowing now. Woodz took his tokes from the two blunts that were now lit up and grabbed his cup of Vodka. He told R-Dee to hold him down while he snatched Lauri and lured her away to the bathroom. J.O. and the rest were too engulfed in smoke to notice that Woodz had disappeared, but J.O. did catch his sister drinking the Vodka she made a ruckus about! "Fuckin' lil bitch . . ." He thought to himself. Everyone was lounging while Woodz went into full L.B. Mode!

Lauri closed the door behind them as Woodz took a seat on the toilet lid. She waltzed over to him and sat on his lap. He took another sip of his drink and their tongues immediately met. Woodz squeezed on her breast while she lifted up her white T-Shirt and exposed them for him. He easily pulled her beige bra over and wasted no time attacking her soft brown C cups with his lips.

He kissed and sucked on her nipples and she moaned with pleasure. She slid back a bit and fondled her way down to his belt and unbuckled it again. She pulled out his dick and the sensation that traveled through Woodz body as Lauri wrapped her tongue around it was like nothing he ever felt before! He didn't know if it was the weed or liquor inducing the feeling, but he felt like he was floating. *Oh shit . . . this one's a pro too*! He said to himself taking short sips of his drink.

About five minutes passed before Tina noticed that Lauri was strangely quiet and missing.

"Annie where this bitch at?" Annie shrugged her shoulders and returned her attention back to Thugged Out who was trying to lay down his mack game. Tina walked out the living room and into the kitchen but only found Capone, Joey and Rabbit at the table with another bottle of booze open. "Where the fuck??" She turned and found the rest of the guys all standing alongside the wall by the bedroom. Now she began to worry. "What the fuck is ya doing to my fuckin' sister?!" She yelled at R-Dee, looked into the bedroom but found no one inside.

"Ain't nobody doing shit to your fuckin' sister!" R-Dee fired back. "Ayo J.O. come control your bitch dogz!"

"Fuck you R-Dee! Ugly crater face mothafucka'!" With only one place left Tina stormed towards the bathroom and found it locked. She began banging on the door. "LAURI! BOOM BOOM BOOM!! LAURI! Let's go bitch!!" Woodz cursed Tina as loud as he could. Lauri stopped and looked up at him smiling. Tina yelled again.

"I'm coming bitch! Relax!" Lauri shouted fixing her bra and shirt.

"Aight c'mon Luv . . . blast me off so we could get up outta here." Lauri swallowed him up one last time and went full steam ahead! Woodz grabbed the back of her head and watched it bounce up and down. His toes curled up as he felt it finally coming. He released it all into her mouth and she took in every last drop.

She stood and spat out whatever was left in the sink and rinsed her mouth. Fixing herself up she giggled at Woodz who looked paralyzed on the toilet he couldn't move a muscle! She kissed him lightly on the lips and told him to get up. She flicked the light off and closed the door behind her half way when she walked out.

Woodz couldn't see a thing but he heard Tina and her sister cursing each other out. He pulled his pants up and heard Ace's voice calling out for him.

"Yo' you aight my nigga'??" Ace and the rest of the fellas smiled broadly when Woodz finally emerged out of the darkness of the bathroom, standing between the door way like a champion gladiator climbing out of a coliseum! He held himself up with the empty cup in his hand and wobbly legs, cracked a big smile and yelled L.B!! The fellas all returned the call proudly though slightly disappointed that they weren't going to get some action as well but that's the way it was, many were called but only a few were chosen!

The scene back in the kitchen was like a house party. The second bottle of Vodka was damn near empty, plastic cups were everywhere, music was still loud and smoke loomed in the air. Rabbit was snapping away with his camera as Woodz rejoined Capone at the table. He refilled his cup and gave Capone a recap of his completed mission. They toasted the L.B. moment and were rolling. Woodz collected his thoughts. It was time to usher in their newest member.

"Yao!! Rabbit c'mon I wanna take this L.B. flick . . . sorry ladies ya' can't be in this one." Everyone huddled around Pretty Boy and Thugged Out with cups, bottles and weed held up high and proud. Rabbit snapped the photo, a picture that would last a lifetime. "Aight yo'! Listen . . ." Woodz sat back down and called for the attention of the squad. "So what ya' think? Is our boy J.O. ready??" The fellas all gave mixed answers of approval and taunt, but all in all everyone approved.

"Aight look Joe . . . this was butter, you came through with the stash and hosted an official meet tonight, but it don't stop here my nigga' . . . you gotta keep it live my nigga' keep showin' nigga's that your swag is up and bitches is gonna be fightin' for you . . . I'm tellin' you dogz . . . it's all about props my nigga'." Woodz words were a bit slurred, "On some real shit." He added. The fellas all greeted their newest L.B. Master. Joey sat next to Woodz.

"Yo' Woodz hold up." He whispered into Woodz ear. "Yo' you was getting' sucked off? Sucked off in my bathroom nigga'!?" Woodz smiled at Joey and sipped on the last of his drink.

"It's what I do my nigga' . . . I had to bless the crib, the fun house my nigga'!" Woodz exclaimed. Joey continued.

"What up tho' my nigga' I wanna' get sucked off too? What's good nigga'!" Woodz looked at J.O. with a doubtful stare.

"Dogz you and me know that won't happen . . ." They were both certain that Tina would not let that go down. Woodz sensed disappointment in Joey's face so he quickly gave him a reassuring look and whispered in his ear. "Not tonight at least!!" The two fools broke into laughter and slapped fives. "Dogz I'm twisted . . . welcome to the family B'." Woodz laid his head on the table next to Capone while Joey walked towards Pretty Boy. "Yo' I'ma go lay down in this nigga's room . . . I'm twisted kid . . . yo' tell this bitch to meet me there in a few minutes aight?" Capone gave Woodz a puzzled look.

"Nigga' you fucked up!" Capone said and laughed.

"Yea . . . my fuckin' head's spinnin' yo' I'm finished for the night." He gave Capone the rest of his empty cup and slowly made his way towards the bedroom. He closed the door behind him and dropped onto the bed, placing his fitted cap over his eyes. He laughed to himself because he expected Lauri to show up at any moment. Then as expected someone knocked on the door and Lauri peeked in finding him laid out on the bed.

Lauri asked him if he was ok as she closed the door and hopped on the bed beside him, grabbing his leg and rubbing on his dick until he was fully aroused again. Woodz ran his hands over her thighs and slipped his hands into her blue *Gap* jeans to squeeze her ass.

"Ready for round two? He asked. Lauri smiled and reached into his pants to grab hold of his hard on.

Woodz maneuvered his hand in between her thighs, felt the hair covering her hood then slipped his middle and index finger into her moist opening. He loved the feel of her warm juices on his fingers and her moaning into his ear. She bit his ear and told him she wanted to fuck him. Suddenly the sound of Thugged Out's voice approached the room and the door swung open.

Thugged Out cracked a big smile while Lauri covered herself up with a blanket. Woodz meanwhile winked at Thugged Out and kept his fingers inside of Lauri. He asked what was up.

"My nigga' it's time to ride out."

"What time is it?" Woodz asked as Lauri placed his cap over his hard on.

"Like 11 o'clock, Ace and Jay wanna' bounce plus her and Tina gotta' be home soon." Woodz caught a glimpse of Annie peeking into the room.

"Aight tell these nigga's to clean up and shit and we out aight." Thugged Out closed the door and made the announcement that it was time to clean up. Lauri left the room also to use the bathroom leaving Woodz alone, until Annie walked into the room and stood aside the bed.

"Why you still layin' in my dad's bed and everyone's cleanin' up? You think you special nigga'?" Woodz scanned Annie from head to toe. She had a gray and pink sweater, tight blue jeans and a pair of size 4 black and pink *Air Max* sneakers. She looked liked a cream puff in Woodz eyes and he wanted a taste.

"What took you so long?" Woodz had told Capone to tell Annie to meet him in the room, no questions asked!

"Nigga'! I just couldn't walk in here! your boy's on my dick!" She laughed and sighed. Thugged Out was driving her crazy. "Anyway," She continued, giving him a devilish look. "I heard about you already hmm." She crossed her arms.

"What you heard?" Woodz asked as innocent as possible. He motioned for her to sit by him on the bed. She perched up one leg on the bed and leaned on him. Then she grabbed his fitted hat off his lap and found his hidden hard on!

"Que esto?!" She laughed and then grabbed and squeezed it. Woodz wrapped his left arm around her waist and drew her closer to him.

"You know . . ." She whispered in his ear. "It was suppose to be me and you in here . . . right?" She kissed his face and gently kissed him on the lips. Woodz reached up and felt Annie's right breast, and gently bit her nipple through her sweater. He was ready to explore further but then Lauri opened the door catching the two of them off guard.

"Bitch He's mine! Get the fuck away from him!" Annie hopped off the bed and the two playfully squared off on the side of the bed. Woodz loved every minute of it. Lauri retreated and lay back next to Woodz, grabbing his lips. "Umm I love your lips!" She gave him hard kisses and hugged him. Annie sat back down beside him and Woodz wrapped his arms around them both. "You know Annie . . . we could share him . . . you know that right Annie?" Woodz gave Lauri a seductive look and then at Annie.

"Bitch I know! You don't have to tell me." Annie's reply didn't surprise Woodz it only excited him even more, but before he could respond Tina barged into the room followed by the whole squad. The party was officially over.

Everybody shot puzzled looks at one another seeing Woodz on the bed with not only Lauri but with Annie as well! The fellas left the room one by one knowing full well that Thugged Out wasn't happy about it. Woodz sensed the tension quickly brewing so he raised himself out of the bed. Thugged Out however was fuming inside and wanted to make a scene. Jealousy quickly filled his heart again. It wasn't the first time Woodz crossed the lines. He eyeballed Annie and called her to him.

"It's time to bounce ya'!" Woodz announced shooting Capone a sinister look. Joey was still basking in his L.B. glory and didn't realize what was going on. While everyone waited by the door to leave Thugged Out and Annie both erupted in an argument by the door.

"Damn nigga'! Get the fuck off my dick! Damn nigga' you ain't my real man nigga'!"

"Get off your dick?? Bitch you probably do gotta' dick bitch!" Tina and Lauri ushered Annie out of the apartment while Rabbit and Ace calmed Thugged Out down. Both Woodz and R-Dee were chuckling.

. . . This nigga's is crazy . . . lika' lil' fuckin' kid. Woodz thought. He loved Thugged Out like a brother but hated the fact that he was a sucker for love.

They all walked up to 99th Street on Third Avenue and dropped off the sisters. Annie and Joey took a cab back home to finish cleaning up before their dad got home. The squad returned back to 109th and called it a night. The night in the fun house would be one that they would never forget.

L.B.Master 1998 Rabbit, Capone,
Thugged Out, Omar, Woodz, J.O.

CHAPTER 3

4 da' luv of money

Woodz first year at **_Park East High School_** didn't go as smooth as he had planned. A few weeks after the fun house episode there was an accident at the Chinese Restaurant on 110th that resulted in him being severely injured on his left hand. His boy Malik got thrown through the plexiglass window of the restaurant by a kid name J Smooth from Park Avenue. As the plexiglass shattered Woodz covered his face from the glass and his hand was cut very bad. Instead of going to the 119th Street Carnival as they planned, he spent the night in the emergency room getting stitched up.

Eventually he needed an operation to repair a torn tendon in his hand. After the operation he sported a cast on his forearm for two months until physical therapy, where an ugly beige hand brace was put on him to help support the operated finger. The therapy was scheduled to last at least six months! It was agony for Woodz who was succumbed to embarrassment by his handicap. He tried to hide the hand by wearing his army jacket over it during every class, everyday! Not only did it hinder his shine at school, but the injury affected his relationship with Maya who criticized him for not showing her the attention she wanted.

The spring of 1998 was underway and as soon as the brace was off it was back to business for Woodz. The summertime was quickly approaching. He filled out the application to work in the summer Housing program and also convinced Thugged Out to sign up too. So together they took on the task of cleaning up Clinton projects.

School was finally over. Woodz successfully completed his first year of High School with a B/C grade point average. Now it was time to clean up Clinton! Despite the unbearable heat and tons of garbage Woodz enjoyed the work and quickly established a respectable report with the seasonal housing vets. Thugged Out however hated the heat, the smell and sight of garbage everyday. The grounds supervisor refused to put up with his attitude so eventually Thugged Out quit and abandoned Woodz to deal with the trash himself.

Money was an issue with Woodz who had learned in the past two summers of how critical it is to have money in your pocket during the summer. He knew that he couldn't depend on Momma Luv, Pedro or anyone for handouts for too long. Halfway into the summer the fling Maya and Woodz had came to a complete end again and he hooked back up with Sonia. He couldn't deny that he was crazy about her, the girl was a challenge and it actually enticed him.

They were sweethearts from that point on and the news their hook up didn't surprise the rest of the squad, what did surprise them though was Woodz unexpected faithfulness to her. So he had his girl and hustled by picking up trash. He swept parks, changed garbage cans, and raked grass it was all about cleaning and he enjoyed it.

As far as the rest of the squad they continued to congregate and watched Woodz in admiration while a few also worked during the summer as well. That is except for Thugged Out who was on a mission for another kind of hustle. He was familiarizing himself with the old timers from Lexington Avenue. Two in particular were hosts of their own Public Access Rap Video show called *The Big Cat & Black Stew Show*. Big Cat and Black Stew hosted the show, promoted parties throughout the five boroughs and quiet as kept, were the two guys to holla at if you were ambitious about getting in the drug game.

During the day Woodz was all about his Housing grind and spending time with his new girl. During the night however he began hanging out on the 109th corner of Lexington with the rest of the night crawlers. He had become known as Shorty with the radio and lil

Tupac. Woodz took his radio everywhere and played mostly Tupac. It blared on the corner all night while he was out there in the mix.

Already a native to the corner was **_J.T_.** a tall skinny Moreno who lived in 1738 and was the official weed man on the block. J.T. took a liking to Woodz who seem to fit in perfectly with the night scene naturally. Woodz had humor, swag, and natural street smarts. The two formed a street corner bond to the point that J.T. asked Woodz if he was interested in dabbling in the drug game. Woodz admitted that he was. It was something him and Thugged Out spoke about a lot lately. So it was no surprise to him while walking out the park after punching out from work that J.T. was waving him over to where he and Big Cat was standing.

Big Cat asked Woodz to walk with him for a minute, curious to meet the lil' guy J.T. spoke to him about.

"I hear a lot about you shorty . . . what they call you Woodz right?" Woodz nodded his head, glancing at the full court basketball game across the street. "You know who I am?" He asked Woodz.

"The Big Cat and Black Stew show no doubt . . . I catch the show when I can oh yea, why ya' neva' shout out 109th Lex Ave or L.B.M? What's up with that Cat?" Big Cat laughed.

"Aight aight I got ya' Woodz. Look here's the deal . . . you may not know it Woodz but you got a lot of juice around here. In fact I know you got a lot of juice out here." Woodz looked up at the six foot giant in awe. He didn't know what to say. "J.T. told me some good thangs' about you and that you thinkin' bout gettin' your hands dirty . . . is that true?" They stopped at the Johnny pump in the middle of the block, turned and walked back towards Lexington. It was a question that Woodz had asked himself a million times, now here was the moment of truth.

"Yea I mean . . . I think about it. I be hollerin' at J and shit . . . J's a cool mothafucka' and um, he told me that he'll show me the ropes. What did he tell you about me?" Woodz asked curiously, grinning up at Cat who was looking up ahead towards the corner.

"Let me worry about that lil bro." He answered casually reaching into his jean pocket. He pulled out a white business card and handed it to Woodz. "This is my cell number call me when you ready to get your hands dirty . . . don't lose it and don't give it to anybody aight?" Big Cat gave Woodz a pound and walked off towards the corner store across the street. Woodz held the card in his hand and let it sink in. *You got a lot of juice round' here* . . . He jogged towards his building with his ego filled, excitement building that he was about to get this money!!

Two weeks later on a sunny Saturday afternoon Woodz hopped in a cab along with Big Cat, destination 145th Lenox Avenue. Woodz thought about how nervous he was while dialing the cell number on the card he was holding in his hand.

"I've been waiting for your call Woodz . . . for a minute I was startin' to think that you was bullshittin'." Woodz smiled at Big Cat who was answering a call on is cell. He sat quietly in the back seat staring out the window deep in thought.

Here we go Woodz . . . time to change the game again. The cab made four or five turns until finally reaching 145th Street, then pulling up to it's destination.

The building was tall, beige and across the street from a school yard. Big Cat paid the cabbie and led Woodz into the building. The elevator reached the fifth floor and Big Cat led the way towards the apt door by the staircase. A musky incense smell hit Woodz as he walked into the large living room. Two long leather black couches, a lazy boy seat and medium sized wooden table. A wall unit with a 30inch T.V. and plastic bags scattered on floor. There was also a small kitchen unit where they entered through.

"Chill out Woodz and make yourself comfortable aight." Woodz sank into the black couch while Big Cat fumbled with bags scattered around his lazy boy in front of the T.V, he sorted through a stack of video cassettes and popped one into the V.C.R. "Yo' I wanna' show you some funny shit ya heard . . . tell me who you see aight Woodz." Big Cat chuckled as he re-winded the video.

It was a party in a club, everybody dressed to impress. The club was dark with music blaring and the camera man focused mainly on the stage that was surrounded by 30 or more men and women all watching a sweaty thick dark chocolate girl shaking her enormous ass! She wasn't wearing anything other than a gold G string tied around her waist with bills stuck into it. Woodz felt his dick getting hard by the second watching the chocolate beauty perform on stage.

He walked over to Big Cat's seat for a closer look and knelt down to conceal his hard on. "See anyone you recognize from Lex.? Look good look . . ." Big Cat grinned waiting for Woodz to spot his mystery Lex Ave comrade.

"I see . . . there's big Jay there I see em' . . . he's twisted too, OK Jay!" Woodz focused his attention back to the girl on the stage built like a house! She twirled her legs in the air, opening and closing them while laying flat on the stage, hypnotizing her audience.

"Yea big jay is twisted . . . watch what he do now tho'." Woodz watched as Big Jay approached the stage where the girl was sitting up now, legs wide open running her fingers around her pussy. He was suddenly face to face with her massive dark sweaty thighs and inches away from her promised land. He was surrounded by the crowd cheering him on until finally thrusting his face into her pussy!

"OH SHIT! This nigga's eatin' the pussy!? That nigga's CRAZY!! Haha!!" Big Cat cracked up along with Woodz, slapping his forehead recalling the night in his head.

"Yo' don't tell big Jay or anybody that you seen this aight . . . crazy right?" Woodz watched the rest of the video as Big Cat walked towards the bedrooms in the back of the apartment. He returned and tossed a small jar at Woodz who took a seat back on the couch. "Smell that baby boy that's some good shit right there." Woodz opened the jar and smelled the smoke. He looked up at Big Cat.

"WOOO! This shit is the truth! This is what you blessin' me with Cat!? This is Haze right??" Woodz analyzed the jar filled with potent hairs and not one seed or stem. The smell quickly filled up the air around him.

"Yup that's purple haze my nigga' but that's not what I got for you tho not yet at least. You wanna' roll up or want me to roll cuz' I'm tryin' to get high baby!" Big Cat tossed Woodz the Philly cigar and he went to work rolling it up. The sound of *DJ Kay Slay Street Sweeper's* C.D. erupted out of the huge speakers that lined Big Cat's wall. Woodz dumped the tobacco into a plastic bag Big Cat gave him and put the finishing touches on the L'. "Spark it up."

Big Cat tossed Woodz a transparent purple lighter and Woodz lit up the blunt. He blew O's of smoke over his head. The Purple Haze was strong but smooth. Woodz bopped his head to the Kay Slay C.D. and watched Big Cat dig into another bag. He guessed that Big Cat had to be at least in his late thirties. Big Cat had the old school swagger, kept a low fro always shaped up. He knew Big Cat was sitting on some money but just never flossed it. He wasn't a flashy dress up type. Instead he wore basic blue jeans, army jacket or sweater and a pair of half new Timberland boots.

"Damn Cat this shit is the truth B' . . . here." Woodz passed the L' after his third pull. Big Cat reached for it and sat back down in his seat. Woodz was too much into the music and buzzed off the Haze to notice that Big Cat pulled out a small scale from the bag. After only three or four tokes Big Cat passed the Haze back to Woodz and motioned for him to kill it.

"Yea this shit is a mothafucka' mellow as fuck . . . do you aight." Woodz had only smoked Purple Haze once before with J.T. while they played *LIVE 99* at his place. Woodz was so high that night that he couldn't focus on the game. He took two long pulls from the L' about the size of a clip now and clipped it. He set it down on the ashtray atop the table.

Finally Big Cat spoke. "Aight Woodz here's the deal . . . basically like I told you that day you got a lot of juice on that block dogs, J.T. told me that you have potential to be strong on 109th . . . now J is my man for years now . . . I've been fuckin' with J for a minute so I respect his word." Woodz listened intensely, staring down at the clip of Haze. His head started feeling funny and light. The Haze had him sky lining!

As Big Cat began explaining the specifics of baggin' up, using the scales and quality of the bag, Woodz mind began to float off.

Why this nigga' still talkin' so much??? Hmmm mothafucka' can't you see that a nigga's chopped right now! Hm hm nah let me chill. Woodz felt silly and hoped that Big Cat didn't notice his aloofness but could'nt help himself. Big Cat was still going on.

"I'm also workin' on settin' up a stash house for nigga's in Johnson somewhere, shit ain't set yet but I'm workin' on it. You cool with Johnson? Any beefs over there that I should know about?" Woodz shook his head no and felt like everything was moving in slow motion. He adjusted himself on the couch, stretched his arms and wiped his face. He tried to focus on what Big Cat was saying. "I'll let you know, it should be soon tho' oh, I wanna' set ya' up with beepers and phones too."

Big Cat lifted his gaze from out of the bag and looked at Woodz, clearing seeing that his little homie was stuck off the Haze. He hoped that Woodz at least absorbed half of everything he had said. "So talk to me baby! You aight? What up? Is you ready to get this paper or what?" Woodz wiped his face again, suddenly feeling extremely thirsty. He needed something to drink, soda, water, juice anything!

"I'm good Cat that was some bomb ass smoke ya heard . . . look man, I'ma tell you like I told this nigga J.T. I'm new to all this, I've been workin' basic bullshit summer jobs since 96—" Woodz paused to swallow wad of spit but it didn't help much against the dry mouth building up. He continued. "But I believe I'm ready for this shit and need it . . . a nigga' need some more loot in his pocket for the summer time, I'ma do my best to get it ya' heard and not get caught up, be part of the team na' mean . . . I go to school so I could bump it there . . . I'ma give it a shot dogz and if it don't work for me I'll let you know and I'll fall back and make sure I don't owe you nuffin' and keep doing me . . ."

Woodz felt like he was rambling for hours and hoped Big Cat didn't ask anymore questions! He was dying of thirst and couldn't hold it no more! "Cat, can I get some water or something nigga'? I'm thirsty lika' mothafucka' over here!" Big Cat sprang out of his seat and flashed Woodz a smile.

"My nigga' say something! He chuckled. "I can't have my new man chokin' on my couch from some Purp! Ha ha" Big Cat gave Woodz a tall cold glass of fruit juice that Woodz savored. The fruit punch hit the spot instantly. He sat back down on the couch cradling the juice and looking down at the clip again thinking about relighting it. He picked it up and put it in his pocket.

Big Cat disappeared back into the bedrooms again and returned seconds later carrying a large *V.I.M.* bag. He reached into the bag and revealed an ounce of weed. It was Woodz first time seeing a whole ounce of smoke first hand. Big Cat also pulled out another zip lock bag filled with clear empty nickel bags, a lot of nickel bags. "I'ma give you 50 baggies for 50 nicks. One ounce is enough for fifty nicks like I showed you before. Bag it up, do the math and bring me back 70% Holla at me thru that cell number I gave you I always keep it on." Wood grabbed the weed and smelled it. What ever it was it didn't smell like the Haze they just smoked.

"What is this Cat, skunk?"

"Commercial Arizona Skunk its good quality shit, just something to start you up with." Woodz was ready to leave and hoped that Big Cat was giving him a ride back to the block.

"Good looks Cat . . . you comin' back to the block too?"

"Oh nah Woodz, I wasn't plannin' to . . . you gonna' be aight takin' that back??" Woodz studied the ounce again and took a whiff of it.

"Yea I got this Cat . . . I got this." Woodz made it back to the block. He was a little paranoid but made it back safely.

Back in home base Woodz devoured a ham and cheese sandwich and guzzled down two huge cups of *Pepsi*. He called Thugged Out as soon as the Pepsi was gone. "Yo'! I'm in the buildin' my nigga'! I got dat!"

"You got it!? Yea nigga'!!" Woodz could hear voices in the background and whoever it was got yelled at by Thugged Out to shut the fuck up.

"Yo I need a place to bag this shit dogz . . . I don't wanna do it here Millie is here."

"Nigga'! Bring that shit ova' here! I got the crib my momz and these bitches aint here, nigga' all these nigga's is here!" In the background Woodz heard Ace, Rabbit, Cypha and a black kid name ***Boobop*** who was also Hakala from Capone's building. "Come ova' so we could sample! I'll send one of these nigga's to meet you downstairs."

With the help of Thugged Out Woodz bagged up fifty decent nickel bags of the Commercial Skunk. In total, 70% that went to Big Cat was exactly $175.00 where as he kept only $75.00. He knew that was going to have to change soon. Of course they stretched most of the bags so they could have at least two nice samples for themselves. Woodz even lit up the clip of Haze that he kept while Cypha and Thugged Out lit up the Skunk and the bunch celebrated the new L.B.M. hustle.

It took Woods two days to bump all 50 bags with some help from Thugged Out who also had his own work to sell. Woodz met up with Big Cat and gave him his 70% took his 30% percent and carelessly spent it on mix tapes and batteries for his radio. He even brought his girl Sonia a pair of gold Door Knocker Earrings!

He kept his hustle a secret from her and their families. Woodz made his second pick up days later and this time Big Cat gave him two ounces and 100 baggies. He transported it back to the block on bike along with Thugged Out and Cypha tagging along. Woodz was enjoying the thrill of hustling on the block and couldn't wait until school started so that he could floss there as well.

At the end of the summer he wrapped up his Housing gig promising to return next summer. His plan was to sign up for the seasonal when he hit eighteen years old, but with the way things were going there was no rush! Now being with Sonia caused him to spend less time with the squad and that didn't sit well with them. The squad missed his presence and wanted Hollywood back on the scene!

The two ounces took him a little longer to move but he did it and paid Big Cat his dues, and this time didn't rush to get hit off with the next ounces. He wanted to wait a week or so when school started officially. He had money for clothes and he spent it! The family didn't suspect anything and weren't on his back so he figured he was doing something right. He looked back at the summer as a success and as far as he knew it was going to get even better.

CHAPTER 4

Change of Hearts

If there was ever a summer filled with love and hate it would have to be the summer of 1998 in Clinton projects. Not only was there a new big Dominican family moving into Capone's building drawing a lot of attention but Woodz and Sonia were still the talk of the block and now Thugged Out's younger sister Clari was trying to get her fifteen minutes of fame! The family consisted of the mother, father and eight children! Six girls and two boys, an army! Capone was first out the squad to meet the new comers and helped them move their property into the 5 Bedroom Apartment on the third floor.

He met up with Woodz in front of 1505 around 8 o'clock that night and gave him the rundown on the Brady Bunch. They both sat on top of an old beat up gray Buick drinking tropical fantasy sodas and eating pizzas from the **Kennedy Fried Chicken** spot on 110th Street Lexington Avenue.

"The oldest sister's name is *Ivette* badd you heard . . . skinny and shit but badd. The cute chubby one name *Maggie* . . . Maggie? Yea Maggie. Then *Angie*, Angie's badd too my nigga' but she look like the type with a fucked up attitude but she's proper, after her is *Melina* they call her Melly, that's who I holla'd at. She's proper too . . . this nigga' Kenny wanna' fuck with her already." Woodz wasn't surprised. He looked over at Capone and shook his head.

"Damn! Already this nigga's thirsty!? Nigga's crazy . . . who the rest of them?" Capone continued.

"The twins but they ain't real twin twins, *Amari* and *Natalia* they call her Flaca Shit, Flaca could be Yvette's twin and Amari Maggie's twin . . . crazy right? Natalia's pretty as hell both of them are . . . they all look good B' and they all look like each other!" Capone paused to take a gulp of his Pink Champagne soda.

"Damn nigga' you like dialing 4-1-1 and shit! You got all the info!" Blurted out Woodz who chuckled and glanced up at the 3rd floor apartment facing Park Avenue. The apartment was filled with voices and activity. "What about the brothers?" He asked licking tomato sauce off his fingers.

"Oh them lil' nigga's is cool ya heard. *Perucho* and *Manolo* them lil' nigga's is wild I'm tellin' you . . ."

* * *

"Damn nigga'! I know this bitch ain't got you whipped like that dogz?!" Thugged Out was well known for his verbal assaults on just about anyone from the block but it was rare to hear him attack Woodz or anyone for that matter. The squad had gathered in their usual post in front of the Bodega on 109th Street on Lexington Avenue. It was a beautiful late Monday afternoon, sunny blue sky with the avenue vibrant with students returning home from their first day of school and the regular rush hour home.

The squad normally met up on the corner, maneuvered over to the stoop in front of an old abandoned building next to the Bodega, made rounds from 116th down to 103rd street through Lexington and Third Avenue, then finally retreat to the park. Woodz was surprised to see them on the corner so early. He just got out of school at a quarter to three and was on his way to pick up Sonia from New York Prep. He had walked her to school that morning and promised to pick her up at 3 o'clock.

As for his first day back at Park East it was nothing less than perfect! He strolled into Park East with his black Panasonic Radio in hand and pocket full of nickel bags of chocolate, filled with confidence with a stride that demanded everyone's attention! The little guy was a giant in his own mind. He was proud of being in his second year of High School at the East and couldn't wait to reunite with his classmates to retell stories from their summer.

He was determined to make up for his embarrassing freshman year due to the accident with his hand, his year had been ruined! Being exposed to the game had only intensified his transformation. He knew he wasn't a big time hustler yet, but just knowing that he possessed swag and juice fortified his attitude.

He was determined to shine throughout the year and it was all good until he found himself on the other end of Thugged Out's petty criticism. Woodz knew that his boy still felt some kind of way about Sonia being his girl over Capone and him, and that he probably still harbored ill feelings about Annie who was totally out the picture now. Capone, Rabbit, J.O. Ace, R-Dee, Cypha and Pretty Boy were all amused by the shots fired by Thugged Out at Woodz and huddled around waiting for Woodz to retaliate, but he didn't seem bothered by it.

"My nigga' fuck this nigga' Kenny what's up B'?" Ace greeted his twin as he greeted the rest. He was a taller version of Woodz, always dressed fresh, had a smooth quiet swag and kept the peace within the squad. "Go head and do what you gotta' do my nigga' you know where we at." Added Ace while Thugged Out stood aside him waiting to see if Woodz was going to fire back . . . finally he did.

"Yoo? Did this nigga' show ya' the new tattoo on his arm?" He asked. Woodz was ready to walk off but decided to check Thugged Out. The fellas all looked at one another and then at Thugged Out shaking their heads, asking him if he gotten a tattoo. Thugged Out immediately grabbed his left arm and shook his head hoping that Woodz wouldn't blow him up.

"Hell no this nigga' wouldn't!" Thugged Out thought.

"Show em' the tat Kenny go head . . . I know you ain't scared nigga' . . . show em' or I'll just tell em'!" Woodz enjoyed watching Thugged Out stick his foot in his mouth. Woodz was the only person who knew of the *S* he branded on his arm with a hot paper clip. The *S* was over his infatuation over Sonia. Thugged Out finally gave in and pulled up the sleeve of his navy blue Mecca sweater revealing the *S* branded on his pimply light skin.

"What the fuck? Dogz fuck is that . . . . a *S*?" Asked R-Dee looking over at Woodz who was nodding his head and grinning.

"Tell em' what the *S* is for Kenny . . . go head." The bunch was all ears waiting for Thugged Out to spill the beans.

". . . Sonia." He finally muttered throwing the squad into an uproar, bellowing in laughter. Woodz was in tears and told them he would see them later. Thugged Out snapped at everyone who was still laughing and called out to Woodz.

"Yo' my nigga'! Let us hold the radio!!" Woodz turned and waved his finger no.

"Hell no!!" He yelled back rewinding the *D.M.X Ruff Ryders Anthem.* "Walk wit' me if you wanna hold the radio!!" Woodz didn't think Thugged Out would walk with him but here he came jogging up towards on 110th street where Woodz waited. "Damn nigga' I was just playing!" Thugged Out snatched the radio from him.

"Nah I gotta' go see my aunt in Jeff and hit her up for some money."

"You gonna' show her your tattoo of—" Thugged Out cut Woodz off before he could finish.

"Fuck you nigga'! That was some bullshit too blown' me up to those nigga's like that." Woodz smiled and bopped his head to the music.

"Mothafucka' now you know neva' to try and shoot at me . . . now raise that up." *STOP! DROP! SHUT EM' DOWN OPEN UP SHOP! OH! WHOA!!*

*   *   *

The beginning of the school year started out smoothly for Woodz until the middle of November when everything seemed to go hay wire around him. He dropped the ball on his last pick up from Big Cat foolishly smoking up most of the smoke him self. Now he was in debt and had to pay him back from out of his own pockets! Woodz was beginning to grow tired of hustling nickels and dimes for Big Cat and hustling period. Not only was the cold weather getting on his nerves, but it was getting real risky outside with police and he dodged capture about two or three times within two weeks.

To compliment the chaos was the drama unfolding throughout Clinton. After Thugged Out's failed attempt to charm and handcuff Melly Capone was able to lure her in with his cool collective demeanor, but her dominating Taurus attitude was too much for his Pisces character to handle. They didn't last a month but she and Clari quickly became best friends during and after her relationship with Ace came to an abrupt end. She was introduced to Melly's family along with her sibling *Bernice*, and the Dominican cuties went on a trail blaze raising their popularity and drawing dislike all over Clinton.

As for the squad animosity between Capone and Thugged Out brewed due to Capone's involvement with Melly. It sent Thugged Out into a jealous frenzy and drew dislike from R-Dee who was annoyed with Thugged Out's mouth. With Woodz attached to Sonia everyday R-Dee spent most of his days now with Rudy, Ace, Pretty Boy and the new comer to the squad *Malcolm*. Malcolm was a six foot Puertorican giant and R-Dee's neighbor who became the looming body of the squad. He was easy going with a smooth personality until his buttons were pushed.

The clashes between R-Dee and Thugged Out became constant and it changed the face of the squad for the worst. Coincidentally this was in synchronization with the turmoil between the N.W.O on the wrestling program who the squad owed their transformation to. They faced an internal conflict, a clash of egos and were ready to implode at any moment. It was all due to the egotistic Hollywood Hogan!

Woodz couldn't believe it as he watched the program at Sonia's place in Lehman Projects along with her two younger brothers.

"Nah . . . its T.V not real life . . . that shit won't happen to us" But it did. During the winter rumors began circulating about Woodz and Melly messing around. The minute Sonia met the family she quickly disliked Melly but liked her sisters Natalia and Amari and immediately asked Woodz to keep away from Melly. Flaca became real tight with Bernice while Amari had Thugged Out chasing her around everywhere.

It only took Sonia a few days to learn of the rumors from her unknown source. She had asked Woodz respectively to keep away from Melly and he'd been hanging around her behind Sonia's back. She planned to find out for herself in due time. Woodz didn't know who was spreading the rumors and didn't care. He never touched or made a move on Melly so the rumors were just he say she say bull shit, but he couldn't deny that their attraction was there and slowly building up.

The Clinton Community Center opened its doors for the kids and teens to participate in fun after school recreational activities. The squad made it their own refuge to escape the cold, but no one was prepared for the scene that was about to take place on a chilly Tuesday night. Sonia made it her business to catch Woodz unexpectedly with Melly and thanks to her unknown source tipping her off about his whereabouts, she made her way towards the center and found her man with Capone, Clari and Melly.

"ANTHONY! Come here now!" The whole gym in the Community Center fell silent as all eyes were on Woodz who sucked his teeth and wondered how Sonia knew he was there. He followed her out the gym and into the lobby of the Center. "Why? Anthony why!?" Sonia asked raising her voice angrily.

"Why what Sonia? What happen now? What am i doing??" Woodz tried to keep his voice low but he had low tolerance for bull shit.

"Why what?? I gotta' be bugging! Why are people telling' me that you fuckin' around wit' that lil' Dominican bitch in there? Is it true!?"

"What? Who Sonia?! Who ever's telling' you that is full of shit and got you buggin' ma' . . . ain't noffin' goin' on wit' me and nobody yo." Woodz did his best to remain calm but inside he was boiling and wanted to know badly who it was feeding his girl lies.

"I don't care about the rumors, I asked you to stay away from that lil' bitch and you been lyin' to me! nigga' you said you love me!!" Tears filled up in Sonia's eyes and dropped onto her black North Face coat. She crossed her arms and shook her leg repeatedly and stared at him. Before Woodz could respond Capone, Clari, Boobop, Flaca and Melly stepped out into the lobby asking what was going on. Melly didn't waste any time not biting her tongue.

"Sonia if this is about me and Ant your man ain't neva' try noffin' wit' me." Sonia eyeballed Melly.

"Whateva' bitch shut the fuck up and mind your own fuckin' business." She twisted her neck and gave Melly the old talk to the hand treatment but Melly fired back.

"ill bitch you don't know me Sonia! Don't fuckin' disrespect me bitch!! You da' bitch! Yea' I'm fuckin' wit Ant! What bitch!?" Clari and Boobop dragged Melly back into the gym before she and Sonia killed each other. Melly continued to hurl words at Sonia who frustratingly looked at her man.

"You happy Anthony? You happy?? You want me to leave? I'll leave and let you go back to her and your lil' friends . . . go head and you don't have to worry about me no more." She wiped the tears flowing down her chubby cheeks. Woodz hated to see girls cry in front of him, but he was fuming and hated more to be made a fool of.

He was going to find out who was back stabbing him but first he needed to get the hell away from Sonia. She watched him turn away from her and her heart shattered into a million little pieces. "I knew it! OH MY GOD!! I knew this lil' bitch was gonna' do this! Fuck you Anthony! Go nigga' ya' deserve each other."

"You don't know shit Sonia! Go the fuck home you fuckin' buggin'." Woodz shook his head and sat on a chair by the window away from her grinding his teeth. "Go home already! Fuck!!" Sonia ran off home while Melly stormed back into the lobby followed by Clari and the rest.

"Ant! You aight!? What that stupid bitch said?! I'll fuck that bitch up for you nigga'! I ain't scared of that bitch let me know! OOOH! This bitch is lucckkeeee!!"

"Ahi Melly shut the fuck up! Bitch you wasn't gonna' do shit!" Said Flaca who laughed and shoved her sister out the way to give Woodz a tight hug. He embraced her and held her with his left arm.

"Awww bendito!" Shouted Clari and everyone laughed.

"My badd Ant . . . if you don't wanna' talk to me no more it's all good I understand." Melly pulled her hair back and gave Woodz a sad puppy face. She had long dark hair, a cute mole on her face and a petite body he loved. He gave her an adoring look.

"Nah we still cool Melly fuck it, let em' keep saying' what they wanna say about us." Melly flashed him a smile.

"That's right nigga'! nigga's is on our dicks damn! Oh my god I can't believe that I just moved out here and already drama yo . . . I'm glad I got my bitch Clari here tho'!" She gave Clari a big hug and they all went back into the gym.

It wouldn't take long for Woodz to find out that someone close to him deliberately started the rumors of Melly and him. The underhanded act would lead to two things happening, more animosity and strife between the squad and his inevitable hook up with the new girl on the block, Melly.

CHAPTER 5

Sucka' 4 Love

Cypha took his forth pull of the Dutch and rotated it to his left hand side into Woodz fingertips. Woodz blew the ash off forming on the tip of the blunt out the window and took a deep long pull of the Chocolate tye. It was his first visit back to the fun house since J.O.'s initiation into L.B.M. As the smoke filled up his lungs he quietly thought about the memorable night gazing out the window of the four story building.

Just like the street below the fun house was quiet. Only noise coming from the tokes of blunts and light coughs they produced. Joining Woodz was Cypha, J.O. and Boobop. They had all cut school on the chilly December morning and rendezvoused at the fun house.

"Yo' Woodz my nigga' what's good dogz?" J.O. asked breaking the silence of their Pow Wow. "Yo'

I heard you and this bitch Sonia broke up you and Melly what happened?" Woodz took his pulls from the second L' glancing up at J.O. from his seat on the floor next to the window.

"Yea . . . somebody was hatin' on the kid hard body my nigga' spreadin' bullshit bout me and Melly and the bitch went for it." Cypha and Boobop exchanged a quick glance. Both were familiar with the details of the story.

"That's fucked up nigga'." J.O. said being passed the first L' again. His olive tone face was quickly showing the effects of the two L's. "Fuck that nigga' L.B. my nigga'!" He shouted before taking a pull from the blunt. Woodz wanted to change the topic.

"Yo' what up wit' Annie and these bitches J.O.?" He asked. Boobop had the answers for him.

"Uhm Annie's livin' wit' her momz now and I think this nigga' said that Tina and Lauri going to school and shit." Woodz nodded his head regretting that he didn't get a chance to really fool around with Annie. He cleared his throat and returned his mind to the cypher.

"J.O. I've been hearing about you too J.O. heard you brought some L.B's to the block and that you gettin' your hands dirty over there in Lehman . . ." J.O. nodded his head and passed Cypha the first L'.

"Yea my nigga' L.Bin' ya heard! I started hangin' wit' this nigga' J-Smooth and nigga's is tryin' to get some dough na' mean!" J.O. reminded Woodz of a white boy trapped in a Puertorican body. He was funny to look at and even funnier to listen to. "Yo' so wussup with you and Melly ya' fuckin' around now don't lie dogz ha ha." The Buddha heads bursted out into laughter. Woodz continued to puff away enjoying the moment with his L.B./Hakala squad.

"Something like that . . . we might fuck around for a minute just to make mothafucka's even more mad." He laughed at the thought of when Flaca exposed Thugged Out as the person behind Sonia finding out about the rumors the night he was in the Center with Melly, and even starting the rumors in the first place!

"Don't tell her I told you nigga'!" Flaca commanded from Woodz in the lobby of 1505. "But . . . Sonia told me and asked me if it was true, I told her noooo . . . but the crazy bitch still did what she did so phew!" She threw her palms up in the air and rejoined Bernice in front of the building leaving Woodz livid!

So as expected he and Melly hit it off and news of their Christmas hook up spread through Clinton like a wildfire! They spent New Years together at a house party in 1485 on Park Avenue, for his Birthday and Easter the couple went to the movies and saw *Big Daddy* starring **Adam Sandler** and *The Matrix* starring **Keanu Reeves**. By Melly's Birthday in late April their relationship had become fully sexual fortifying their union to one another.

Woodz couldn't understand how but he was crazy about Melly and she was falling in love with him. They broke nights over the phone, wrote letters to each other and he even participated in her sister's Yvette wedding as a grooms man with Melly as his partner.

There didn't seem to be any stopping the two lovebirds. When she was sick and cooped up in the hospital Woodz was there. Melly even brought a $100 gold name plate chain with their names on it. Their open affection was driving everyone crazy and while their passion continued to intensify, the fling between Thugged Out and Amari ended just as quickly as it started.

Amari remained a close ally to Sonia who she knew despised her sister Melly. Sonia blamed Melly for their breakup in the Community Center, now Amari and her watched Melly's obsession with him and it made them sick! Animosity between Amari and Melly eventually developed due to her association with Sonia and watching sisters bicker with one another was like watching a fuse ready to explode!

Even though Sonia was still bitter from their break up she still loved Woodz and vowed to get him back. Until then she kept Amari close by her side and Thugged Out on a long leash. He was still infatuated with her so she teased him to keep him glued on to entertain herself, and to be her eyes and ears in Clinton. The situation in Clinton caused R-Dee, Ace, Malcolm and the rest to steer away and stay amongst them selves. Pretty Boy was in and out the picture with his own wifey Crystal from Washington Projects and even Rabbit was incognito watching the drama unfold from the sidelines also.

That left Capone and Thugged Out standing alone in the cold, both disapproving of Woodz commitment to Melly. Woodz never revealed Thugged Out's act of treachery to anyone or Capone, instead he put them and the rest of the squad on the back burner again. In all actuality, he was jeering them both of being out swagged yet again! It only escalated the tension between Thugged Out and R-Dee who also couldn't stand Melly. He and Thugged Out were at arms with each other every time their paths crossed.

The tension finally split L.B.M down the middle while Woodz was blinded with his new love Melly. In the mist of the squad's split Capone had suddenly become deeply attracted to Clari and was now trying to establish a relationship with her. He failed to win Clari's heart instead she began dating a kid who she went to school with, *Mark* from 1485 on Park Avenue. He was a young and upcoming flamboyant pretty boy himself, He was always dressed with the newest Jordan's, Timberlands, fitted caps and Pelle Pelle gear. Mark was quietly planting his flag on 109th street.

He helped Clari upgrade her wardrobe, self esteem and swagger altogether. Even though her mother Belky wasn't too excited about her daughter dating a black kid as almost all middle aged Spanish speaking women who were brought up during the 60s through the 80s. They were taught by their parents not to inter-mix outside of their culture or race, but within the end of the millennium approaching American culture had evolved into an inter mixing melting pot.

Since their fallout at the Community Center Woodz hardly saw or heard about Sonia except that she was now going out with a kid name *Ivan* he knew. He wasn't thinking about Sonia. At Park East he was shining, passing his classes and receiving welcomed attention from the girls from wearing the *Melly Loves Anthony* chain proudly for all to see. Gym class was always the best for Woodz, he loved admiring the girls playing volleyball. A big boned Puertorican girl named *Jaylin* who lived in his building greeted him with a big hug and kiss very close to his lips. Little did Woodz know that she was about to ruin his day.

Jaylin immediately eyeballed the lengthy Melly loves Anthony chain.

"Ooh! Let me see that shit!" She playfully demanded holding the gold name plate in her hands. "Wow . . . this shit is nice I like this . . . damn nigga' you got that bitch on your dick like that?!" Woodz shook his head and rested his chain back with his other two chains. He smiled smugly at Jaylin who he knew didn't like Melly. In fact, no girl on the block other than Clari liked Melly . . . and not even she was liked!

"That's my boo you heard." He said coolly still focused on the girls playing volleyball.

"Your boo or baby? Let me find out!?" She reached to pinch Woodz neck but he flinched back.

"Chill Jay you wildin'."

"What? Your lil' girlfriend's gonna' get mad if she sees hickeys on your neck?? Kia! Grab his arms!" Woodz didn't know there was someone behind him and now he was trapped between a rock and hard place! *Kia* was another big boned girl and she bear hugged him while Jaylin pinched his neck until the hickeys formed on his light skin. "Ahi! Oh my god . . . Ant I'm sorry! Ahii nigga' I didn't know you had sensitive skin like that . . . Kia look at his neck!" Woodz turned his neck so Kia could look at it and his smile quickly vanish seeing Kia's horrid expression.

"Oh shit." She blurted out and turned away from both Jaylin and him. Woodz felt on his neck and cautiously looked at Jaylin who was shaking her head.

"Jay? Please tell me you didn't violate??" He asked coldly.

"Nigga' I'm sorry! I didn't mean it! If your girl says something just tell her it was me just make sure she watch what she says cuz' I'll fuck her skinny ass up! And you know my cousin Littlez don't like her either and already wanna' fuck her up too." She walked away from Woodz who rushed out the gym to find a mirror.

When he did find one he couldn't believe the damage she had done to his neck. Jaylin's fat fingers left him three huge ugly hickeys! Woodz tried everything in the book to get them off when he got home, brushing his neck with a comb, the flat side of a spoon, even rubbing a lip stick cap over them but nothing worked!

He tried to conceal his neck from her because he knew she wouldn't believe that someone pinched his neck, and the last thing he needed was his girl getting into a confrontation with Jaylin, Littlez or anyone from the block who he knew would whip Melly's ass. Yet it's the story he ran with and it broke Melly's heart she didn't believe it at all. So just like that the lovebirds came crashing down from their high ride.

After two weeks of their first breakup. Melly gave him the benefit of a doubt after her best friend Taisha confided in her that Woodz was miserable about what happened. She realized that she loved Woodz too much to just throw it all away, and decided to move past the situation and take him back. However their relationship was never the same. Melly's attitude had changed dramatically and she began to try and control Woodz to dominate the relationship.

She was jealous if he even spoke to any other girl and put him in positions where he had to end close friendships with girls just to appease her! Her change of attitude irritated him greatly and just when she thought he was submitting to her whim a phone call one Monday night changed it all for good.

"Yao who this?" Woodz answered on the second ring. He put the *Resident Evil* game on paused and waited for a voice to speak. Finally it did.

". . . Anthony?" The whispering voice asked, immediately recognized by Woodz.

"Sonia?? This is Sonia?" He asked shocked.

"Yea It's me . . . I hope I'm not callin' at a bad time." Woodz stood up and looked out his window with the cordless phone in hand.

"Nah . . . nah it's aight I was just playin' Play Station and shit . . . whats up? You aight? Kinda' sounds like you cryin' . . . you aight?" Even though he and Sonia broke up on bad terms he couldn't help but feel concerned about the mouthy Gemini.

"No Anthony I'm not aight." She quickly replied. Woodz didn't know what to make of the call. "I need to talk to you . . . I'm downstairs in my cousins crib." She added.

"Come upstairs I'll meet you in the hallway." Woodz met Sonia by the staircase in black chancletas, gray sweat pants and gray sleeveless Hard Knock Life shirt and brought her inside. Momma' Luv' was resting and Big Tee had gone out so they were practically all alone. Woodz got her a glass of water and sat next to her on the cream colored sofa in the living room.

Sonia began revealing disturbing details about almost being raped inside her building when she was returning home Friday night drunk and alone. A tall Spanish guy tried to force her inside her elevator but luckily she knew guys hustling in front of her building and was able to convince one of the guys to ride with her upstairs. Her quick thinking scared off the predator and she made it home safe, but was still shaken up by the experience.

Her face was red and puffy from crying as she cried in Woodz arms. Woodz felt a huge wave of empathy hit him. He gently stroked her brown hair on his shoulder totally speechless. He thanked god that she wasn't hurt when just a few weeks before a girl from Capone's building was supposedly followed home from school and raped inside 1505. It had the entire L.B.C on the hunt for the rapo.

"Sonia . . . I don't know what to say, you gotta' be careful yo' what the fuck is you doing going home drunk and dolo!? Where the fuck was that nigga' Ivan? Where was he?"

"You stupid I don't fuck with Ivan no more we been broke up." Woodz stared at Sonia's face laid on his shoulders.

"You got me fucked up right now . . . you definitely ain't walkin' home dolo tonight fuck that! Damn Sonia I would've went crazy if some shit like that happened to you . . . word." Sonia lifted her head off Woodz shoulder and gazed into his eyes, then kissed him softly on his lips. She missed Woodz so much but her pride wouldn't allow her to admit it.

She knew that he missed her too . . . Woodz just didn't realize it . . . until now and she intended on making it clear for him. Woodz kissed Sonia back and felt another surge of emotion build inside of him. He realized that he not only desired Sonia still physically, but he was still in love with her. They locked their arms around one another and exploded on the sofa. Woodz lied on top of Sonia's body and allowed his tongue to do the rest of the talking. He kissed her face, neck and slowly unbuttoned her blue blouse revealing the black bra covering her massive D-Cup breast.

He worked his tongue downward to her breast and gently squeezed them with his hands and snapped of the bra. Woodz licked around her harden brownish nipples while his hand caressed her thighs until finally reaching in between them. He rubbed between her thighs over her black jeans until finally sliding his fingers underneath her jeans and black panties.

Woodz didn't know what possessed him and he didn't care! All he knew is that he had to have Sonia no matter what! Strapped with a kitchen knife he walked her home with a fire burning intensely in him. Sonia returned to his place the following night and from the second she stepped into his room it was on!

Woodz made love to Sonia that Tuesday night, a night when he was expecting Melly to show up at around nine P.M. Sonia arrived around seven thirty and surrendered her body to Woodz, and allowed him to explore her naked body. Woodz caressed it and dove into her private paradise. He loved the smell and taste of her juices and swollen juicy lips, most of all her hairy bush covering her hood since he had a fetish for a hairy vagina. So when she welcomed his lips and tongue covered with her juices and pubic hairs back to her mouth, it drove him even crazier. It was in that moment of pleasure that Woodz totally forgot about his commitment to Melly, all he wanted was to conquer Sonia's body.

When they were finally done it was about eight thirty so she exited and headed to Maya's apartment just in time to evade Melly on her way upstairs. Woodz had about ten minutes to clean up, change the sheets and wash up. Suddenly while staring into the bathroom mirror he felt a feeling that he hadn't felt in a long time . . . it was daring, exciting it was back, he was back! The L.B. Master was back!

He'd been blind all along, why was he settling for just one prize when he had the power to enjoy both!? Woodz felt reawakened and reunited with his first true love, L.B.C! Oh how he missed the thrill of it all! He didn't even bother washing himself up instead he greeted Melly with the same lips and tongue that had just finished swimming around in Sonia's pool of love juices, feeling no regret! Woodz was back and all bets were off!

Melly was never aware that her man was secretly meeting with Sonia behind her back. Instead she was still under the impression that they were soul mates. Woodz however was on a mission to reclaim his L.B. glory in 1999. In his mind the beginning of the New Year was filled with too much drama and chaos. Everyone was too emotionally warped by end of the world theories for the year 2000 and we're neglecting the three P's of life, Pussy, Power and Paper!

Sonia and Woodz enjoyed their last moment of perversion in the staircase of her hallway. Woodz loved the staircase setting it was where he performed some of his classic feats! He was having his cake and eating it too and nothing could ruin the fun he was having . . . until he received another phone call from Sonia . . . this time informing him that she was pregnant!

"Pregnant?! Pregnant!!? How dogz?! I used mothafuckin' condoms!!" Woodz shouted at Capone who was sitting in his room blown away by the revelation he was hearing.

"Dogz, you's a fuckin' beast nigga'! How the fuck!? Nah, fuck that right now, you gotta' find out if she tellin' the truth . . . she could be bull shittin' just to make you and Melly break up." Woodz thought about it and met up with Sonia that same night at her place. They spoke in the hallway for privacy and she told him that she missed her period, was feeling pains and to conceal it from her aunt Nancy she played it off as regular stomach aches.

Woodz didn't know what to say or do. Sonia felt as if she knew what he was thinking so she emphasized it clearly for him.

"And don't think I'ma kill my baby cuz' I'm not . . . abortions don't rock in my family." Just as quick as Woodz found his mojo again and was riding the high tide, that quick he hit rock bottom again.

Melly eventually learned of Sonia's alleged pregnancy days later and was devastated, and scrutinized by Clari and her family about him. Woodz on the other hand was on the hot seat with both Pedro and Big Tee after he confessed to them about possibly getting Sonia pregnant.

"Well guess we gonna' be uncles right Big Tee?" Pedro joked. He was lost for words to express how angry he really was with his little brother.

"Hey we could put a crib right here in the room with you and she could live here too lika' big happy family." Woodz quietly sat on his bed with a stoic demeanor. Big tee and Pedro's sarcasm wasn't helping his situation. He knew they were pissed off but why crack jokes about it? His life would be over and he never felt so depressed. Yet he pondered . . . strangely the subject of a baby hadn't surfaced with her aunt who he was certain would chew him out as soon as she learned her niece was pregnant.

"Maybe Pone's right? She's just doing it to break up me and this bitch . . . or maybe she just ain't tell her yet . . . fuck!!" He continued to ponder while Pedro and Big Tee continued to joke and drill him about being irresponsible, out of control and a sorry ass father to be.

For the next few days Woodz walked by Park Avenue on his way to Sonia's building and saw Melly with the rest of the bunch. Her face always filled with heartache and tears every time she saw him. It was driving Woodz crazy and he finally realized that he didn't want to be with Sonia . . . or did he? He decided to admit it to her as well, baby or no baby.

"Ugh Anthony you still love that lil' bitch??" Sonia bluntly asked tired of the funny vibes she felt from him for days. Plus it was obvious to her after he called her Melly not once but twice two days in a row! Woodz stared down the quiet gloomy project hallway trying to make sense of his feelings.

"I dunno' I think so . . . but it's not only about Melly its about you, me . . . and—" Sonia raised her hand before he could continue.

"Ahi go Anthony go . . . go back to her or who eva' you want . . . I'm sorry I fucked up your life again you don't have to worry . . . me and the baby gonna' be just fine." Woodz didn't respond, he turned and walked towards the staircase and down the stairs he went into the night.

CHAPTER 6

Keep It In The Family

Things had finally begun to cool down in Clinton but the summer of 1999 had arrived and it was expected to be a hot one! School was finally out, the pools and beaches would be open soon, and it was back to work for Woodz with his Housing gig. Now that his dream of becoming a big time hustler was officially a bust, he would pay Big Cat the hundred bucks he owed and really enjoy his summer.

His first priority before anything was resurrecting his L.B.M squad that was still in shambles. The year long soap opera with Sonia and Melly had tore the squad apart and he couldn't believe the coincidence of the N.W.O on T.V. now comprised of two separate factions after splitting apart also. There was now a Wolf pack N.W.O, the rebellious side going against

Hollywood Hogan and his regime. R-Dee and his circle were that same Wolf pack.

Woodz realized it wouldn't be easy while he took refuge in the Bronx with Pedro at his home base in Sound View. It was his chance to not only get focused again but to get away from Clinton and while Pedro tried to school his little brother on the importance of being responsible, the word came from Clinton that Sonia was back on the scene, out and about along with Amari and apparently not pregnant at all . . . it was music to Woodz ears!

Upon his return from Sound View he never heard anything about a baby from Sonia or anyone so it seemed that his prayers were answered! Once he began working and getting back in his groove he actually tried to reconcile things with Melly. Unfortunately Melly wasn't the same lovable sweetheart he once knew. She had enough of Woodz. His games and lies not only broke her heart, they scarred her forever.

Instead of retreating and licking her wounds Melly was determined to face the summer head on. So along with her best friend Clari she began familiarizing herself with the older crowd of females from Thugged Out's building. The new crowd embraced her and Clari and quickly influenced a change of attitude in both of them.

They imbedded in Melly's mind that she had to leave the past behind and pay no mind to the haters. Especially Clari who was the envy of all the girls in Clinton for being Mark's wifey when they were all trying to lure him away. These wise females of Lexington Avenue explained to Melly that guys like Woodz were only good for one thing, dick. So she regarded him as a booty call and built an icebox around her heart for him. Melly paraded around Clinton with a more stubborn, bitchy and cockier new attitude. She even acted more seductive as she attracted guys in and outside of Clinton to satisfy her growing sexual appetite. She even helped transform Clari into a certified smoke head and alchy also!

Woodz was also leaving the past behind and finally getting Melly out of his system. They would occasionally answer the booty call but it would lack all the passion they once shared. By the end of the summer his squad was finally beginning to reassemble just as the N.W.O on T.V. were. Then after finally paying Big Cat the pocket change he owed Woodz decided to treat himself so he brought a lengthy $100 gold chain with a $100 diamond cut crucifix piece that caught everyone's eye!

He also brought Flaca her own gold name chain for her fifteenth birthday. Flaca and Woodz were still very close even after the fiasco with her sister. He figured he'd splurge some on his favorite make believe little sister. He was still liked by most of their family. Both Perucho and Manolo were part of the L.B. and loose cannons. Certified smoke heads also but the squad loved their asses.

Amari was also celebrating her birthday. Woodz wasn't as close to her as he was with Flaca so he didn't buy her a gold name chain. What he did do being that she was a Buddha head now too was spark a birthday blunt up for her! Which in any true smoke head's right mind, was just as valuable as a gold chain if not more!

"DAAAGGGGG . . . I can't believe how much your room's changed since the last time I was here yo'. Damn nigga' your shit is hooked up!" She exclaimed admiring the vast number of posters, pictures and stickers covering all four walls of Woodz room. She took two quick drags of her third birthday blunt of the afternoon and passed it to Woodz who was sitting on his wooden bar stool by the window.

It was a beautiful day outside perfect for a blunt of *Hawaiian Haze*, then again what day wasn't! The sun was shining, sky was clear blue and Momma' Luv' was in the Bronx visiting family with Big Tee so he had home base all to himself. It was also Woodz last week of working with Housing for the summer. He couldn't wait to work Seasonal for Housing so he could stack his money and get his own apartment.

"OH THAT'S MY SHIT!! Raise that up nigga'!" Amari shouted and started dancing in front of the huge mirror Woodz had standing against his wall. He raised the volume on his Pioneer Stereo and the **Jay-Z** and **Amil's** *Can I get a what what* song blasted in his room. Amari continued bouncing to the song as Woodz passed the dutchy back to her.

"Yo' so you don't have no plans for tonight? Mom dukes ain't cookin' ya' noffin'? No party? Cake?? No boyfriend to take you out or noffin'?" He asked grinning lowering the volume of the stereo. He hated when his neighbors banged on the walls to complain about the loud music.

"Nah nigga' you know my momz is broke ha ha nah, they might cut me and Flaca a cake and shit . . . a party would be dope probably next year . . . you gonna' come sing happy birthday to us?" She asked wishfully.

"HELL NO! ha ha your pops probably kill my lil' ass if he caught me up in there. Tell your man from Lehman to come sing for you ha ha." He laughed and Amari rolled her eyes.

"I wish nigga'. I was fuckin' wit' that nigga' in Lehman for lika' week but he played madd games and shit." She passed Woodz the Haze.

"What about Kenny?" He asked laughing and almost choking on the smoke.

"OH MY GOD! Please don't tell me about Kenny! That nigga' yo' . . . Kenny's too much, that's my boy tho' but I can't fuck wit' Kenny's ass you crazy . . . YOOO!! wussup wit' this shit my sister's been sayin' about you?! I know you heard about it right??" Woodz smiled and slowly nodded his head passing the Haze back to the Birthday girl. He knew full well of the gossip Melly was spreading around to slander his reputation.

"And what did you hear Amari??" He asked suspiciously grinning. Amari looked out the window through red chinky eyes and back at him from her peripheral with a smile.

"Thaaaaatt . . . you cried when she broke up wit' you the first time, you begged her to take you back when ya' broke up again and . . ." She paused to inhale the trees and passed the half dutchy back to him. "And that you need Viagra to get your dick up!!" She blurted and laughed trying to cover her mouth with both hands to muffle her amusement. "I'm sorry my nigga' I didn't mean to laugh like that . . . shit is funny you can't front, Melly is fuckin' stupid." Woodz didn't mind her laughing it was funny. He smirked as he took one last pull of the smoke.

"And you believe it!?" He asked shockingly. Amari didn't respond. Instead she took a long pull of the L' and gave Woodz an innocent look. "Enjoy birthday girl I'ma get us some Ice Tea to drink." He rose from the bar stool and gingerly made his way down his hallway towards the kitchen to fetch the needed refreshments. "I need Viagra . . . heh bitch is crazy." He mumbled to himself. He couldn't deny the absurd accusations struck a nerve, but after a while it not only made him more eminent throughout Clinton but it also made Jaylin and the other girls from 109th want to whip Melly's ass more than ever now! Clari especially who was still despised because of Mark being her hubby.

Woodz returned to the room with Ice Teas and a huge bag of Doritos Cool Ranch Nachos Momma' Luv' brought from *MET Supermarket*. Amari had killed the L' just as he walked in and thanked him for the drink. Woodz plugged in his black fan and sprayed some of his Baby Powder cologne in the room and in the hallway to kill the Haze smell.

He sat down on his bed and helped himself to a handful of *Cool Ranch Doritos* while Amari who was listening to **Lauryn Hills'** *That Thang'* record did the same.

"Yo' so you didn't answer my question . . ." He said eating crumbs of Doritos off his red and black Jordan jersey. He looked over at her and continued. "Do you believe that shit your sister's sayin' about me?" Amari sat the glass of Ice Tea down next to the stereo.

"Ahi yaya toda via!? Ha ha nah you wanna' know the truth?" Woodz nodded his head and munched on a handful of Doritos. "Hell nah nigga' everybody know my sister was on your shit crazy, ya' was together for lika' year . . . then this crazy bitch Sonia was on your dick too?? Damn nigga' what the fuck you be doing to these bitches on this block!?" She laughed again and sat on Woodz burgundy leather swivel chair. He shrugged his shoulders and took his Braves fitted cap off to rub his head then leaned back on his pillow.

He felt the Haze working its magic and started to zone out while Amari continued. "And you treated my sister good nigga' well, until you started fuckin' wit' Sonia again . . . she's fuckin' wit' some nigga' name Ivan or was I don't know now, I don't be chillin' wit' her like that anymore . . . but I be seeing her sometimes . . . anyway, what was I saying? Oh yea' ha ha yo good looks for that blunt nigga' that shit got me feelin' niicee . . . but yea' before that all my sister used to talk about was you . . . damn yo' why I can't find a nigga' like that? To take me to movies, buy me shit . . . tell me the truth Ant, why you picked Melly out of all of us? You don't think I'm pretty??" Amari question snapped Woodz out of his zone and back to reality.

"What?? What you mean why I picked Melly? I didn't pick Melly . . . me and Melly just happened and what you mean if you pretty?? Of course I do." Woodz meant it, the six Bolina sisters were all beautiful.

"You don't think I'm ugly?" She asked seriously sitting up on the leather swivel seat to pull her hair behind her ears. Woodz sat back up too and put his fitted back on. He wiped his face and scanned Amari from head to toe. She looked very pretty in her white T-shirt, tight blue jeans and white New Balance sneakers.

Just as Capone had reported to him last summer Amari was a cutie and could easily pass for her older sister Maggie's twin. Her hair was long like Melly's but lighter brown. She was petite also maybe just meatier than Melly with potential to grow thicker. She had a healthy sense of humor that was easily tickled, always full of hugs and smiles, smiles that always revealed the chipped tooth she had. Amari was two years younger than Melly but mature in her own unique way.

"Ugly?!" Woodz finally uttered. "Hell no you crazy!?" He smiled at her. "You's a cutie Amari, you don't think nigga's on this block wanna' fuck wit' you?" He stood up to stretch his back and arms and wondered if it was the Hawaiian stirring up the tingly sensation in his body.

"Fuck outta' here! For real?" She asked curiously. "Like who? And don't play yourself and say Kenny again nigga'!" They both laughed and Woodz gulped the rest of his Ice tea.

"You know I can't blow nigga's up like that but trust me you know em' and see em' everyday." Amari observed Woodz closely in his Chicago Bulls jersey. He set his empty glass down besides hers and looked out the window. Finally he sat back down on the bar stool and looked at her. His eyes were as red as the jersey!

"You not gonna' tell me nigga'? That's fucked up yo' . . . I thought we were peoples!" She smiled and stood up to stretch also while Woodz eyeballed her. He was beginning to really enjoy her company.

"Look at that smile of yours . . . how can a nigga' not like that smile you got?? I think it's the chipped tooth that really does the trick you heard." Amari covered her mouth with her hands and stared at him wide eyed.

"Don't make fun of my tooth nigga'! You so mean!!" She teased with her hand still covering her mouth hiding her smile. Amari was enjoying being with Woodz and wondered if it was wrong to feel the feelings she felt being that he was her sister's ex-man, but she couldn't resist.

"I'm not makin' fun of your tooth I love your smile girl . . . come here." He stretched out his arms to give her a big hug and Amari happily met his embrace with a hug of her own. Woodz inhaled the smell of her hair, it was refreshing and the feel of her B-cup breast pressing against his chest was arousing him.

"Happy Birthday Amari . . . damn you always smell this good yo'?" She thanked him and smiled while inhaling the scent of his Baby Powder cologne. "You know what??" He whispered in her ear. "Only cuz' it's your B-day right I'll tell you one person who I know wants to fuck wit' you . . . you wanna' know?" Amari pulled away and looked at Woodz through brown reddish eyes.

"Who??" She asked conspicuously. They were still holding each other and she wasn't sure if she wanted him to let go. Woodz licked his lips and slowly pulled her towards him.

"Me." He answered smoothly and kissed Amari on her lips. He had a feeling she was feeling the magic of the Haze too . . . the Hawaiian never fails! Amari wrapped her arms around him and allowed her tongue to dance along with his as he caressed and squeezed her lower tenderloins.

A few seconds passed before she finally pulled away suddenly feeling a wave of guilt. Was she crazy!??

"Damn nigga' we can't do this . . . you was my sister's man and you was like my brother you crazy nigga'!" Woodz shrugged his shoulders and held her waist.

"Fuck that . . . I was your sister's boy friend and never your real brother . . . maybe only make believe . . . but if you want me to stop and let you go just say the word." He looked into her chinky eyes and ran his hands along her sides. "Or . . ." He added. "We could give Melly somethin' really worth talkin' about." Amari smiled and let his arms pull her back towards him. She grabbed the Braves fitted off his head and put it on hers then caressed the sides of his head.

The bulge underneath his blue Pe'Pe jean shorts grew more and more and finally got Amari attention. She glanced down and grinned at him.

"Didn't need Viagra for that huh??" She laughed and bit her lips before kissing Woodz lips again.

"Wanna' see it?" He asked her and the question only made her grin more. She let go of his neck to pull back her hair again. Amari gave Woodz a devilish look and tugged on his chain until his face was close to hers. She nodded her head yea . . . so he showed her.

Just when everybody thought Woodz was down for the count they were completely caught off guard with the move he managed to pull off this time! No one was prepared to see Amari and him as a couple, not in this lifetime! The hate came from not just Melly and her family, but also from the squad and damn near the whole Clinton projects!

No one was convinced that the two were serious about each other though especially Thugged Out and Capone who were sure it was Woodz way of getting back at Melly for trying to defame him. They were appalled by Woodz blatant disrespect, but despite all the ridicule and criticism he made sure they all saw Amari and him together. He was keeping it in the family, love it or hate it!

After two weeks of seeing the new couple together the criticism began to subside just a bit and the two were starting to be recognized as a real couple. In fact all eyes were on Amari now who looked a lot more appealing in the eyes of the fellas on the block. She wasn't Melly's little oddball sister or Sonia's sidekick, she was Woodz girl now so her stock value had rapidly increased!

Amari didn't have Melly's unpopular attitude or act anything like her so the other girls in Clinton liked her. Thanks to an upgrade of her wardrobe, the fellas couldn't help notice her petite but protruding figure that was looking better than Melly's! Her hook up with Woodz infuriated Melly and made her not only loathe him and her younger sister more, but now she really wanted to kill her!

With a few days remaining in the summer the parks in Clinton were alive and active until the wee hours of the night. After learning of the buzz Woodz was causing with his new girl R-Dee, Rudy and the rest were curious to see what other tricks he had up his sleeves and surprisingly they liked Amari and preferred her rather than Melly and Sonia hands down. She was easier to get along with and Woodz seemed content about keeping her as his girl, but not even he was sure about that.

There was too much tension between the sisters because of him and it was only a matter of time before they ripped each other heads off! He did enjoy being with Amari and didn't mind at all having her sit on his lap in the park on the cool September night. He had his new girl his squad in high spirits, and even Thugged Out and R-Dee were getting along for once. Nothing or no one could spoil the evening for him . . . well except Melly of course.

"NATALIA! AMARI! Mami said to come inside now!!" Melly Shouted from her bedroom window facing the park. She'd been watching her sister straddle Woodz lap for the past ten minutes and made it her business to inform their mother that it was getting too late for her sisters to be outside with a bunch of boys.

"C'mon Amari say goodbye to your boyfriend, man whateva' . . . before papi comes out again with the correa." Joked Flaca who was laughing with Bernice but Woodz knew she was dead serious. The fellas teased Amari who didn't budge off Woodz lap. Instead she wrapped her arms around his neck and kissed him passionately. "Look at you, you lil' slut!" Flaca playfully shouted at her twin sister as the fellas cheered her on.

Amari stuck her middle finger at Flaca and sucked on Woodz lips giggling.

"Look at that lil' bitch Clari . . . oooh this nigga' got fuckin' balls yo' right in front of my window . . . NATALIA AND AMARI!! Mami said to come inside now!!" Melly yelled again but this time Amari responded.

"We don't need you to let us know when to come inside Melina!!! Your not our fuckin' motha'!" She knew Melly was trying to embarrass her in front of Woodz and it annoyed her. "Mami knows me and Flaca in the park! So let her call us inside when she wants us!!" The fellas all laughed and shot unfriendly words at Melly. Woodz just shook his head and chuckled to himself. It was obvious the two sisters were at war and he wondered which one of the two could really hold their own.

"Amari! C'mon! before this crazy bitch runs and tells papi and that nigga' comes out here buggin' the fuck out!" Flaca pleaded. She knew he would and so did Woodz who witnessed their father go berserk on the bunch when they wouldn't listen.

"Better go inside before Melly comes out here and fucks you up." He said and grinned at Amari

Anthony 'A-Class' Quinones

who sucked her teeth glancing through her peripheral towards the window.

"Fuck outta' here . . . I already fucked that bitch up once." Woodz chuckled and rubbed her back. Flaca asked him to convince her to go inside but she wasn't budging. Amari refused to let Melly show her up.

"Nah fuck that!" She yelled out loud. Enough for not only Melly to hear but for the whole block! "That bitch is just mad cuz' you my new man now!! Fuck herrrr!!! Let her tell papi! It's not that late and that bitch is hatin'!! Why you hatin' bitch?!! Mad cuz' I'm out here kissin' Anthony and you not!?!"

Ah fuck . . . Woodz thought. He knew Melly all too well and was positive she wouldn't let her little sister have the last word.

"What the fuck you said Amari?!! Don't play yourself bitch! Don't make me go out there and fuck you up in front of your fake ass boyfriend! Lil' hoe!!" Woodz tried to keep his girl calm but she hopped off his lap and challenged Melly to come out.

"Whateva' bitch!! Come out here and say it to my face! I bet you I'll fuck you up again! You pussy Melly!! You can't fight!! That's why you were scared to fight Sonia! She had you shook nigga'! She was gonna' fuck you up!!" Flaca tried telling Clari not to let Melly come outside but it was too late, she had already disappeared from the window and was heading towards the park. Flaca argued with Amari then with R-Dee who was rooting Amari on and taunting Melly.

Woodz was going to try and get Amari out of the park but it was too late. Melly charged into the park with Clari trailing behind her.

"I'm out here now! What bitch?! What was all that shit you was talkin'?!" Melly stepped right to her sister who didn't back down one bit! Woodz didn't do or say anything except watch along with the others as Melly and Amari began mushing each others faces. Melly finally grabbed two fists full of Amari's hair and tried to knock her down to the ground but she underestimated her little sister who got her hands on Melly's long hair also and tugged at it hard!

"Flaca pleaded and yelled for them to let go of each other and tried to break them apart but Capone and R-Dee held her back so she wouldn't get hit by the hay makers both sisters were launching wildly at each other now! Amari was a little shorter than Melly but she stood her ground and went head to head with her even as Melly landed a few side punches on her. However Amari would get the upper hand on Melly by knocking her to the ground while Melly was off balance from swinging wildly.

Flaca screamed desperately towards the window for one of her sisters to come out and stop them from brawling. Nobody in the park dared to. They all watched Amari pin Melly to the ground and pummel her with punches repeatedly across her face. Melly did her best to shield herself but her sister was relentless! The fellas finally separated the two before Amari killed Melly. Woodz grabbed his girl from behind while Thugged Out and Capone helped Melly off the ground, cursing her sister out.

"YOU FUCKIN' BITCH!! You gonna' fight me for that bum ass nigga'?!! I'm your sister!! FUCKIN LIL' BITCH!!" Melly continued to launch words at Amari who was being hauled away by Woodz.

"Yo you crazy Amari! You fucked her ass up!!" He said in her ear, pinning her against the gate to keep her from lunging at Melly.

"Whateva' bitch!! That's why you got fucked up!! Who's the pussy now?!" She yelled over Woodz shoulder.

"Aight chill . . . chill out ma' you won its ova' champ! Let me check your face and hands." She had a few bruises but nothing major. Perucho, Capone and Angie dragged Melly inside while Maggie came for Amari. Woodz wanted to boast about Melly getting her ass whipped so badly but he decided to keep it to himself for now.

No one was thrilled to learn that the two sisters slugged it out over a boy, over Woodz for that matter! He didn't scope the damage done to Melly but it had to be more than the few scratches Amari had. Woodz loved ending the summer on a high note but the finale for this summer was just too much . . . talk about ending the summer with a bang!

CHAPTER 7
The Window

The golden bright rays of sunlight penetrated through the slightly drawn royal blue curtains in Woodz room as the sun ascended over the windy Spanish Harlem area. Woodz awoke on the mid October Saturday afternoon to the sounds of children playing in the park across the street and car horns blaring aloud. *It was all a dream*?? He mumbled under his breath sitting up and facing towards the direction of the sunlight splashing across his face. "It was a mothafuckin' dream . . . Ha ha."

He let out a raspy laugh still picturing the image of the dreams he was having only moments ago. He and Sonia were in the park pushing a baby carriage when Melly came with her own carriage talking shit. Then out of nowhere Amari showed up and the three of them began clawing at him then each other right in front of the babies! Luckily for Woodz it was just a dream where as a few months and weeks the images were more like a nightmare!

The brawl between Amari and her sister Melly put a definite end to her short lived affair with Woodz and made Melly the butt of everyone's joke in Clinton. Amari excuse for fighting her was strictly because of Melly's mouth and not over him, but everyone knew the real story. Woodz kind of missed Amari company but knew that he had to keep marching forward and not let the soap opera with the feuding sisters hold him back any longer.

He wasn't a vindictive person by nature and didn't care what drama Melly or any of them found them selves in. As the summer came to a close he wasted no time and rounded up the squad to squash any minute beefs and patch up all differences. He knew he had let them down so he had to make sure they bounced back and reestablished their trust in one another.

As his senior year at Park East got underway he learned of a new phenomenon sweeping across Spanish Harlem and New York City in whole. C.B. radios/walkie talkies, he began seeing people walking up and down the street talking into the hand radio devices. He and Thugged Out knew they had to get their hands on a set, and it didn't take long for the duo to get them.

Woodz couldn't believe how the C.B. was creating an underground world in the palm of your hands.

Woodz studied the Cobra walkie talky Thugged Out gave him. The black device was just like the walkies he'd seen on T.V. There were fourteen different channels available to chat. Fourteen different channels to rule and conquer thought Woodz. He saw this new phenomenon as another way for him to resurrect his L.B. squad. The walkie was like a drug, once you plugged in you was hooked!

Day and night Thugged Out and Woodz stormed the airwaves meeting people from all over Harlem and the Bronx. Channel one was the Times Square of the C.B. world where everyone congregated. Woodz declared it Hollywood's channel and channel ten as the L.B. channel. They all learned the C.B. lingo and made an immediate impact in the C.B. world . . . Hollywood had struck again!

Woodz switched on the walkie talky he had on his window ledge as he drew his royal blue curtains open and gazed down at Lexington Avenue. He had one of the best views in Clinton. Every one loved looking out his window. No gates on his window so it made looking out his window feel like a balcony, portal and even a throne.

He washed up and fixed himself a quick brunch of cheese eggs with toast and relaxed in his room enjoying the tranquility in home base watching re-run movies on FOX. Woodz loved the privacy of having his own room after years of sharing it with Tito. The two brothers didn't share the same closeness that he and Pedro had.

Big Tee was the more serious brother out of the three, he was the man of the house who made sure all the bills were paid and that they were all right. Now with school back in session waiting for Woodz to return home was becoming an everyday problem for him and Momma Luv. Every night was a gamble if whether or not Woodz would return home safely or at all.

Woodz admired himself in front of the 6 foot 3 mirror standing against the wall in his room. Maria had left him a brand new T.V. stand, mirror and clothes cabinet. He had four new surround sound wall unit speakers, adjustable lighting, new furniture and even a fresh paint job that he did himself.

Completing his sanctuary were the posters and pictures that he covered all four walls with. His prized picture was an autograph Dead Presidents soundtrack picture signed by *Jay-Z* himself when he visited a teacher he knew at New York Prep. Woodz made sure that his room met Hollywood standards.

Woodz applied lotion on his 125lb cut up frame wondering why he didn't gain any weight. Then again as far as he was concerned he was bigger than life already and if the ladies didn't complain, then why would he? His home base on 109th was the L.B.M headquarters and the spot period!

His window was his watchtower and some what of an attraction in Clinton. You never knew who or what you would see when you looked up at his window. Loud music, flashy lights and of course the infamous black blog covering up the L.B.M tag under his window ledge. Little did Woodz know that his window would once again be glorified and attain praises on this particular afternoon.

While he devoured the remaining cheese eggs he listened for any incoming calls over the walkie talky and at about 12:50 on channel 1 he received an unexpected call.

"Hollywood pick it up . . . Hollywood pick up . . ." Woodz heard the female's voice and fumbled with names in his head. He waited for her to call again. *"HOLLEEEEWOOOD! Where you at nigga'! pick it up for L.E.S. Hollywood!"*

"L.E.S.?" He repeated to himself then smiled. The mystery voice was *Jerilyn* from the Lower East Side. He met Jerilyn few weeks ago on Lexington Avenue while he and Malcolm were walking past the Kennedy Fried Chicken spot. Jerilyn was walking down towards 110th with a friend of hers. Woodz showed her his window from downstairs and told her if she was ever in the neighborhood again to call out for him.

"Yooo' . . . this is Woodz what up? Who's this callin' me like they know me and shit?" He finally replied.

"Nigga'! Look out your window." Woodz peeked out from behind his curtain and spotted L.E.S. cordially walking by the Pawn Shop across the street from 1760.

"Yaooo! What up ma!" He exclaimed now drawing his curtains wide open to reveal himself.

"What's up? What chu' doing?"

"Just got out the shower and shit . . . bustin' down some eggs . . . what's good?"

"I'm comin' up alright?" Woodz wiped his mouth and grinned. She was walking past the store now staring up at him.

"Aight that's a copy ya' heard." He gave her the intercom number and buzzed her in as soon as she called.

Other people began calling for him on the channel but he disregarded the calls and went to unlock the door for her to come inside. He waited in he room with the music blaring until she finally knocked and let herself inside. L.E.S slowly made her way towards the room and met him with a big hug and kiss. Woodz grabbed her wide ass with his hands and squeezed on it. While he waited for her Woodz realized that the visit was exactly what the doctor ordered. In the aftermath of dealing with Melly and Sonia he hadn't had any real playtime with any L.B. on or off the block.

"I like your room nigga'." L.E.S was impressed by the flashy look of his room most guys she knew had filthy rooms. She admired his C. D.s hung on the wall by thumb tacks, all the pictures, stickers and posters symmetrically placed all over the walls. The fellas always loved his room, his neatness and taste of class always received praises. He watched her admire the room in awe while he lusted over her ass.

"So what's up with you? Missed me huh?" He asked grinning, leaning on his swivel seat still lusting over her while she studied his autographed *Jay-Z* picture. She finally turned towards him and followed what his eyes were staring at. She threw her jacket on his bed and leaned against his body. She felt the bulge under his sweat pants and squeezed on it with her left hand.

"Nooo . . . just passin' by from my step pops house and wanted to see if your lil' ass was around." Jerilyn resembled both Sonia and Melly, Woodz thought with the exception that she was taller than the two, had a long face covered with light freckles and bigger breast and ass.

She stuck her tongue down his throat as he ran his hand over her breast, thighs, and slid his hands down her pants to squeeze her butt cheeks. Woodz was about to unbutton her jeans when Thugged Out's voice came alive over the C.B. radio. He didn't even know it was still on.

"Holleeeeewooood . . . pick it up nigga . . . what you doing up there Woodz??" Jerilyn and him both laughed hearing Thugged Out's altered voice. Woodz peeked through the curtain and saw that he wasn't alone. Joining him downstairs in front of the window were Ace, Rabbit, Mark and his boy *Greg* from Foster projects. They had all gathered next to the blue and white garbage dumpsters listening to Greg play his new Juvenile tape.

As they all stared up at the window Thugged Out hailed Woodz again. *"Woodz!? Who's up there wit' you??"* Woodz couldn't help it but laugh Thugged Out knew him too well. He gave L.E.S. the walkie and told her to answer him back.

"Thugged Out pick up for L.E.S."

"L.E.S.? This be Thugged Out L.E.S. who you be?" He curiously asked unfamiliar with L.E.S. The fellas all listened in. *"L.E.S. whats your twenty right now?"* Woodz motioned for her to reveal herself out the window. Rabbit saw her first and tapped Thugged out on his shoulder so he could look up and see her too. L.E.S stared down at the group with the walkie in her hand and answered back.

"Uhh I'm the one in the window . . . hi." She giggled and watched Rabbit try to grab the C.B. away from Thugged Out. He fought him off and hopped on the dumpster for safety.

"L.E.S this be Thugged Out again, what's Woodz doing??" L.E.S checked behind her. Woodz was returning from the bathroom. He leaned over her back and grabbed the C.B.

"Thugged Out whats crackin' my nigga'!!"

"Yo' Woodz! Why you ain't say nuffin' . . . you gotta' let nigga's know that your L.B.in' nigga' is you L.B.in'??"

"And you know this! MAN!!" The group reacted with shouts and declarations of L.B.! Woodz smiled at Jerilyn.

"Ya' nigga's is so retarded . . . what's L.B.?" She looked downstairs again and laughed her ass off seeing Thugged Out shaking his ass in Rabbits face from atop the dumpster. Rabbit wasn't so enthused however. Woodz suddenly had an idea and decided to have some fun with L.E.S and the fellas. With all they had been through in the last few months the moment called for a treat . . . Hollywood style.

"Ayo Thugged Out . . . ya' wanna' see what I'm workin' with?" Thugged Out looked up and was puzzled by Woodz question.

"Uhh I don't copy Woodz I don't copy . . . what you said?" The fellas gazed up at the gate less window clueless about what Woodz meant.

Woodz positioned himself behind Jerilyn's ass and kissed on her neck while caressing her breast.

"Umm, what you doing?" She asked seductively. Woodz didn't answer instead he began loosening her Bra. "Nigga' what you doin'!?" She asked again this time in disapproval. Woodz kissed her again and cupped her beast in his hands, trying to sound as persuasive as he can.

"Chill sexy chill . . . lets give em' a show to really go crazy about . . . you want Hollywood right? Well let me give it to you . . . trust me I got you." L.E.S kissed him back and returned her gaze back down at the fellas who were all looking upstairs. She didn't know why but she trusted Woodz.

He got her to slowly sway side to side like a belly dancer and unbuttoned her blue blouse, then flashed her massive D-Cup breast at the fellas who went into a frenzy! They were howling, wooing and slapping fives while L.E.S and Woodz both laughed peeking from behind the curtains.

Mark grabbed the C.B. away from Thugged Out who was gleaming over the huge titties he saw out the window. After he had transformed Clari into an overnight celebrity in Clinton by upgrading her style and swag, he assembled his own squad in Clinton called the Cash Money Boyz and they made an immediate presence in Clinton. Even though he was Thugged Out's sister's boyfriend, he still flaunted his charm and was under close watch by her and for good reason. Mark was a bachelor at heart before anything!

"Yo' Ant I mean Woodz, Hollywood shit, my bad my nigga' . . . yo' what's good B'? what up with those big ass titties my nigga'! Is you serious!?" He cracked up along with Greg as Thugged Out snatched the hand radio back.

"Shut the fuck up!" *"Yo' Woodz my nigga' that was beautiful but some of us didn't get to see, the fuckin' sun dog I . . . we need to see that again you copy?"* Woodz peeked out the window to make sure none of the family was catching the live peep show he had going on at the window. Convinced that the coast was clear L.E.S. flashed their audience again.

Mark spotted two of his fellow Cash Money Boyz *C.J.* and *Taino* across the street and called them over. The two stepbrothers crossed the street wondering what everybody was excited about.

"*L.E.S pick up ma.*" Mark called out.

"*Yeesss?*" She answered.

"*Yo' my two manz just came ova' here and they don't believe that you did what you just did, can you please shut these nigga's up ma?*" Jeralin looked over at Woodz.

"See what you started??" Woodz chuckled.

"Aight give em' one more peak then it's a wrap." L.E.S thought about saying no for a second but with Woodz holding her from behind she couldn't refuse. She couldn't believe how she had guys who she didn't know from a hole in the wall in the palm of her hands. It gave her a sense of power and Woodz made her feel it . . . Hollywood just like he said.

She flashed the fellas one more time this time jingling and bouncing her goodies for a better show. The fools went bananas! One by one they marched towards 1738.

"Hollywood! Nigga's is comin' up to meet flash!" L.E.S and Woodz both fell onto the bed laughing. He held her and kissed her bosom. He buttoned up her blouse without her Bra on that he wore around his neck like a chain. Together they went out to the hallway to meet the fellas by the elevator.

The elevator door opened and the boys all stepped out. Taino and C.J wanted to smoke so they all spilled into the staircase. Woodz stood against the wall with Jerilyn leaning on him facing the fellas who all sat and stood by the steps.

"How old is you shorty?" Taino asked, L.E.S answered that she was eighteen and slowly swayed against Woodz waist.

"Yo . . ." blurted out Greg who couldn't resist. "Yo' you got some nice ass fat titties damn!!" Everyone laughed and the L's were lit.

"Fellas this is my L.E.S girl . . . we had a feeling ya' was gonna' enjoy the show." Jerilyn felt Woodz bulge again and enjoyed the attention she was receiving. Back at home she didn't receive attention like this, so she couldn't resist either.

"Ya' wanna' see one more time??" Woodz coughed off the smoke and passed the L' back to C.J.

"Aight I think its time to bounce."

"Nah! Hold up nigga'!" Both Taino and Greg interjected. Woodz pinched L.E.S on her ass. "One more close up at them thangs ain't gonna' hurt nigga'." Woodz nodded his head and gave the fellas a devilish look. He felt powerful and realized that his peers still respected his swag, more than ever now! He wrapped his arms around her tight waist.

"It's up to L.E.S she knows what it is . . ." Without hesitation Jerilyn unbuttoned her navy blue and white blouse and gave them the close up they wanted. Woodz held the massive breast in his hands and squeezed her nipples softly watching the expressions on their faces, they were all practically drooling!

C.J. sucked his teeth loving and hating the fact Woodz would be the one enjoying her goodies and not him or the others. Taino and Greg got as close as they can for an even closer look and just when Greg lifted his hand to attempt a touch Woodz squeezed her left breast and she quickly covered up. She turned her back to the fellas and buried her face into Woodz shoulder. He pointed to her ass and squeezed on the fat booty. He flashed the L.B. sign and the fellas could only stare and admire nodding their hands.

The show was officially over so he told L.E.S to wait for him inside so he could talk with his boys. He gave everyone pounds and huddled with Mark and Thugged Out.

"Yo' you about to smash that right my nigga'?" Mark asked.

"Straight cheese B' I'll see ya in a lil' while." He gave Thugged Out another pound and went back inside. He found L.E.S on his bed with her belt unbuckled, sneakers and blouse off. Woodz closed the window and drew the curtains shut, raised the volume on his stereo and joined her on the bed. It was time for his show now.

The show in the window was the talk of the day. News of a mystery girl in Woodz window flashing her tits spread through Clinton. Even Melly got wind of it and tried to act as if it meant nothing to her but it struck her nerves and she knew it. At around 6 o'clock Woodz finally emerged from the building after Jerilyn's departure. He walked out the back door passed the park and was summoned by *Littlez* his ex girlfriend who was sitting on the bench alongside the gate.

She watched her two younger sisters playing in the park as Woodz greeted her with a kiss on her cheek.

"What up Littlez?" Their history stemmed back to late 1994 where they met. She lived two floors above him and used to over hear his conversations with Maya. Their relationship only lasted about a year but they maintained a friendship that sometimes crossed the line. Her little sister Laura had a crush on Woodz and rushed towards him to hug him as soon as he sat down next to Littlez.

Littlez shooed Laura away and gave Woodz a naughty look.

"Hmm . . . I heard about you . . . why you got half naked bitches hangin' out your window??" Woodz ducked a playful slap to the back of his head and denied any wrong doing.

"Chill Littlez I don't know what you talking about . . . you the only girl I wanna' have half naked anywhere." They both laughed and he noticed Littlez was blushing. He squeezed on her right thick thigh and she tried to kick him with her other leg but Woodz hopped off the bench and exited out the park. "Love you Littlez!"

He crossed the street into the other park and found Capone and Thugged Out sitting on the bench. The trio chilled and spoke about the squad, L.B.'s and ofcourse the show in the window today. At around 9:30 Thugged Out and Woodz met up with Mark in 1485. He was in the staircase on his floor with Greg already cracking two dutches and dumping the tobacco all over the floor.

"Whats good my nigga's?" Thugged Out and Woodz gave pounds to Mark and Greg and began rolling up their own dutch. They all listened to the **L.O.X** *We Are The Streets* tape. Mark and Greg became cool with Woodz after he had a fight with Taino. The scuffle was over a girl name Rosy and Woodz surprised many and even him self when he proved that he was strong enough to tussle with the bigger Taino.

Greg was a new face in Clinton and knew Mark since Junior High School. He was from Foster Projects and was the comedian of the two, whereas Mark was the quieter one. Greg wasn't as flashy as his boy but he always kept fresh cornrow braids and money in his pocket. Greg and Mark were complete opposites but they were best friends, and both were dying to know about Woodz new girl flash and when she was coming back.

"Yo Woodz what up with the big titty bitch? She a L.B.?" The four of them sat in the staircase rotating the L's counter clockwise. Woodz took a long toke from his L' and passed it to Mark.

"I guess so but she's on a nigga's dick hard body ya' heard so I told her to start bringing some friends up here for all of ya'." Greg nodded his head and chuckled.

"Yo' I never met a lil' nigga' like you . . . no offense my nigga' you know what I mean." Woodz nodded his head. Greg Continued. "I could fuck wit' ya' L.B. nigga's word." Mark was tired of listening to Greg.

"Nigga'! Pass the fuckin' dutch damn nigga'! And get off my man's joint B'! Straight cheese!"

"Fuck you nigga'!" They all laughed and stayed in the hallway for about twenty more minutes before they finally wrapped it up and bounced. After they rode the elevator downstairs Mark and Greg sparked up their New Port Cigarettes to boost up their highs. Woodz took one too but not Thugged Out. Greg blasted the **L.O.X** tape and the group made their way towards Lexington Avenue.

It was a good day for Woodz so to cap the night off he smoked an L' upstairs with his brother Pedro. Woodz placed a towel under his door and lit up the clip of Skunk he had in his stash. He retold the window episode to Pedro who couldn't stop laughing.

"Yo' mo' you the illest . . . ya' nigga's is crazy and where shorty from?" Pedro asked Woodz who passed him the L'.

"She from L.E.S. Yo' Pay I had these nigga's thirsty B' word . . . shit was crazy." Woodz stared at the smoke that Pedro was blowing out the window and smiled to himself. He listened to Pedro strike up a convo with a female over the walkie name Purple Haze. He knew who she was and while his brother spoke to her he thought about the rest of the year and felt very optimistic.

Pedro left minutes later and Woodz watched his brother walk under the trees towards the train station. He stayed in the window talking on the walkie and felt at peace at his window. His window was the gateway to his world . . . Hollywood's world.

Woodz live on the mic! 109th Street 1999

CHAPTER 8

The Chase

The wind slammed against Woodz face as he turned around to look back at the unmarked vehicle pursuing him up 113th Street towards Pleasant Avenue. His heart was pounding and adrenaline rushed through his body, but he rode the stolen *Honda Elite* moped like a true rider! The looks on the Detectives faces were stone cold and nothing less than grim. They knew all too well that any hoodlum riding around on a moped only meant one thing, robbery.

The two middle aged Caucasian men hoped that Woodz hit a speed bump, cat, or just crashed! However that wouldn't be the case tonight. The Jefferson Park entrance on Pleasant Avenue was up ahead and Woodz wasn't thinking twice about jumping the curb. He just prayed that he would be able to maneuver through the metal pillars that stood parallel from each other. The wrong bounce could mean disaster for him.

He braced himself, sat up slightly and crouched over the steering bars and made the jump! ***Vroooom!!*** A group of guys standing in front of a Bodega on 114th Street on the corner across the street all shouted and cheered him on as they watch the moped fly through the air avoiding capture from the detectives.

The black *Crown Royal* came to a screeching stop as Woodz successfully jumped the curb and rode perfectly through the metal pillars evading capture. He quickly rode the moped aside the deserted football field, looking back at his pursuers who had stopped and were now changing course. Neither he nor the detectives could believe he had made the jump.

"Fuck ya' mothafucka's! Ha ha." He enjoyed his moment of triumph but victory wasn't his yet. Now he had to make it back to Clinton! "This wasn't part of the fuckin' plan man fuck!!"

*   *   *

The breezy Friday began downtown at City Hall. Woodz tagged along with Thugged Out and his cousin *Luigi* from 117th Street. Thugged Out was picking up a certificate of completion from 2 days of community service. Luigi resembled the actor *John Leguizamo* and was always teased and bullied by Woodz and the others. He was Thugged Out's little man and wanted to establish some props by cutting school and rolling with him and Woodz downtown.

They made their way towards the train station and as they descended down the stairs they were pulled over by a Truancy officer who was posted behind an office door on the platform. The officer asked for their I. D.s and both Woodz and Thugged Out produced their school I. D.s Unfortunately the 14year old Luigi didn't have a school I.D. and was taken away on a bus filled with other traunties. Woodz couldn't stop laughing.

"Ha ha yo' that was crazy! You see all them lil' nigga's on the bus?! Ha ha that's good for Luigi's lil' stupid ass!"

"Chill nigga'! That shit ain't funny dogz! His pops is gonna' bust his ass for this, damn!" Thugged Out was fuming while Woodz continue to snigger. A messenger riding by on a moped suddenly caught Thugged Out's attention and gave him a brilliant idea . . . they needed a moped! "Yo' let's walk back to the block." He suggested. His eyes still fixed on the moped stopping at the red light about 20 ft. away from them. Woodz twisted his face.

"Walk?? K' I don't feel like walkin' back . . ." Thugged Out pointed at the moped riding off before Woodz could finish his rebuttal. Woodz quickly got the picture. "Nigga' . . . you serious?"

"I got this dogz c'mon." Thugged Out was infamous for stealing mopeds, bikes and even cars when he was lucky. The duo started the trek up

Broadway, scanning every street and alley for a parked or mobile moped. By the time they reached **Madison Square Garden** Woodz legs started aching and hunger was kicking in.

"Yo' buy some chips or something I'm starvin' nigga'." He stood in front of a gift shop while Thugged Out went into a Grocery Store to purchase something for them to snack on. They stood in front of the gift shop eating Little Debbie cakes sharing an Orangina juice. "Yo' you got us walkin' for noffin' nigga'. We ain't see a scooter yet yo', snatch a bike or car or somethin' nigga' fuck it!" Woodz was impatient but Thugged Out didn't respond. He kept his eyes focused on the area for mopeds and Truancy officers.

They resumed their trek up the avenue and after walking up about 20 more blocks Thugged Out finally spotted his prize pulling up to an office building across the street.

"I told you nigga'! That's us right there!" He exclaimed.

"You's a lucky mothafucka' K'." Woodz could only laugh. They watched an Asian messenger hop off leaving the moped parked in between two large delivery trucks as he disappeared into the giant office building. Another huge truck pulled up also at the red light giving them an excellent block. Woodz was hesitant but ran across the street behind Thugged out to get it over with. Thugged Out tried to pop the steering break off and did, but couldn't start it.

"Hop on!" He shouted at Woodz. "I'ma wheel this shit across the street."

"What?!" Woodz shot back. "Nigga' you buggin'! Is broad daylight out here!" He was hesitant again but hopped on as they both kicked pushed the moped across the street. "Nigga' you crazy."

"Fuck that! Aight move." Woodz hopped off and kept a look out as Thugged Out hot wired the moped. It took a couple of seconds before it came to life. "Hop on nigga'! We out!" Woodz held on to Thugged Out's shoulder and the two sped off towards the east side, quickly reaching 5th Avenue then Madison and Park Avenue. "Yea nigga'! I told you we was gonna' ride home!"

They made it back uptown and stashed the moped in Woodz room to buy some time eating Pops cereal. The gasoline smell was too much in the apartment so they brought the moped back downstairs to ride around in the basketball court until the rest of the squad assembled. People crowded in the basketball court asking Thugged Out for rides. Having a moped on the block was like having a Benz or Beamer!

L.J. was Woodz boy from 108th Street on Madison Avenue. The 6 ft. light skinned black and Puertorican Madison native went to New York Prep, graduated along with Woodz and was now attending Park East High School also. He had been a part of the N.W.O. craze that gave birth to L.B.M. so they had a good comradery and friendship. L.J. had a well liked personality through out Clinton. With his sense of humor, excellent ball skills, he was admired and the fellas loved smoking and drinking with him or just hanging out with him period.

L.J. was part of F.E.B so he was also well respected by both friends and foes. He strolled into the basketball court to where Woodz was standing watching Thugged Out ride two kids from the block on the moped.

"Ya' nigga's is sick. Who's shit is that Ant? That's ya' shit?" Woodz turned and greeted L.J. cracking a wide smile.

"Yea it's us, what up? Wanna ride?"

"Shit yea. I wanna' ride to the smoke spot right quick, ask this crazy nigga' to let you hold it for a minute and take the ride with me."

"He'll let you rock ask em'. Plus we need someone to take it off our hands for a minute." L.J. really didn't get along with Thugged Out but he didn't feel like walking all the way to 124th Street. He approached Thugged Out who had come to a halt on the moped.

"Kenny what up nigga', let me get a quick ride to the smoke spot. I'll bring the shit right back ya' heard." Thugged Out didn't trust L.J. with the moped, not after they lost a moped in Madison after stashing it in L. J's old abandoned apartment.

"What spot L'?"

"Second Ave nigga' I ain't going far, I'll be right back." Thugged Out looked over at Woodz who nodded his head in approval and climbed off the moped to hand it to L.J. "Yo' Ant ride wit' me c'mon." Woodz agreed to tag along only to put Thugged Out at ease. He knew that Thugged Out didn't trust L.J. with the ride but he did.

"K' I'll call you down when we get back aight?" Thugged Out nodded his head and jogged off towards his building. L.J. rode down 110th Street towards First Avenue. "L' I thought you said Second Ave?"

"Yea nigga' but I didn't say what street! Fuck you Kenny! Ha ha." They both laughed as L.J. sped and cut through traffic while Woodz kept an eye out for *pepa*/police.

It took L.J. a few minutes to handle his biz inside the Caribbean spot on 124th Street. He rode them towards New York Prep and parked in front of the school.

"Why we comin' here for?" Asked Woodz.

"I need to holla at this nigga' Ern real quick." Ern was their old gym teacher *Ernest.* Woodz circled the dead end street until L.J. came back out. "Yo' let's ride through Park East real quick, see what bitches is out there." Woodz was for it and enjoyed the ride over to the East.

It was about 2:45 and students had begun spilling out of the school. He and L.J. greeted a few people then decided to head back to the block. They hit Third Avenue where Woodz spotted his boy *Virgilio* aka **Gigilo** walking home along with his sister and cousins.

Gigilo raised his hands in the air as they flew by on the moped. Woodz loved the attention they were getting.

They finally returned to Clinton and L.J. parked the moped in front of 1760.

"Yo' what up, wanna' smoke wit' me nigga'?" He asked Woodz.

"I'm good L' good lookin', I'ma wait for this nigga' to come get this shit." L.J. thanked Woodz and made his way back to Madison Avenue. Woodz called Thugged Out from the intercom and by the time he came downstairs, Ace, Rabbit and a few other people were outside waiting for their rides on the moped.

*   *   *

Night fell over the Barrio and both Thugged Out and Woodz needed to stash their stolen ride before it got too late. The duo rode over to Jefferson projects where Thugged Out's goon *Troy* aka **T-Roy** lived. Thugged Out knocked on his first floor window. The night was chilly and damped so he and Woodz wanted to be back on the block pronto. T-Roy finally appeared in his window, but half naked.

"Put some clothes on nigga'! Crackhead lookin' ass mothafucka'!" Woodz laughed as T-Roy put on a pair of sweat pants and cursed out Thugged Out. He was Thugged Out's number one henchman, a lanky, goofy lookin' Moreno. "Come outside and take this scooter in your room for the night . . . I'll come get it tomorrow my nigga'." T-Roy quickly shook his head no.

"Nah nigga' my pops is here, he aint' gonna' let me keep that shit in here hell naw!" Woodz relaxed on the moped on the sidewalk listening to the two fools argue, until he felt a car pulling up behind him. He looked over his shoulder and quickly recognized the black unmarked vehicle.

"Oh shit!" He uttered and kick started the moped, riding off through the parking lot on 112th Street. Thugged Out stood frozen in front of T-Roy's window who wasted no time disappearing from view. He watched the black Crown Royal drive up onto the sidewalk and speed through the projects towards First Avenue, then yelled at T-Roy to go to sleep and followed the car hoping that Woodz got away safely

*   *   *

Just when Woodz thought the hard part was over now he had to abandon the moped, dodge pepa and make it back home! He laid the moped under the F.D.R Drive bridge and ran down towards 106th Street as fast as he could. He reached the entrance of a schoolyard and peeked from behind the wall of the building and spotted a blue and white police cruiser parked in the middle of the street facing First Avenue!

He cursed under his breath and tried to remain calm, realizing that leaving the moped behind was a smart move. It was completely dark inside the schoolyard so he decided to kneel down and tip toed his way over to a cluster of benches and tables for cover. He made it over and squatted down taking deep breaths. "Aight . . . they'll break out . . . c'mon bounce already mothafucka's."

The blue and white cruiser finally pulled away about ten minutes later, slowly turning the corner of First Avenue and driving off. Woodz didn't waste any time. He jogged towards the entrance and out the yard, and sprinted through Franklin Plaza. He ran all the way to his building like a thief in the night and flew up the ten flights of stairs, quickly opening his door. Big Tee was sitting in the living room watching T.V. and looked up at the clock on the wall.

"Uhhh your late." He plainly stated. Woodz relaxed and took a seat next to his big brother, he never felt so good seeing Big Tee as he did at the moment.

"Damn . . . 12:30? Damn I got caught up with the girls Tee, you know how it is." He threw playful punches at his brother and stood up to go to his room.

"There's food for you in the kitchen if you hungry!" Big Tee yelled out. He relaxed as his younger brother walked into the kitchen. Another late night but he was safe.

Woodz looked out his window feeling the breeze of the night. Suddenly he spotted Thugged Out walking down towards Lexington from Park Avenue walkie talky in hand. Woodz switched his mic on.

"Yo' Hollywood that's you?"

"Yea nigga'!" Thugged Out began jumping up and down frantically.

"My nigga'! How the fuck you get away!?" Woodz waived him upstairs. Thugged Out made it upstairs and Woodz wasted no time retelling the story of how he got away.

"Damn nigga' I had to leave the scooter behind dogz . . . let's go check in the morning to see if it's still there."

"Fuck that scooter my nigga' we'll just get another one you know how we do." They ate some left over Arroz con Pollo before Thugged Out went home.

Woodz thought about the night he had. Was it cleverness, luck or fate how he gotten away? He stared out the window and it never felt so good inhaling the air into his lungs and taking sips of his Pepsi. He knew that he flirted with danger tonight, but he felt excited! The rush and thrill of danger that a soldier at war probably felt, he thought to himself. He took a long hot shower then spoke on the mic afterward until he fell asleep. The chase was done for the night, but it was far from over.

CHAPTER 9

2000

"10! 9! 8! 7! 6! 5! 4! 3! 2! 1! HAPPY NEW YEAR!!"
Woodz and his family welcomed New Year's in with
excitement and tears of joy. The year 2000 had finally
arrived! The Y2K Bug rumor was the talk of the world
but the electricity didn't shut off, and the world didn't
explode. The new millennium was at hand and for
Woodz it meant time to look towards the future and
leave the past behind.

His L.B.M. squad made it through another year
sustaining bumps and bruises along the way but
remained in tact. The New Year meant new grinds,
swag, and elevating to a higher level. Technology was
evolving, the Internet was changing the world, and the
dirty south was taking over Hip-Hop! In the aftermath
of the east coast/west coast rap war, upcoming new
artist like *Ludacris* and *Nelly* were kicking down the

door of Southern Hip-Hop other artists had slowly opened in the past. Best of all, Woodz was turning 18 in two months!

On hand celebrating New Years was his uncle *Guidi*, Pedro, Momma Luv, Big Tee and a few L.B. Masters. 1999 had been a roller coaster year for Woodz. His relationships with both Sonia and Melly, his hustle with Big Cat turning sour, ducking jail a few times, and his bumpy year at Park East where his grades were the poorest they've ever been in his life.

His crummy senior year was the result of him hanging out late, sometimes all night! And not only smoking and drinking, but from taking part in the new craze for him on 109th robbing and beating up Mexicans. They called it *catchin' a vic* and it was becoming a trend on not only Lexington and Park Avenue, but pretty much all around the city. His disregard for he rules at home kept him in constant drama with Momma Luv and his brothers and sisters.

Margarita found herself too overwhelmed to deal with Woodz and his rebellious ways. She knew they didn't have the life of the rich and famous but she did her best to make sure her son had clothes on his back, food in his stomach, and a roof over his head.

Unfortunately there was only so much she can do. Woodz realized by early march that he wasn't going to graduate from High School with the Class Of 2000. His G.P.A. was below his average and he was failing almost five classes every semester. His failure bothered him deeply and enraged both Pedro and Tito, but he ignored the stress and scrutiny and focused his attention on upcoming Birthdays. Thugged Out, Rabbit, and Capone's were all in late February/mid March, where as his fell on March 23rd. The three of them were Pisces and he was an Aries. His Birthday was always proven to be the icing on the cake.

*Jacob **Jakkes** Lopez* lived on the 5th floor in Woodz building with his mother and two brothers. He was the third oldest of four and the jester of Clinton projects. A young chubby John Candy looking Puertorican kid who you did not want to banter with! He was relentless with jokes and had established his comedic reputation from the second he moved into Clinton. Jakkes began hanging out with Woodz steadily after Capone and him made cassette tapes of secrets about everybody in Clinton. If anybody loved to gossip it was him!

Although Woodz' birthday fell on a cold night in March the streets were hot, so they remained upstairs celebrating. Woodz kept the word about his B-Day on the low and only invited Jakkes, Capone, and Rabbit. Big Tee presented the birthday boy with a fresh bottle of **Bacardi Limon** to compliment the bottle of **Smirnoff Vodka** that Capone's cousin *Lisette* purchased for them. After a brief talk with both Pedro and Tito, Woodz relaxed with the fellas who were listening to *Hot 97*, and filling cups up with their *Vodka.*

Woodz took sips of the **Vodka** enjoying their company. Tito and Pedro had drilled him again about his lack of responsibility and the session left him feeling gloomy. He was snapped out of this zone by Tito's voice calling him.

"Someone's at the door for you!!" Woodz turned down the music that drowned Tito's voice. Tito repeated it again.

"Who is it Tee!?" Now it was the barks of the two dogs they had that made it impossible to hear anything. Big Tee escorted the unannounced visitor towards the room as the fellas asked Woodz who it was. Woodz wasn't looking forward for anybody else showing up, but before he could open the door himself three young ladies appeared in his doorway. It was Jerilyn and she wasn't alone!

Woodz started howling and wooing. He couldn't believe Jerilyn's timing, he had to be the luckiest bastard in the world! *Oh, I gotta' be da' fuckin' man boy!* He thought to himself, looking over at the fellas who were stuck off the girls. Jakkes began grabbing and pulling on Capone asking him if he knew who the girls were. Woodz finally addressed his guest.

"Jerilyn! What da fluck is you doin' here?" He smiled from ear to ear feeling the drinks take effect. He sipped his drink and wiped his mouth.

"Nigga'! What happened to your phone? I be calling you and you neva' pick the shit up . . . the voice mail always pick it up." Woodz forgot about the blue *Motorola* flip phone that he bought from a girl in

Thugged Out's building name *Jezzy*. The phone was stolen so he only had it for less than a month.

"Oh . . . damn ma' I been got rid of that shit, shit was hot ya heard? My bad . . ." Woodz quickly turned his attention to her two friends who were looking around the room, awaiting their introductions. "Jerilyn, introduce these two lovely girlfriends of yours." Jerilyn pointed to her brown skinned friend name *Cristina* and her other friend's name was *Angela*. Both girls were Dominican and very attractive. "Aight ok, well ladies these are three of my partners in crime. That's Melvin, Chris, and that's Jacob."

As the fellas greeted the girls Capone fixed his gaze on Cristina who was noticing the bottles of *Bacardi* and *Smirnoff*. She asked Woodz if they were having a party. "Well Cristina . . . it just so happens that we're in the middle of a toast . . . it's my birthday." Jerilyn's eyes bulged as she smiled at Woodz.

She tossed her coat on the bed and grabbed his drink out of his hand to sit on his lap. She kissed him and glanced up at her friends who looked at one another and took their jackets off also.

"Rabbit pour the girls a drink and let em' get comfy." said Woodz. Rabbit did and cranked up the music, then raised his glass up and proposed the birthday toast for the birthday boy.

"Happy Birthday my nigga'! L.B.!" The fellas and girls raised their glasses and the party was on. The tunes of **Beenie Man** flowed through the speakers and filled Woodz room. Jerilyn grind her ass on Woodz lap while he tried to hold on to his drink. Jakkes tried to get Angela to dance and Capone had Cristina's ear running his game on her.

Rabbit floated around the room feeling out of place but enjoyed watching his idol at work, cracking up watching Angela fight off Jakkes. She called him crazy and planted herself back on the bed chiming into Capone's and Cristina's conversation. The girl's got open off the drinks but gave Jakkes no play. He finally gave up and decided to get some air outside.

"Yo Hollywood I'ma go downstairs I'll be back" Woodz quickly interjected.

"Nah Jakkes! If you bounce don't come back up . . . ain't no revolving doors up here tonight." Woodz clearly saw that his boy wasn't getting any play and neither was Rabbit, but they knew the rules to the game. Rabbit motioned to Woodz that he was leaving also. Jakkes gave Capone a pound and Woodz a bear hug.

"I'm out ya' be easy, you coming Rab?" Rabbit followed Jakkes out the door. Angela walked over to the window while Woodz scanned her body from head to toe. *Damn shorty is right.* Jerilyn stepped off to the bathroom giving him a moment to examine her lovely associates. Angela had curly light brown hair and a deep Dominican accent. Cristina had straight dark hair that touched her shoulder's, both had full lips, hips, and beautiful faces the total package! It was why Woodz loved Dominican girls.

Cristina was teasing Capone and started dancing with Jerilyn when she returned to the room. They took shots of Bacardi while Capone nodded his head at Woodz who was keeping Angela company by the window.

"Angela whut up? You aight?" She shrugged her shoulders.

"I don't know . . . I feel a lil' outta place now . . . I like yo view nigga." Woodz needed to get somebody up there quick to even things up with the girls before Angela spoiled it for Capone and him, but who!? He looked out the window inhaling Angela's perfume and spotted Greg on the corner with his radio. It was worth a shot he thought.

"GEE! What up my nigga'!!

"Yo'! It's my birthday nigga' holla!" yelled Greg.

"Mines too nigga'! What up?! Come up!" Woodz replied. Greg wouldn't have mind going upstairs but Mark and him had plans.

"Yo' come down! We got liqs' me and Mark nigga'!" Woodz still motioned for Greg to come upstairs as Angela left him to refill her drink. "I'm with Mark! We bout to go do us!" Greg repeated again to Woodz who kept waving him upstairs. Greg hollered at Mark who was standing in front of the Liquor store on the corner, he told Greg to hold on while he worked on getting their bottle of Hennessy for them. Woodz realized that he had to use some bait to lure Greg upstairs.

He grabbed Angela by the waist and pulled her back over to the window drink in hand and told her to say hi to Greg. Greg laughed and waved back also. He wasn't surprised to see a girl in Woodz window but then he saw another girl stand by Woodz other side!

Jerilyn had walked over to the window to be nosy and started waving at Gee also. Woodz began bouncing to the music playing from the stereo, palming the girl's asses with his hands. He knew fully well that he had Gees full attention now. Capone emerged from the other window then allowed Cristina to stick her head out also and call out to Gee. All three girls yelled out his name giggling and sipping on their drinks as Gee's jaw dropped seeing the girls waving to him from Woodz window.

"Last chance nigga' you coming up!?" Woodz asked. It didn't take Gee long to make up his mind now.

"I'll be right up!" He answered. Gee yelled something at Mark who was still inside the liquor store and made his way towards Woodz building. Woodz heard the chihuahuas barking in the hallway indicating that Gee had arrived. The Taco Bell chihuahua chased Gee down the hall way until he opened Woodz door. He quickly scanned the girl's sitting around and smiled then greeted Woodz. "Happy Birthday my nigga'!" Gee handed Woodz a bottle of **Long Island Ice Tea**, one of Woodz favorite drinks!

He took a better look at the girls and immediately recognized Jerilyn sitting by the window. "Oh shit big titties is here? What up girl!" Jerilyn and the girls broke out laughing as he gave her a hug. Woodz realized that Gee was the perfect fit to complete the trio. Gee revealed two already rolled up L's and the party was on again! Woodz sparked up the first L' as Gee took his seat next to Angela and they immediately hit it off.

The light was dimmed and the blunt was passed around and everyone took pulls by the window. The bunch mellowed down and the mood became more intimate. Jerilyn took her seat on Woodz lap again kissing him and exposing her breast for him to suck on. She worked her hand down his jeans and pulled out his hard on. Woodz sat back as she lowered her head and wrapped her tongue around his shaft. He scanned the dark cloudy room as Jerilyn's head bopped up and down on his lap, noticing that not only was Capone and Cristina submerged underneath jackets and his quilt, but so was Gee and Angela!

Suddenly he smelled a familiar odor mixed in with the liquor and weed aroma. It was sex, someone was fucking!

"Yo'? Which one of ya' is fuckin' in there man!" He laughed and watched the submerged bodies squirm around hearing moans and laughter.

The party was over about an hour later and the bunch headed downstairs to get some air. Jakkes rejoined them as Gee and Woodz sparked the other blunt in the park. The girls eventually hopped into a cab and returned home. For Woodz it couldn't have been a sweeter birthday . . . it was his best B-day thus far!

*   *   *

As expected Woodz failed to graduate from High School so he would have to repeat his senior year once the summer was over. After his birthday he missed about 50 days of school due to always being too hung over from drinking and smoking, and stressed over Momma' Luv getting sick. It caused arguments between him and his siblings because they kept him in the dark about her illness and about their family history in all. One day of missing school quickly multiplied and it cost him big time.

The early summer of 2000 was filled with all sorts of peaks and valleys. Rapper **Big Pun** had died, the N.W.O. had officially disbanded, and his L.B.M. Squad was once again facing adversity. R-Dee and Thugged Out were clashing once again and it was affecting everyone. Missing in action was Rabbit who was now involved with a girl name *Maria* from Woodz building and who he knew very well. No one knew what J.O.'s story was. He was still hustling and smoking his life away totally disconnected from the squad in all.

The rest of the pack had followed R-Dee to 111th street between Lexington and Third Avenue to take over. Eventually Woodz and Thugged Out followed suit and had no problem in making 111th their new stomping grounds. The natives of 111th had already embraced Rudy, Pretty Boy, Malcolm and Isaiah but Woodz and Thugged Out weren't concerned about being welcomed, all they were concerned about was finding new L.B. Material!

Of course it didn't take long for the dynamic duo to make their mark. Thugged Out hit it off with a lovely slim Puertorican girl name *Desiree*. Whereas Woodz started messing around with Desiree's best friend *Nina*, a short cutie with a baby face but the bad girl attitude Woodz loved.

Back in Clinton Thugged Out began making moves with a kid name *Jasper* who had just moved into his building from the Bronx. Jasper a blancito Puertorican wasn't so social with anybody from Clinton except Thugged Out who he purchased his smoke from. He drove a red Suzuki Jeep, which became his trademark in Clinton and eventually Thugged Out and Woodz bat mobile!

Jasper became an unofficial L.B. Master who was embraced by most of the squad then introduced and spoiled Thugged Out to the joys of driving.

*   *   *

The **_Puerto Rican Day Festival_** and **Parade** arrived in June and Thugged Out made moves to be a part of the parade. All he needed was a vehicle to supply music for the Baton Dancers and escort an important representative of Puerto Rico so he convinced Jasper to come along and provide his jeep. Jasper invited his younger brother Louie to tag along and Thugged Out included Woodz and Rabbit in the event. It was a dream come true for Woodz who saw it as an opportunity to enhance not only his swag, but more so his reign in his Hollywood world.

They arrived on 43rd street an hour before the parade was scheduled to begin on the hot sticky June morning. There were floats and dancers everywhere. Vehicles were lined up the block towards 5th Avenue and the temperature was expected to hit the mid 90s!

"Damn it's fuckin' hot yo'!" Woodz exclaimed. He and the fellas hung around the jeep observing the scene around them in the scorching heat. Luckily for them water and ice cups was being handed out by parade organizers. Jasper sat in his jeep with a wet towel wrapped around his bald white head.

"Yo nigga' I can't believe I let you talk me in this shit bro." He said to Thugged Out. "I'm hot and fuckin' tired dogs! I worked all night yesterday and wanted to stay in bed today nigga' . . . I'm fuckin' twisted right now." Thugged Out poured his cup of ice cold water over his towel and told him to cool off. Woodz laughed and shook his head. He wasn't complaining about the heat and ignored whoever was complaining, as far as he knew he was where he belonged in the spot light. He scanned the cluttered street hoping to see celebrities but the only celebrity they met was **D.J. Tony Touch** from Brooklyn.

The parade was finally underway so they all hopped on the jeep wooing and shouting at the top of their lungs. Woodz and Thugged Out took off their shirts and wrapped them around their heads. Woodz also placed a bunch of mini Puertorican flags into the shirt on his head, he was psyched! They reached the corner of 5th Avenue and as they awaited the signal to join the parade two girls ran up to the jeep hollering for Woodz to give them one of his flags. He gave them both a flag and watched as they giggled and jumped up and down thanking him frantically. Louie laughed.

"Yo kid, you got groupies already!" Woodz gave him an embarrassed look. When he turned his attention to the sea of people around him all he could do was look in awe. The parade was full of life! There were screams, laughter, love, flags and endless energy all simmering in 90 degrees of pure heat! The jeep slowly made its way down 5th Avenue driving behind their coordinator and the kids dancing to the classic **Hector Lavoe** song, *El Cantante*. The fellas jumped around, yelled, laughed and waved their flags. Woodz had loved it when his family used to attend the parades every year, now it seemed as if they lost their passion for the celebration and had become too lazy to even watch it on T.V.

For Woodz and the fellas it was a dream come true to be part of the parade. Thugged Out was actually Dominican but he showed Boriqua love anyway. Twenty minutes into their march The Baton Dancers were too hot to dance and began to lose steam. They were walking more rather than dancing and Woodz was feeling the same, but was really getting tired of the Hector Lavoe song playing over and over. The heat was taking its toll on all of them except for Louie who was getting upset that the fellas were losing their steam as well.

"Ayo ya' nigga's is wack what up!? Ya' tired? Hot?? We in the P.R. Parade nigga's! Ya' nigga's . . ." Woodz knew Louie was right and had an idea.

"Yo' this is fuckin' up my moment man . . . Jasp' throw on that Kool Kirk C.D." Woodz placed his hand on Louie's shoulder. "You ready to wild out and make it live my nigga'? Let's turn up the heat!"

"Lets do it nigga'! Boriqua baby!" Louie answered. Woodz splashed his cup of water across his face.

"Jasp blast that shit!" He shouted and in seconds the sound of *Swizz Beatz* and the *L.O.X.'s* *Wild Out* song blended with *Black Rob's* *Whoa*!! song cranked out the jeep's speakers. The crowd seem confused at first but as soon as the fellas started rocking the jeep from side to side yelling out *PUERTO RICO* and *BORIQUA!* It sent the crowd into a frenzy. Rabbit hopped off the jeep and grabbed a huge Puerto Rico flag then began circling the jeep waving the flag, he slapped fives with the crowd as Woodz and the fellas continued to wile them up.

No one in the crowd knew the guys in the red jeep, but they were having fun and representing Puerto Rico so they loved it. The girls in the crowd were going crazy and the jeep was now surrounded by other marchers who were holding up huge posters and banners of Big Pun. Even the kids were dancing and having fun again and their guest in the jeep who was quietly waving at the crowd seem to enjoy their hysteria. Woodz and Louie nodded their heads in satisfaction, they were losing their voices but it was worth it!

Woodz wished that he had a microphone or bullhorn. He had hundreds if not thousands of people cheering him on like a superstar . . . it was the greatest moment of his life. Up ahead a girl wearing a tight red dancing uniform was running towards the jeep. She was part of a dance group that had left her behind now she hoped to tag along with the mystery red jeep that was electrifying the crowd. Woodz looked behind him where she was trailing the jeep.

"Needa' ride?!" He asked. The pretty tanned girl smiled up at him biting her lips. Woodz did a double take and realized that the girl was gorgeous! Thugged Out and Louie looked at each other clueless but Woodz didn't think twice. He reached down and grabbed her hand while Rabbit boosted her up from behind. She wrapped her arms around him giggling and exhausted from the heat. Jasper continued ascending up 5th Avenue honking his horn with a wide smile across his face. Woodz took a quick time out to meet their lovely hitch hiker.

"What's your name!"

"*Vanessa*! Wooo!!" She answered snatching his last flag from his shirt to wave it.

"What happened?! You got left behind?!" He asked flashing a quick smile at Louie who continued to holler at the crowd.

"Yeaaa but I'm glad I did now! You cute you know that?! BORIQUA!!" Woodz cracked a big smile and looked around at the thousands of people on 5th Avenue. He hoped that they were being recorded on T.V. Thugged Out tapped his right arm and pointed towards the crowd on the corner of 65th Street. He spotted Cypha, Boobop, and *Brian* a skinny black kid who lived in Thugged Out's building. The three of them were waving their hands yelling out L.B.

With the jeep making abrupt stops Woodz told Vanessa to stand in front of him so she wouldn't fall off the jeep. She stood in front of him while he held onto the jeep's roof top feeling the heat of her body.

"Yo don't get mad at me if you feel something pokin' you aight? It's hot as a motha'fucka' and so are you ma!" He whispered in her ear. Vanessa turned her head back at him and smiled.

"I won't!" She answered. Jasper repeated the **Kool Kirk** *Wild Out* mix again as the jeep made its way towards 86th Street. They all started rocking the jeep again while Vanessa and Woodz bodies grind on one another. The crowd cheered them on as she fed him ice from a cup that Thugged Out passed her. Woodz had stolen the show!

No unauthorized vehicles were allowed to drive down 86th Street so the Puerto Rico representative who rode in the passenger side had to get out the jeep and walk along with the Baton Girls. The fellas wished they could finish the ride with them.

"Senora we hope that you didn't mind us having a little fun!" Said Woodz, glued onto Vanessa.

"Ahi no mijo I had a fabulous time . . . you all get home safe okay?" Senora Martinez slammed the jeep's door behind her and Jasper drove off up 5th Avenue. They all laughed and regained their composure as they zoomed towards 96th Street. Jasper drove down to Madison Avenue feeling totally out of energy but proud of the experience.

"Yea nigga's! That's what the fuck I'm talkin' about! Ya' saw how hype we had everybody?!" Louie exclaimed. His voice was just about completely gone and so was Woodz, who spoke quietly into Vanessa's ear.

"Gotta' man?"

"Uhm sort of . . . yea." Answered Vanessa regretfully.

"Can I call you? Holla' at you? What up we can't end it like this." Jasper sped off towards 3rd Avenue with the *Kool Kirk* C.D. blasting while the fellas continued yelling at the people both returning and heading to the parade. Vanessa turned her body to face Woodz. She held onto his arms and smiled at him.

"I do gotta' man sweetie and I'm not that type of girl . . . I had fun with you all of ya', pero no puedo." Woodz scanned Vanessa's brown glistening perspired body trying to accept the fact that he may never see her again. He smiled at her and nodded his head in respect to her position. He was having too much of a perfect day to let getting shot down by her ruin everything. They reached 111th Street and parked on the corner of 3rd Avenue where Vanessa hopped out the jeep and thanked the fellas.

"I'm going to Taino Towers so I could walk." She looked at Woodz one more time and read his mind. "I'm sorry sweetie . . . I'll never forget you alright . . ." She blew a kiss at Woodz and disappeared through the crowd.

Jasper dropped off Thugged Out, Rabbit and Woodz then gave his brother Louie the Keys to the jeep.

"I'm going upstairs to sleep fuck that." Louie thanked the fellas for an incredible day and drove off. Woodz thought about the day all night. It was the highest point of his life thus far, Hollywoodz life! Although he didn't get to capture Vanessa he was more than satisfied with the experience of actually being a part of the **Puerto Rican Day Parade.**

CHAPTER 10

Struggle For Power

With the summer over Woodz was getting ready to repeat the 12th grade and would have to attend night school on 96th street on First Avenue. He needed to make up two credits if he was hoping to make a 2001 graduation possible. It was bittersweet news in the aftermath of Thugged Out and him having their first real fight a few weeks before school started. Woodz sat in Science class replaying the events that led up to the fight in his head.

Thugged Out and Capone met some girls over the C.B. radio from Taft projects. A short baby face Puertorican girl name *Katie* aka **Mami Chula** and *Jenny* aka **Foxy**. Jenny was also short, thick and a lot feistier than Katie. Capone met both girls face to face but was attracted more to the easy going baby face Mamichula. He arranged to meet Katie on 110th

on Park Avenue and brought Woodz along so that he could maybe hit it off with one of her friends.

Woodz played the sideline watching his boy tower over his new shorty getting his swerve on. Katie had light brown and reddish hair down to her shoulders, She was dressed fly and was a very cute Puertorican blancita Woodz thought, impressed with Capone's fine catch.

Woodz didn't hit it off with any of her friends but did take a liking to her cousin *Cali* aka ***White Thong***. Thugged out also met White Thong and immediately was infatuated with the brown skinned beauty. He maintained his relationship with Desiree and secretly formed one also with White Thong who had no clue about his girl Desiree.

Woodz and Nina's relationship had fizzled out but he kept a friendship with Desiree who unknown to him had her own infatuation with him! Eventually rumors began floating around about Desiree having feelings for him while other rumors of Woodz and White Thong messing around also started surfacing.

It didn't take long for White Thong to find out about Desiree and she put Thugged Out in a position to either choose between Desiree and her. Thugged Out believed that Woodz was behind his spot being blown up and it was the last straw for him! It would all hit the fan on a Saturday afternoon when Woodz, R-Dee, Ace and Rabbit were walking down 109th towards Lexington Avenue discussing a fight that had just taken place on Park Avenue with F.E.B. and L.B.C. R-Dee spotted Thugged Out across the street walking towards Park Avenue and shot a few caring words for him.

"What up bitch ass nigga'! Can't say what up?! Don't go to Park cuz' they might fuck you up too!" The fellas laughed but Thugged Out wasn't laughing.

"Suck my dick R-Dee! And if that lil' bitch finds that funny he could suck my dick too!" Thugged Out replied and stared right at Woodz who stopped dead in his tracks and returned the stare. The fellas slowed down and didn't know what was going on. Woodz surveyed the block and realized there were too many people around. He wanted to deal with Thugged Out privately.

"Yo'! Your floor! Five minutes! So I could show you who's the lil' bitch!" Woodz had enough of Thugged Out's mouth and couldn't allow him to continue disrespecting him blatantly and behind his back . . . enough was enough!

"Yo' Woodz what the fuck going on? Where you going?" Ace asked who was unaware of the war going on between both of them.

"Nah fuck that! This nigga's mouth is loose so I'm going to meet him on is floor and break the shit off for him . . . if ya' comin' come if not break out and don't say shit . . ."

R-Dee worked Woodz up more as they entered 1760 not knowing if Woodz was serious about fighting. Woodz shot up the stairs to Thugged Out's floor and the rest followed. Rabbit remained silent. He was nervous about the situation and didn't want to see Thugged Out and Woodz clash, but he couldn't deny the tension brewing between them because of Desiree and White Thong.

"Hollywood cabron fuck that shit nigga' don't let—" Woodz quickly cut Rabbit off.

". . . The fuck up Rabbit . . . break out if you don't wanna' see this any of ya' I'ma duff this nigga' out as soon as he come out that elevator." The fellas all exchanged puzzled looks. It was a side of Woodz that they had never seen!

The sound of the elevator bell rang as it slowly ascended up, getting closer to the eighth floor. Woodz could feel Thugged Out on the elevator and stood aside the door with his fist balled up. The door finally opened and just when he was ready to nail Thugged Out, R-Dee and Ace both stopped him.

"Nah Woodz! Hold up! Hold up!" Thugged Out instinctively ducked down as he stepped out the elevator to avoid the cheap shot that was held back, Woodz held back the punch and backed off from the elevator. "Listen if ya' nigga's is gonna' thump it's gonna' be a clean one on one no dirty shit, stompin' out, clean ya' heard? Ya' nigga's is best friends so don't forget that?" Ace's words registered in both their minds as they faced each other just a few feet away from one another.

Woodz was having second thoughts until Thugged Out blurted out "C'mon nigga'! Let's go!" With both of his fist balled up also, he stepped towards Woodz who slowly charged him with one thing in mind . . . *Hit this nigga' with all your power Woodz.*

Ace, R-Dee and Rabbit watched as Thugged Out threw a left hay maker at Woodz who gracefully ducked the punch like a professional boxer and landed a massive right hook on the side of Thugged Out's left eye. The impact of the punch was loud and made the fellas jump and let out "oohs and O's" For Woodz it was years of frustration being taken out on Thugged Out's face.

He followed the punch by driving Thugged Out's back against the wall as hard as he could. The impact broke Thugged Out from out the daze and he landed a quick jab across Woodz mouth busting his lip open. Woodz tasted the blood on his lip, ducked his head and gave Thugged Out a series of knees to his groin and stomach, Thugged Out countered by landing punches repeatedly on Woodz head until he finally backed off him.

The sound of a door opening caught their attention. Woodz stared at Thugged Out who frantically raised his hands again.

"That's it nigga'? C'mon!" He swiped his hand across his left eye and became furious at the sight of his own blood.

"Fight's over." Said Woodz who didn't know how to feel but who wanted to get the hell out of there before things got real ugly. He turned and walked towards the staircase while Ace and R-Dee followed him downstairs. He heard the sound of Bernice's voice calling her mother and Clari as he descended down the stairs. Thugged Out's mother stepped out into the hallway and asked her son what was going on. Then she began to panic when she saw his face dripping with blood.

"Pero que paso chulo!?? Ahi! Quien te rrompio tu sojo Kenny!?? Melveen que paso!??" Clari also asked Rabbit what had happened while Thugged Out argued with his mother.

"Ant did that?!! Oh Shit!!" She laughed out loud but behind her brother's back.

Woodz sucked on his busted lip. His head ached and as he walked out the building people noticed the blood on his sky blue Housing shirt and asked him what happened. When he didn't answer they asked both R-Dee and Ace if Woodz had a fight and who won.

"Who ya' think won?" R-Dee replied pointing at Woodz who marched towards his building ignoring the calls for him. The fight with Thugged Out reopened the old wounds of L.B.M but delivered justice for Woodz in his opinion. The word of their fight spread quickly and was made official when Thugged Out sported a big Band-Aid on his face for a few days. He denied claims of losing the fight while Woodz never spoke about it.

A part of him felt good whereas another part of him felt guilty about fighting Thugged Out. He shook off the feeling and tried to focus on school. His goal was to land that Seasonal Housing position by next summer and work to get his own place, maybe even a car, but he needed to graduate and was determine to do so!

In the aftermath of the fight the squad grew apart again. Capone and Katie broke up after only a few months so he got into his school mode also. R-Dee and Ace stayed around 111th with the rest, while Woodz spent most of his time with Jakkes. Winter was approaching and he detached himself from the streets and the squad, doing most of his socializing over the walkie talky. Unknown to Capone Woodz and Katie had become good friends and the two spent a lot of time together on and off the walkie.

Woodz would've never imagined that Katie had secretly fallen for him that same night on the corner of 110th and he for her. Along with Katie he personally met with Foxy on the walkie one breezy Saturday morning in September. He found her while riding his bike by the Marketa on 115th on Park Avenue.

Woodz tried to spend time with both of them as much as possible with out them finding out about each other. He picked them up from school, hung out with them in Taft and had them coming to Clinton to see him. He gave Foxy her first kiss in Central park inside the Botanical Garden and worked his way into Katie's heart.

"This can't be life . . . this can't be love . . .
This can't be right there's gotta' be
more this can't be us . . ."

Woodz listened to his favorite track off his bootleg **Jay-Z** *Dynasty* album during fourth period math class. He had his boy Cool Breeze's C.D. player that was equipped with exterior speakers so he didn't need any headphones, allowing him to play his tunes freely while trying to understand Algebra.

He continued pondering about his fight with Thugged Out and his relationships with both Mamichula and Foxy. He contemplated cutting it off with Foxy and get serious with Katie whom he was more attracted to. The period finally ended so he posted up at his usual spot between the third and fourth floors of Park East. It was where he and his boy *Gigilo* always met up before lunch to kick it.

"What up my nigga'?" Gigilo greeted Woodz finding him nodding his head to the Dynasty album. Gigilo was from Jefferson projects, a chubby Puertorican kid who was friends with Woodz even before their Hakala days. They never planned on both landing in Park East but loved that it happened. They also both got left back and were even taking the same night school classes together . . . they were brothers for life.

"Same shit B' . . . waitin' to see if I see Nicki ass around." Woodz answered.

"Oh shorty from your block right? Big titties? I ain't see her . . . yo' let me hold the C.D. player for Music class." Woodz handed Gigilo the C.D. player and proceeded to class, while keeping an eye out for *Nicki*.

Nicki was from Carver Projects on Park Avenue, she was a brown skinned Puertorican girl about the same height as Woodz, with a smile that lit up the darkest room. They met during the end of the summer through Capone who was trying to hook up with her cousin Myra. He was unsuccessful, but Nicki and Woodz hit it off and remained good friends.

Woodz even knew that she talked over the walky but she wouldn't reveal her handle to him. If he really wanted to know he would have to find out somehow she told him. Woodz loved it and found her in days. Her handle was **Fresca** over the airwaves. He had become more attracted to her from that point on, not only was she beautiful with a body to complete the package she was fly, had a job and was about her biz. Woodz swore that Nicki was his gift from god, she was certified wifey material hands down!

He knew Nicki had the kind of mind set to upgrade his swagger but his only problem was his feelings for Katie who he was craving to be with! Just when he thought things couldn't get more confusing it did. At 2:45 classes were over and Woodz walked with Gigilo and his sister Chinny and their cousins who also attended Park East.

He finally spotted Nicki walking across the street with her cousin *Myra* so he left Gigilo and the rest and started singing his Dynasty song out loud pretending not to see her. She called his name a few times before he finally turned to her and flashed a big smile.

"Nigga'! I know you heard me lil' asshole!" Woodz raised his hands in the air and walked towards her.

"Hey! What up sexy?! What's good yo'? I ain't see you all day . . . where you was hiding at?" Nicki chuckled.

"I wasn't hiding I actually go to class nigga' somethin' you should be doing instead of watchin' girls play volleyball all fuckin' day!" Woodz smiled watching the two beauties laugh out loud. He walked beside her, grabbing and swinging her hand.

"So what's good? When can I get my kiss you owe me?" Nicki gave Woodz a baffled look and snatched her hand away.

"Your kiss?? What kiss nigga'!? Myra you hear this shit?!" She laughed and Woodz bit his lip. He enjoyed playing the game with Nicki. He walked the two beautiful cousins up to the corner of 108th and gave Nicki a hug then smirk. "See . . ." She said flashing him a playful stare. "Until you tell me why you won't get no kiss . . ." She winked at Woodz and walked off with her cousin. Woodz smiled and made his way to 1738.

He reached the building and bumped into Mark who flashed him a Dutch cigar. Woodz accepted the invite and led the way upstairs to home base to spark up. Mark greeted Momma Luv' in the kitchen when they entered and followed Woodz to the room.

"Roll up my nigga'? Straight cheese?" Woodz nodded his head and passed Mark the wastebasket to dump the Dutch out in. He laid his towel under the door while Mark rolled up the **Indica** bud. He grabbed Woodz C.B. radio from the window and struck up a conversation with someone name *Playgirl*.

"What up ma'? This be Cash money ya' heard?!" Playgirl didn't respond so Mark placed the radio down and lit up the dutchy. He took three pulls of his favorite bud and passed it to Woodz who was laid back on his bed watching videos on **B.E.T's The Bassment**. He thought about Katie while Mark looked out the window and spotted Capone waking with L.J. and his girl from Park East. Capone told Mark to let Woodz know he was on his way up. He arrived minutes later and was surprised to enter the smoke filled room. He made himself comfy and even accepted a few tokes of the L'.

"Yo' . . ." Capone took one last pull and passed it to Woodz who was focused on the **Ruff Ryders WW3** video. Capone continued "Yo' dogz I started rhymin'!"

Mark killed the smoke and looked at Capone and so did Woodz.

"What??" Woodz uttered letting out a laugh as he grabbed his baby Powder cologne to spray it around the room.

"I don't know B' . . . the other night I'm listening to this nigga' Kiss and I got hype and just started writin' my own shit . . . word I think I got potential nigga'." Mark didn't comment but shot a look over at Woodz who seemed to be stuck off the Indica or just stuck on stupid.

"Aight! So spit somethin' my nigga'! Straight cheese." Blurted out Mark. Capone rubbed his chin and after a few seconds recited a few bars he memorized. Woodz couldn't believe it.

"And I already got a name . . . I'ma call myself Talent . . . I might, I dunno' yet." Woodz repeated the name to him self and shook his head.

"Its definitely original . . . it's aight I guess." Mark announced he was leaving so Woodz escorted him to the door. He returned to the room with two glasses of soda for Capone and him "Chris you serious? You wanna' be a rapper now nigga'?" Woodz jeered.

"I mean, I'ma fuck with it . . . I might get better and stick with it . . . nigga' its betta' than runnin' around and fuckin' with this corny shit all day." Capone said bluntly picking up the walky talky and shooting a look at Woodz who just smiled smugly.

He didn't appreciate the cheap shot but chuckled at it and wiped his mouth, still feeling the effects of the bud. He decided to change the subject.

"So what's up other than that twin? I see you and your boy Kenny still be runnin' around."

"Nigga' when is ya' gonna' squash ya' beef and talk already?? Ya' nigga's is actin' like lil' bitches my nigga'." Woodz wasn't going to bite his tongue this time.

"Nigga' hold up! You got a lot of fuckin' nerve B' . . . I fought that mothafucka' not only because I wanted to duff his ass out, but because of that shit he did that night with the B.B. Guns with Papo and these nigga's . . . yea nigga' I fought that mothafucka' for you too! I'm tired of hearin' all ya' nigga's talk shit like lil' bitches damn!" Woodz had exploded and he felt good letting it out.

A few weeks before the fight with Thugged Out, Woodz and Capone and returned from seeing a movie on 42nd Street and when they arrived on the block the L.B.C. accused Capone of shooting Pops in the arm with Woodz B.B. Gun! After Woodz and Capone explained and proved where they had been Pops revealed Thugged Out as their accuser and it resulted in a huge argument between Thugged Out and Capone then with Woodz who tried to smack Thugged Out's head off but was held back.

"Nah nigga' this nigga' apologized for that shit . . . you fought him cuz' ya' beefin' over these bitches . . .

you buggin' dogz this is why I don't chill no more I'm out yo' later." Capone let himself out leaving Wood fuming! Woodz called up R-Dee and shared with him what had taken place. R-Dee came over that night and vowed to deal with Capone as soon as he saw him. The tension between the squad was getting ready to escalate again!

Woodz & Ace on 110th Street Lexington Avenue 2000

CHAPTER 11

Keep It In The Family Pt. 2

The royal blue curtains were drawn shut and *Hot 97* could faintly be heard from the speakers of Woodz wall unit. It was a breezy Wednesday afternoon and he had convinced Chula to swing by home base instead of heading home after school. Even though she had to be at an appointment with her mother at around 3:30, she sat on Woodz lap kissing him as they both were feeling each other up.

"Puta you know I gotta' go soon . . . you tryin' to get me in trouble!" Woodz heard her whining but he was too focused on massaging and sucking on Chula's B cup breast to care about appointments or anything. He wanted to eat Chula up!

"You know I like when you call me puta right? So when your late to meet with your moms is gonna' be your fault!" Katie laughed but continued to nag about having to get home in between her moans of pleasure which only excited Woodz even more!

She was also nervous about being seen in Woodz building and felt funny about messing around with him after her break up with Capone. However Woodz convinced her that it was nothing to worry about. He believed what Capone didn't know couldn't hurt him and if he did find out about them . . . oh well. "Puta it's almost 2:30 I gotta' go!" Chula giggled and moaned as Woodz kissed her passionately, grabbing her hand and sticking it down his pants. She grabbed his manhood loving the feel of it. She wanted to get more intimate with Woodz right there and then, but her mother was going to kill her if she was late!

Woodz wrapped his arms around her and stood up to reach into his top drawer. Still holding her in his arms he pulled a condom out the drawer and she immediately grabbed his hand.

"Nigga' you crazy! I gotta' meet her like in twenty minutes!" Woodz smiled and bit the condom wrapper open.

"Be easy puto . . . just blast me off this time . . . next time tho' this ass is mine." He replied squeezing her ass. She smiled and rolled the condom over his dick and jerked him off while he maneuvered his hand into her panties and inserted his middle finger into her moist opening. When he finally came he chuckled in pleasure and pulled his hand out of her pants. Chula looked into his eyes biting on her lip, she couldn't figure Woodz out. One minute he was brave and animated then the next he would be gentle and full of compassion.

"You's a shy boy puta . . ." Chula said standing and grabbing her Bra off the bed. She stood by the window and peeked through the curtain while putting her Bra on. Woodz tossed the condom into the wastebasket and walked over to put the Bra on for her. He drew the curtains open fully and opened the window as she buttoned her blouse. "Yo!? You want everybody to see me gettin' dressed stupid?" She asked startled and cautious about being seen in the window.

"What? Scared Chris might see us? I don't care if he sees us . . . look I think that's him in his window now!" Chula laughed and turned to bury her face into his chest.

"Oh my god you are crazy nigga'!" Woodz really didn't care about Capone or anyone seeing Katie with him it was open season as far as he was concerned. He escorted Chula downstairs and to her building hoping that Capone did see them from his window.

After the episode with Capone his feelings for his right hand man were on thin ice. To further show up both him and Thugged Out Woodz began congregating with two blood brothers from Taft projects he chilled with sometimes. The blood brothers were *Teddy* and *Tyrell*, twin brothers who had a wild but respectable reputation around Harlem.

They were loose canons but took a liking to Woodz and even tried to *bring him home*.

Woodz had no interest of turning blood. He enjoyed smoking and drinking with the twins and knew full well that they intimidated Capone and Thugged Out. It was a message that he wanted to get across to his opposing L.B brethren and the message they got! Halloween had arrived and Capone wanted to round up the squad so that they could venture downtown to the Halloween parade in the village. Woodz agreed to go on one condition Thugged Out had to stay out of his way!

So with the exemption of J.O. and Malcolm the entire squad journeyed down to the village, met up with their Hakala set and enjoyed a fun night. They met some girls, smoked and didn't cross paths with any of the rowdy gay villagers. Joining the squad also was their new member **Romeo** from Madison Avenue. Woodz met Romeo one morning on his way to school and introduced him to R-Dee who actually already knew his sister.

The following Saturday morning Woodz wanted to stay in bed until the late afternoon after staying up all night on the walky with Chula and also others, but was awakened by the dogs barking and door being opened and slammed shut. "Who da' fuck . . ." He muttered to himself drifting in and out of sleep. He heard the footsteps walking towards the door then the door open. When he peeked from under his covers he saw the pretty pale face of his favorite L.B. *Francine*.

Francine and Woodz met back at the end of 1999 when he used to pick up his then girl Melly at her school on 104th on Madison Avenue. Woodz would always see her huddled with her friends and giggling at him so he knew they liked him but Melly hated them. *"I'ma fuck one of these bitches up watch!"* She would always yell at the girls who she knew were hawking her man. Francine and Woodz would finally speak in his building when she was hanging out with one of her friends from school who lived in his building. Not only did Woodz find out that her friend named *Melo* was crazy about him, but she talked on the walky also and always listened to him at night.

Woodz never got to talk to Francine's friend but he took a liking to her and one night ended up hanging out on 111th between Lexington and Park Avenue. There he got to meet the real Francine. She sucked his dick on the steps of P.S. 101 under a scaffold in front of people driving and walking by and the fellas across the street! Woodz never let her go after that.

As he remained under the covers Francine stood over the bed and reached to pull the covers off him.

"Wake up sleepy head . . . time to get up." Woodz sucked his teeth and fought to keep the covers over him until he finally stuck his head out. He snarled at Francine but was happy as hell to see her! Francine was a pretty white Puertorican girl who always wore her **Yankees** hat or **Derek Jeter** shirt. "Wake up Anthony it's time to get up!" Woodz felt her body next to his and startled her by pulling off the covers, revealing his half naked body. "Hey sexy . . ." She said attempting to kiss him.

"France my breath is on fire right now . . ." Woodz chuckled and wiped his eyes.

"I don't care . . . sexy." She kissed him and stuck her tongue in his morning mouth and loved it. Woodz stretched out as she began kissing his neck and chest, working her way down to his stomach. He was quickly aroused as her face hovered over the hard on under his boxers. He let out a soft moan feeling Francine's mouth wrap around his dick. *Damn! I love this bitch!* He thought grabbing the back of his head and watching hers slowly bounce up and down.

Woodz steered her head to speed up until he was ready to explode. He finally came and Francine took it all into her mouth, every last drop! She got up and stepped into the bathroom to rinse out her mouth. Woodz was still paralyzed from satisfaction on the bed when she lay down next to him. He unbuttoned her jeans and began finger popping her. He listened to her moans and kissed her neck, then finally had enough of the fingering.

"Take your shit off . . . I need some of this hot ass pussy yo' c'mon." Francine removed all her garments quickly and popped her ass in the air while Woodz reached into his top drawer for a jimmy, then mounted her backside.

*   *   *

Thanksgiving was always a feast for Woodz and the family. This year they celebrated at his sister's Maria's new apartment in Franklin Plaza where she resided with her fiance *Ivan* and their beautiful baby daughter *Brianna*. Woodz loved the feeling of being an uncle again. He had Millie's son *Jason* in California and now Bri. He loved Brianna's huge eyes that glowed when she stared at you.

They had much to be thankful for this year especially Woodz. He was excelling in school, getting along with the family, but his L.B.M family was in disarray again. He and Thugged Out had cut off all communication and it was hurting the squad again. They didn't say a word to each other at the Halloween parade disappointing the rest of the squad. Capone even invited Woodz to his home base for Thanksgiving to mend their differences and Woodz came over. The two patched things up but Woodz didn't have anything to say about Thugged Out, and Capone didn't bring up Katie either.

The following week Capone introduced Woodz to some girls from his school and Woodz was very impressed. Their names were *Jessika* and *Jennifer* and according to Capone they were cousins and very promiscuous. Woodz had to agree the girls were gorgeous! Jennifer was short and brown skinned, wore tight cornrows and had the cutest dimples Woodz ever saw. She was very playful and had a nice thick body. Jessika was light skinned, slim and an inch taller than Woodz. She had big dark eyes, thick eyebrows and cornrows in her hair also. Woodz loved her eyes.

Capone tried to lure in the playful Jennifer with his always smooth and playful approach. Jessika meanwhile was the serious one and connected with Woodz from the jump. Capone and Woodz convinced the girls to escape the cold weather with them upstairs where there was a fresh left over bottle of **Long Island Ice Tea** from Thanksgiving awaiting them.

Reminiscent of his birthday Woodz played host for the bunch. Joining them was Jakkes as well. Woodz didn't mind Jakkes tagging along for some entertainment, the girls were ready to drink and he was already in L.B. mode. The lights were dimmed as **Hot 97** played through the speakers in Woodz room. The bottle of Long Island Ice Tea was flowing and Jakkes had the girls rolling. Jennifer was busy fighting off Capone who was trying to seduce her on Woodz bed and also Jakkes who was trying relentlessly to get her to dance with him.

Woodz meanwhile had Jessika secluded by the window, both guzzling down their cups of Long Island. After her second cup Jennifer wanted to run downstairs to the store for some candy.

"Yo' bitch we need to go to the store I want some candy! And I gotta' call back this number." She said looking down at her red beeper.

"Use Woodz phone." Capone said, massaging the back of her neck with his left hand.

"NO!" Jennifer shouted shaking off his hand from her neck. Capone knew that was her spot and she knew he did. "I want some candy!" She squealed and sprung from the bed blushing and sipping the rest of her drink. She yelled at Jessika again who was swaying on Woodz waist to the rhythm of **Sean Paul's** Deport Dem record. "Jessika bitch!!"

"What!? Crazy drunk bitch!" Both girls laughed at each other. "Go with one of them!" She told her cousin who shot back a look of shock at Jessika. Jennifer flashed a wicked smile and grabbed her black North Face coat.

"You gonna' come with me Chris? Pleeease Chris . . ." She grabbed Capone's hands and placed them over her breast for him to feel on, she had nice round full breast that Woodz was scoping too. Capone didn't want to go but realized that he had no choice. He looked at Woodz who flashed him his smug smile. Capone grabbed his coat and led Jennifer down the hall followed by Jakkes who knew what time it was.

With Jessika and him all alone at last, Woodz knew he didn't have much time before they returned from the store. He walked over to Jessika who was in front of his mirror analyzing her slim image. Woodz stood behind her and wrapped his arms around her waist.

"Hmm . . . we look good together don't we?" Jessika sucked her teeth then smile. She ran her right hand across his cheek.

"You think so?" She asked turning around to face him.

"Nah . . . I know so." He answered, and met her lips with his. They locked arms and maneuvered over to the bed where she laid on her back and pulled him on her. Woodz unbuttoned her shirt to look at her titties, they were small, firm and bite size. He practically ripped off the Bra and scarfed down her nipples with his mouth.

He kissed her stomach and couldn't believe that she had six pack abs like him! *She gotta' six pack?!* They both breathed heavily as they tongue wrestled each other with the music stimulating there senses. Woodz pulled his covers over them and finally worked his hand down between her thighs feeling the heat between her legs. He unbuckled her belt, unbuttoned her jeans and quickly slid his fingers under her thong finding her special place soaked and on fire!

They continued to kiss as she worked her way into his jeans. Woodz unbuckled his own belt and his jeans dropped down to his ankles. She grabbed his package and squeezed it smiling at him while their tongues danced. She started jerking him off slowly and it was driving Woodz wild. Finally he started sliding off her jeans but she stopped him.

"What? Why not??" He asked catching his breath, startled by the abrupt stop.

"We ain't got enough time for that . . ." Jessika answered softly biting her lip. She was still smiling and holding his nuts in her hand. "They'll be here any minute . . . next time cutie . . ."

Damn! Fuck! Woodz shouted in his head. He sucked his teeth and attempted to get off her but Jessika held his arms.

"No let's keep going! Please! C'mon . . ." Woodz stared down at her, she was even more beautiful horny and drunk! He licked his lips and reinserted his fingers into her slippery snatch, slowly thrusting his fingers into her, loving the sounds of her moans and the faces she made. What she did next almost made him explode! Jessika pulled his sticky hand covered with her juices from out her pussy and sucked her own juices off his fingers!

"Oh shit . . . I fuckin' love you!" They both laughed. He licked her juices off his fingers also and was ready for blast off!

"Keep jerking me off . . . Blast me off c'mon." He said smiling. Jessika grabbed his rock hard dick again and jerked it like if she was trying to pull it out his pelvis!

Woodz thrust his fingers in and out of her and felt it coming. He didn't care about not having a condom on he just wanted to feel that pleasure and he did, finally cumming in his boxers grunting in pleasure Jessika kissed and caressed his sacs feeling more turned on by Woodz than she had ever been by any guy in her life.

They remained under his quilt hot and sweaty licking her pussy juice off Woodz fingers unaware that Capone, Jakkes and Jennifer were at the door. Jennifer opened the door and immediately smelled sex in the air.

"Why it smells like ya' fuckin in here?!" She uttered holding a bag full of candy in her hand. Woodz lifted the quilt off Jessika and him and saw the looks of shock across their faces. Jessika was pulling her pants up and grabbed Jennifer to run in the bathroom so she could put her Bra back on.

"You crazy bitch! Ya' was fuckin'!?" Jennifer asked in the bathroom.

"Almost if ya' nigga's didn't fuck it up!" Answered Jessica.

They stayed in the bathroom as Capone and Jakkes smacked fives and screamed L.B. trying to talk to Woodz who didn't say a word. He just stood by his swivel seat quiet, shaking his head as poured himself another drink.

The girls returned to the room and Jennifer was checking her beeper every five minutes. Jessika was quiet and Woodz stood by the window pissed off at how the night played out. Jennifer asked Woodz to use his phone and he let her. He was fuming that he didn't get to handle his business. *These nigga's is some cock blockers for real . . . and that fuckin' beeper yo'.* Jessika could tell that he was angry and walked over to him.

"Oh! Our ride's here bitch time to bounce!" Jennifer announced as her beeper came alive again. Jessika turned back towards Woodz and playfully punched his jaw.

"What's wrong? Don't be mad . . . I'ma come back nigga' . . . I have to come back . . ." She whispered into his ear and planted a juicy kiss on his lips. Jennifer gave Woodz a soft hug and mischievous stare that he returned with a wink of an eye. Jakkes gave Woodz dap and led the girls out the door followed by Capone who told Woodz he was coming back.

Woodz didn't move. He stood by the window with his drink in his hand and stared at his messy bed, still in disbelief on how the night ended. "Fuckin' cock blockin' mothafucka's!". . . He said out loud as Capone returned to the room and walked towards the window.

"You aight nigga'?" Capone asked Woodz who grumpily spun the empty cup in his hand. He nodded his head never taking his eyes off the cup. "There they go." Capone announced watching the girls rush across the street towards their ride home. Woodz turned around and looked downstairs to catch a last glimpse of Jessika, but instead he his eyes were fixed on the red car they were jumping into. He recognized that car anywhere!

"Who's driving these bitches home?" He asked Capone, hoping that it wasn't who he knew it was. Capone yelled to the driver who opened the driver side door, it was Thugged Out! Woodz couldn't believe it.

"What the fuck?! That's Thugged Out's whip?! Thugged Out's their ride?? Where the fuck did Kenny get a car from!!?" Woodz was enraged and was ready to lose his mind.

"Yea nigga'." Capone answered in his own cocky manor. "You ain't know K had the whip?? You know we had to keep it in the family . . ." Capone answered smugly and patted Woodz on his shoulder exiting the room with a smile on his face. Where as Woodz was livid!

"Keep it in the family??" He repeated loudly to himself. "Dis' nigga' played himself . . . aight ya' got this one!" Woodz spent the rest of the night in bed with his walky. He listened to Chula and Fresca over the airwaves dwelling on the turn of events of the night, and vowed to have the last laugh.

Kenny Thugged Out Medina 2000

CHAPTER 12

The Fun house Pt.2

Winter hit Spanish Harlem with full force blanketing the streets with almost five feet of snow in a matter of hours, but despite the snowy weather night school was going smooth for Woodz who enjoyed his walks to 96th street for his evening classes. Not only were Gigilo and him making good progress, he was meeting beautiful girls from the West side, Washington Heights and all over Manhattan!

So despite all of his blunders and devilish behavior the egotistic eighteen year old seemed to have his life under control and moving on to the next phase of his life. The teachers at Park East saw potential in Woodz and encouraged him to stay focus, but the question was would Woodz see it and stay focused?

A cold snowy Monday night kept the streets deserted but the C.B. air waves lively. After two hours of playing **Nintendo 64** Woodz and R-Dee took to the streets for some air and entering 1738 as they were exiting were *Sylvia* and *Christina* from Madison Avenue. Sylvia was Romeo's sister and Christina was their cousin. The cousins were on their way upstairs to smoke at a friend's house and promised Woodz and R-Dee to be back downstairs in half an hour. The lonely masters waited in the lobby for about 45 minutes until R-Dee got tired of waiting.

"Yo' fuck these bitches dogz lets go back upstairs and play the 64." He whined but Woodz didn't want to be cooped upstairs either.

"Nah man I'm tired of bustin' your ass in **N.W.O. Revenge** nigga' . . . lets walk around or somethin'."

"To where?!" R-Dee replied. "This shit is dead out here nigga'!" He said pointing out to the empty snow covered streets. Woodz convinced him to walk anyway and so the two slowly trekked down the snowy Lexington Avenue. Reaching 105th street they made their way down towards Third Avenue and then made their way back up towards 110th. Woodz told R-Dee about the night with Jessika and the under handed games played by both Capone and Thugged Out as they approached 109th and that's when R-Dee had an idea.

"Yo' fuck it c'mon lets troop to Pammy's crib."

"Pammy? Who the fuck is that?" Woodz asked. He didn't recall ever hearing of a *Pammy*.

"Pammy nigga' . . . Pamela dogz, Pammy who lives in Jeff, you know Pammy dogz she be dancin' in the carnivals and shit." Woodz tried to match the name with a face but he was clueless.

"You be going up there on the reg?" He asked R-Dee.

"Yea nigga'." R-Dee quickly answered as they crossed 112th street towards Pammy's building on the corner. "I live up there . . . Pammy's my bitch c'mon nigga' trust me." R-Dee regretted not bringing Woodz to meet Pammy sooner but she was his little secret and her place was his own little fun house that he wanted to conceal from Thugged Out and the rest.

Woodz was skeptical about the whole thing but rolled with his road dog. It beat the blistery cold or playing Nintendo 64 all night. R-Dee yelled up to the fourth floor of the building and told Pammy to toss down the key for the door downstairs. They made their way up four flights of stairs until reaching Pammy's floor. Woodz didn't know what to expect as R-Dee knocked on the door. It opened and Pammy appeared and she immediately scanned Woodz as she greeted R-Dee. She invited them inside and yelled out to her mother that they had company.

Woodz was beginning to remember Pammy now from the carnivals. She was a little taller than him, pale skinned with short brown hair and huge breast! He followed R-Dee into the living room and was finally introduced.

"Aight Pammy this is my road dog Woodz, Woodz Pammy, my future baby momma . . . now that we acquainted Pammy let's go to your room so that I can fuck you in thee ass! Ha ha." Woodz tried not to laugh but he couldn't help it. Pammy called R-Dee retarded and smiled at Woodz, happy that R-Dee had brought him upstairs.

She yelled out to her mother again who finally emerged out of a back room and entered the living room. *Oooo . . . mom duke's looks aight.* Woodz thought to himself glancing over at a white cat rolling around on the sofa by the windows.

"Woodz this beautiful lady is Pammy's moms Carmela, Carmela this is my right hand man from Clinton, the L.B.M. general himself Ant aka Woodz! West Side! West Side!" Woodz chuckled at R-Dee's foolish introduction while the mention of his name caught *Carmela's* full attention.

"Woodz? Woodz short for like . . . Hollywoodz?" She asked giving him a suspicious stare.

"Uh yup . . . that be I, that's me." Woodz felt his ego rising again.

"Wait!" Said Pammy grinning at her mother. "Your Hollywood? The Hollywood on the walky talky that all the girls be callin'?" Woodz smiled and looked over at Carmela.

"I wouldn't say . . . all the girls."

"White Chocolate?? Oh my god ma' it's Hollywood!" Pammy was beaming, leaving Woodz feeling renowned. If she knew him as White Chocolate, then she's spoken to him personally over the C.B. He enjoyed his moment or praise and vowed to reward R-Dee for it.

"Hollywood you don't recognize my voice? I spoke to you a few nights ago." Carmela said as she placed her hand on her hip. Woodz tried to remember the voice but he couldn't pin point it. "Let me help you out sweetie ok . . . *Halleeewooood Halleeeewooood . . . pick it up for Lady Love.*"

"Lady Love??" Woodz repeated. He knew who Lady Love was now! "Lady Love . . . me and you spoke the other night almost all night too . . . oh shit, I was talkin' to another girl too and left her to talk to you." Woodz couldn't believe the coincidence. He scanned Lady Love up and down again and began realizing why his road dog brought him up there. She had her dark hair wrapped in a bun, stood at about 5'1 and had a shapely body for an older female. Her sensuous voice was appealing to Woodz. *I'll beat . . . R-Dee you's a funny nigga'.* He thought to himself turning his attention back to Pammy. "Pammy you be on the walky too right?"

"Yeeaa . . . you know who I am?"

"Yea . . . your name is—" He paused and looked over at the cat again licking itself. "*Kitty Kat.*"

"Wow! You know my name!" Pammy Exclaimed. R-Dee shook his head and looked over at Woodz who wasn't too crazy about Pammy's face, but body wise she was right and could get it too!

Woodz was given a brief tour of the apartment and learned of a younger brother named *Eddie*, older sister name *Jaqueline* and younger sister name *Denise*. He took a seat on the cream colored sofa joined by Pammy who asked him more questions about himself. R-Dee floated around the apartment while Lady Love took a seat on the other sofa to chat with Woodz also.

Moments later the door opened and a miniature Slim Shady ran into the apartment passed the living room and into the back towards the bedrooms. Behind him came a pretty, slim young girl carrying plastic bags into the kitchen. Woodz watched from the couch as Lady Love joined her in the kitchen and Pammy walk over to R-Dee who was trying to turn the stereo on.

Hmm . . . that must be Eddie and Denise damn shorty is pretty as hell. He thought to himself listening to Pretty Boy on the walky talky. Eddie walked into the kitchen asking his mother who the kid on the sofa was.

"That's Hollywood?!" Woodz heard Eddie yell running out the kitchen towards him on the couch. "Oh shit what up Woodz! My bad I didn't know it was you . . . what you doing in my crib yo?!" Woodz gave Eddie a pound.

"I'm here wit' R-Dee that's my right hand man ya' heard . . . I like the Slim Shady look B' you look just like that nigga' yo'." Eddie thanked Woodz and slapped him another five then ran over to the T.V. Woodz watched him switch on the T.V. and **Sony PlayStation** then suddenly felt someone watching him, he turned his face and spotted Denise staring at him standing by the kitchen doorway.

They locked eyes for a few seconds until she looked away and walked towards Eddie who was playing **WWF Smack Down**! Woodz continued to stare not believing how attractive she was. *Damn . . . how old is shorty??* He wondered until Lady Love called him over to the kitchen. Denise watched him walk over to the kitchen and smiled to herself. Inside the kitchen Woodz sat next to R-Dee and across from Pammy at the glass kitchen table.

"Hollywood you wanna' drink something sweetie?" Lady Love asked.

"Yea, I'll take a glass of milk."

"Milk??" Pammy replied standing to open the fridge. She laughed and poured him a glass of milk and took a seat between him and R-Dee.

"It's good for the body ain't it?" Woodz said looking over to Lady Love.

"You must have a nice body then huh?" She responded. Woodz blushed and grinned. *Oh this old bitch is a freak!* He thought to himself gulping down the milk in one shot.

Pammy continue to nag Woodz as Lady Love walked out the kitchen and towards her bedroom. R-Dee meanwhile just sat there and listened until Lady

Love called him from her bedroom. When he returned to the kitchen he whispered into Woodz ear that she wanted him to come to her room. Woodz shot R-Dee an unsure look then made his way towards Lady Love's bedroom.

He knocked on the door and was waved inside by the 40 year old Puertorican mother of four.

"Sit." She said to Woodz patting her queen size bed that was covered with all kinds of stuffed animals. Woodz sat and looked around the room noticing pictures on her dresser and mirror. The room had a cozy feeling to it helping Woodz feel more at ease with Lady Love. "How old are you Hollywood?" She asked standing by the dresser.

"Um I'm 18 . . . I'll be 19 in March." Lady Love nodded her head and took a seat on the bed next to him, crossing her legs lying down on her side. Woodz watched her hand slide up and down the tight black jeans she was wearing as she rubbed her thighs, and started feeling more aroused than nervous.

"Tell me . . . why Hollywood? Why you choose that name out of all the names?" Woodz smiled, he never been asked that by any female before.

"Hmm . . ." He rubbed his chin and smiled at Lady Love, laying back on the bed a little himself. "Who don't wanna' be a star? Live the life? But instead of just talkin' it I'm really tryin' to live it Luv . . . basically." Lady Love smiled at him. She was quickly taking a liking to Woodz. He was smooth, funny and very handsome she thought.

"And what kinda' girls you like? She asked. Woodz was beginning to like Lady Love also her deep Spanish accent was alluring and the lady was fine as wine!

"Girls? I don't discriminate . . . big, small I love em' all." She grinned at Woodz.

"Okay well . . . I like my man to be full of energy . . . I like to please my man so I like guys who . . . who keep it up and not the guys who cum too fast . . . know what I mean?" Woodz was stuck! *R-Dee you mothafucka'!* He thought. Nodding his head slowly and looking around at the stuffed animals on the bed trying to come up with a good reply and quick! He cleared his throat and smiled at Lady Love, he felt like he was ready to melt in her hand but he had to keep his cool!

"I know what you mean and um . . . believe me . . . I'm one of those guys who could keep it up as long as he wants . . . feel me?" He replied smoothly tossing a stuffed bear at her chest. Lady Love laughed softly and swiped her hand across his cheek.

"Your so adorable . . . come." She led him back to the kitchen and offered something to drink again. Woodz declined and he walked over to R-Dee on the sofa next to Pammy. They were watching Eddie and Denise playing *PlayStation*, while Woodz was feeling a rush after being in Lady Love's room. His mind was racing and he turned to go back to the room but then came to a haul, seeing that Denise was now playing the *PlayStation* by her self.

He decided to meet the younger sister so he took a seat by her on the in front of the T.V.

"Press reset and lets see what you got." He said picking up the vacant controller.

"Okay . . . but I'm the best in the house . . . I don't lose." Denise replied

"Well I'm just thee best so lets get it on aight'." Denise selected the steel cage match and the **Undertaker** as her player. Woodz selected **The Rock** and the two battled! They both climbed up to the top of the steel cage and began slugging it out. Woodz realized that she was a good player but he was determined not to lose.

The **Smack Down** game wasn't new to him being that he played it at Jakkes place all the time. He delivered the *Rock Bottom* on her and thought it was over, but the **Undertaker** quickly recovered and Denise planted the Tombstone Pile Driver on him sending **The Rock** through the cage top. Woodz landed on the mat where she pinned him and secured the victory.

"OH! That was bullshit! I had you beat!" He hollered smiling at her. "I let you win." Denise sucked her teeth.

"Yea whatever . . . I told you . . ." She stood up and changed the game to **Grand Theft Auto**. "Now this is my game here." She added. Woodz nodded his head and examined her curvy body closely. He didn't know how old she was and a part of him didn't care!

R-Dee waltzed back into the living room and rushed Denise for the controller.

"Let me play pimp squeak! Move yo' ass!" Denise sucked her teeth and called him an asshole. She took a seat on the sofa alongside of the white cat while Woodz got up also to take a seat next to Pammy and snatched the walky out her hand.

Woodz and R-Dee said their good byes and left the apartment at around 10:30. Woodz promised to return . . . he was looking forward to it! Pammy gave them big hugs and asked Woodz if he was going to be on the walky later on, he answered yea playfully smacking her thighs. She laughed and told him that he better come back. He yelled at Denise about playing a rematch when he did return.

"When eva' you ready!" She yelled from the sofa. The duo made their way downstairs and Woodz needed answers!

"You motha' fuck why you never told me about Pammy and her freaky ass momz nigga'! You's a funny nigga' R-Dee."

"I told you to trust me dogz they stay talkin' about you, "Hollywood" up in there."

"Ayo, how old is Denise's lil' ass?" R-Dee chuckled. He had a feeling that Woodz would also ask that.

"She's a lil' cutie right?? He asked Woodz who nodded his head. "Well forget it nigga'! She's a lil' thirteen year old loose bitch!" He exclaimed.

Damn . . . Woodz thought to himself. He was blown away with how pretty Denise was. She looked like a model! R-Dee and Woodz walked out of Jefferson projects and gave each other dap.

"Be on the mic tonight Hollywood!" Lady Love yelled from the kitchen window.

"Damn nigga' they on your dick already!" Woodz waved up at her and noticed someone else staring down at him through the other window. It was Denise and he was certain that they would have their rematch very soon.

CHAPTER 13

Forbidden Fruit

As New Years rapidly approached the whole world seem to be changing by the second. *Gorge Bush* was preparing to declare war against the Middle East after stealing the presidential election away from *Al Gore* and the world around Spanish Harlem was that a corporate take over was underway. Private corporations were supposedly buying up all the vacant lots and property to renovate buildings to drive residents out of Spanish Harlem. It was called *Gentrification.*

It was serious times but Woodz was only concerned about his grind with or with out L.B.M. Moving out of home base had become his short term goal, moving out of the Barrio was his long term goal. Despite all of his hard work he continued to get entangled in the street life.

Woodz was getting high every night and having wicked thoughts and the strangest dreams while he slept. Whether it was paranoia or insomnia his thoughts were haunting him, something was getting ready to happen to him and he didn't know what or when. All he knew was that he felt like if his time was running out and it left him feeling uncomfortable every night.

He did his best to shake off the eerie feelings. Aside from the streets he was doing excellent in school and meeting Lady Love had rejuvenated his swag. As for the squad they kept their strong hold on 111th street and just a few days before New Year's they found themselves in a defying moment.

One of the young bloods from there was running for his life claiming to almost have been killed by a wild group of Mexicans.

"Yo'! Them nigga's tried to kill me!" **Dee** shouted frantically as everyone listened to him retell the story of the group of Mexicans stabbing him on his side and chasing his boy Louie and him out of P.S. 117 playground. It wasn't the first time Woodz had heard about Mexicans chasing people out of that park . . . were they trying to take over??

He and the rest decided to take a walk and get revenge on the first Mexican they saw. Thugged Out led the group with a wooden bat concealed under his black Flight Jacket as they all strolled up and down Third Avenue but there was no one out, the streets were deserted!

They finally made their way towards 110th on Lexington and posted up in front of the Community Center. After waiting about ten minutes two drunk Mexicans stumbled out of the restaurant across the street and stopped by a phone about twenty feet away.

"Oh! These nigga's is food!" Declared Dee who brought along Louie and a tall God Body kid name *Jay* who was always eager to stir up trouble. Thugged Out, R-Dee, Ace, Malcolm and Woodz kept an eye out for Pepa as Dee, Louie and Jay stepped off in the direction of the two Mexicans. Jay and Dee grabbed up the two Mexicans then slapped, punched and slammed both men against the phone onto a pile of garbage by the telephone pole.

Both Mexicans let out cries of pain calling out for help. Woodz and the rest decided to get Dee and Jay away from the pummeled Mexicans before they were killed. Woodz however wanted a piece of the action so he straggled behind the squad and grabbed the wooden bat from Thugged Out to strike both of the Mexicans.

"TOMA! Mothafucka's! don't fuck wit' mi' juentes!!" The two Mexicans squealed in pain as Woodz walked off towards the rest of the group. Jay, Dee and Louie loved it. They couldn't believe that Woodz had struck with such vengeance. They all rushed towards Thugged Out's building where Woodz tossed him the bat and where Jezzy was standing in front of the building with her peoples watching them attack the Mexicans shaking her head.

"Ya' nigga's is wildin' . . . ya' gonna' fuck up the wrong person one day." She warned holding a New Port cigarette between her fingers. Woodz turned and raised his arms in the air as Thugged Out grabbed his bat and disappeared into his building.

"We can't be stopped ma'! Who's gonna' stop us?" The group reached the corner and sprinted towards Ace's building on Park Avenue. They ran into the building and caught their breaths by the back door.

"Yo' ya' nigga's is crazy! I could fuck wit' ya' nigga's all day! Woodz!? What da' fuck was that my nigga'?! You tryin' to catch bodies nigga'!!" Jay exclaimed trying to catch his breath. Woodz was out of breath also but cracked a mild smile.

"I tried to hit a home run ya' heard." They all laughed except for Ace who shook his head and announced that he was going upstairs and left Woodz and the others by the back door. As everyone parted ways Woodz was relieved to have gotten away with the stunt. He spotted an ambulance and cop cars on 110th as he walked into his building. He made it upstairs and looked out the window at the cops on 110th. He chuckled and grabbed his walky talky hoping to find Fresca or Chula on the airwaves somewhere, not at all concerned about the Mexicans downstairs.

* * *

New Year's finally arrived on a chilly January morning. Woodz, Jakkes, R-Dee and Malcolm stood on the corner with other Lexington Avenue natives celebrating and launching snowballs everywhere. In front of Thugged Out's building there were Belvedere and Hennessy bottles flowing and Thugged Out, Capone, Ace, Pretty Boy and Cypha were joining the festivities. The two groups joined forces on the corner of 109th and all eyes were on Thugged Out and Woodz, but they greeted each other nonchalantly and that was that.

The following day Woodz and R-Dee decided to visit their new fun house at around 6 o' clock. They were both already saucy and hoped to get some L.B. action this time. Pammy tossed them the key to the door downstairs and the two road dogs made their way upstairs.

They walked in the apartment and were surprised to find three familiar faces already sitting in the living room it was Mark, Gee, and Rabbit! R-Dee didn't know about Woodz but he wasn't excited at all about finding the trio there.

"What the fuck is ya' nigga's doin' in my crib? Pammy! Fuck is you doin' wit' nigga's up in here huh?!" Shouted R-Dee jokingly, he greeted Mark, Gee, and gave Rabbit two middle fingers.

"ill R-Dee! Shut the fuck up! Who the fuck is you nigga'! Hollywood's here ma!" Pammy yelled. Woodz smiled at Mark who wasn't feeling R-Dee's vibe at all.

He greeted Woodz who gave Gee dap and Rabbit a long drunken stare.

"Ain't see you in a while . . . what up?" Rabbit shrugged his shoulders and flashed Woodz a cautious smile. He didn't know what to say. He could tell that Woodz was twisted and still couldn't believe that he had showed up with R-Dee. Carmela walked into the living room and said hi to R-Dee and Woodz. R-Dee pulled Woodz into the kitchen while Pammy kept Mark and the others company.

"Listen my nigga' we gotta' get these nigga's outta' here dogz." Woodz nodded his head and peeked out the kitchen, flashing Rabbit a wicked smile.

"Do what you gotta' do B." He told R-Dee who wasted no time. R-Dee's plan was to harass Pammy until it annoyed her unwanted guest. He turned the stereo on and grabbed her to dance with him.

"Stop R-Dee . . . alright R-DEE!! R-Dee!? What the fuck is wrong with you! Alright stopppp!!" Woodz sat on the sofa laughing his ass off but Mark and Gee weren't laughing, and announced that they were leaving. Mark asked Woodz to step out into the hallway with him and he did while R-Dee celebrated his scheme actually working by tormenting Pammy even more.

"What's good nigga' ya fuckin' with this bitch and the mom's too? L.B.?" Mark Asked. His eyes were bloodshot red, all of their eyes were!

"I was about to ask you the same shit B . . . what ya' doing up in there?" Mark pulled a clipped L' out of his pocket and lit it up.

"Nah I fucks with Pammy's home girl downstairs. Nigga' I know Pammy for years already . . . big titty bitch." He laughed and passed the L' to Greg who was rewinding his **D.M.X.** tape in his radio. Rabbit took a few tokes of the chocolate then passed it over to Woodz. He was quiet as always but asked Woodz how he'd been.

"I'm chillin' nigga' damn Mark, this shit is the truth." Pammy finally came out to the hallway to be nosy. She was wearing a white T-shirt, black spandex tights and $2.00 slippers on her feet.

"OOH I know ya' nigga's ain't smokin' in my hallway?? Ya' nigga's is buggin' . . . police be . . ."

"Chill Pammy! Damn!" Mark said cutting her off. "We bout to bounce anyway . . . big ass titties ha ha." They all started laughing as Pammy wrapped her arms around Woodz neck. The fellas teased Woodz who flashed them the L.B. sign, taking his last pull of the clip.

"Hollywood you smoke too?' Woodz squeezed her thighs, his high was boosted and now it was show time!

"We out Pammy, see ya' nigga's later." They returned into the apartment, the fun house was all theirs. Woodz normally didn't eat at anyone's place but Carmela offered both of them food so tonight he made an exception. He was high as hell and starving! R-Dee on the other hand would eat you out your home then ask for seconds. He chomped down the roast beef and white rice.

"Carmela what ya' do for New Years'? Had family over?" Woodz chuckled watching R-Dee devour his plate.

"No we went to my mother's house for a little bit. I like to spend quiet nights at home." R-Dee nodded his head, scraping off the last slab of beef and grains of rice off the china.

"Hmm . . . hey where your other rug rats at? And Carmela can I have seconds?" Carmela and Woodz cracked up as Pammy annoyingly grabbed his plate and served him more food.

She sat back down next to Woodz who was almost done with his plate of food. She watched him eat and asked him if he wanted seconds. He shook his head no finally finishing his plate.

"Oh shit." Carmela blurted out realizing the time. She retrieved the walky talky from her room and called out for her daughter Denise. *"Loca pick it up for Lady Love."*

"What channel she be on?" Asked Woodz assuming it was Denise she was hailing as he took a sip of the cold glass of fruit juice.

"Channel seven my channel. *LOCA! Pick it up now!!"* She yelled.

"I hear you ma! We on our way up now!"

"*Hurry up cuz' its gettin' dark out side.*" Ordered Lady Love, Woodz asked her for the walky.

"*Yea hurry up so I could get my rematch!*" He hollered into the walky.

"*Hollywood? That's you? Your at my house?*"

"*Yea bustin' down Lady Love's food ya' heard, me and R-Dee so you better hurry up before he eats the rest of the food up!*" Woodz handed Carmela back the walky. She asked him about the rematch and he explained about the game, but she knew all about the game already. What caught her attention was her daughter's change of attitude when she heard Woodz.

After R-Dee ate his third plate they all sat in the living room where he laid his head on Pammy's lap. Woodz was waiting for Lady Love to give him some kind of signal but she wasn't. Instead she gave him a weird vibe almost ignoring him but he didn't let it ruin his high. He decided to play the Play Station with Denise when she finally arrived home.

She finally arrived and Woodz eyes were glued on the baby face model. He tried to stop staring at her but he couldn't resist. Denise had her long dark hair done in Indian Braids, she had a beautiful smile under a cute serious demeanor and a body shaped like an hourglass. She asked him if he was ready and switched on the game.

Woodz wobbled over and sat by her in front of the T.V. R-Dee cheered him on as he lay on Pammy's lap feeling up on her breast. Woodz won the first game he and Denise played.

"Been practicing huh?" She asked as they started the second match. She played Woodz harder and had the upper hand on him but he cheated by swiping at her joystick causing her to laugh and lose the match. "That's not fair! You cheater!" She whined but still laughing. Woodz was rolling and raised his arms in victory.

"I told you that I let you win last time." He stood up and wobbled his way towards the bathroom to pee and splash some water on his face. Lady Love came out her room when he stepped out the bathroom and they exchanged looks and a quick smile.

"You okay Hollywood?" She asked. Woodz nodded his head yea. "Don't go home too late sweetie ok." She added and stepped into the bathroom closing the door behind her. Woodz didn't know why she was acting funny but he didn't care.

He asked Pammy for another glass of juice and took a seat in the kitchen.

"Juice no milk today?" She jeered pouring him a half glass of fruit juice. Woodz gulped it in one swig and sat back down in the living room. R-Dee walked into the kitchen as Woodz relaxed on the sofa enjoying the buzz he had. Denise had went to change her clothes and now walked back into the living room wearing a long white V-neck Tee shirt, bright yellow spandex tights and colorful socks on her feet. *Ah man* . . .

Woodz said to himself standing and walking over to the window.

He turned and looked at her sitting Indian style on the corner of the sofa talking on her walky. Woodz was having crazy feelings and thoughts so he didn't even want to sit near her! He knew that he was capable of doing something crazy despite the rules of the game and his reputation that he had to uphold.

Ah fuck it. He thought to himself cordially approaching the other end of the sofa and sank into it.

"You ok?" Denise asked as she began slowly shaking her left leg. Woodz nodded his head and wiped his mouth. He needed to be strong.

"I'm twisted you heard . . ." He answered chuckling locking eyes with her again. He felt a funny feeling in his stomach and wanted to get up but he couldn't move! He slumped over on his right side, the room felt like it was spinning.

"You sure you ok??" Denise asked again smirking to herself.

"Yo . . . my head is spinnin' . . . I need you to do me a favor." Said Woodz who realized that he was about to play with fire but he didn't care.

"What?" She asked suspiciously.

"Rub my head for me." He slowly muttered looking over at her. She laid her walky on the glass table and looked at him. *Baby I'll rub whatever you want.* She thought to herself and flashed him a smile.

"You sure?" She asked him. Woodz sat up and said yea. "Okay, if that's what you want." Woodz took off his black and blue *Mets* fitted to rub his freshly faded head and squirming his body towards Denise. He laid back with his head resting in front of her legs. He didn't care about Pammy or R-Dee catching them, the hell with the rules!

Denise began rubbing his head with her slender fingers. Her gentle touch sent a sensation through Woodz body. She adjusted herself to be more comfortable as he placed his fitted cap over his zipper feeling his manhood rising quick.

Woodz slid his body back closer to her forcing Denise to spread her legs apart wider as he practically pushed in between them until his head was up against her stomach. He inhaled her scent and it had him in a trance. He opened his eyes and looked up at Denise who was staring down at him with her lips parted. She looked like an angel watching over him.

Woodz body was electrified by her touch and he was ready to cross that line then and there! He was rock hard under his fitted as he ran his hand over her calves then across her face. "Damn you beautiful . . ." He heard himself utter out wanting and ready to kiss her. Denise wanted to kiss and taste his juicy lips just as much as he did hers. Their faces drew closer but before their lips could meet the sound of R-Dee's voice snapped Woodz out of the spell he was under.

He quickly sat up and rubbed his face leaving Denise frozen on the sofa. Woodz rushed towards the kitchen and found R-Dee standing near Pammy who was sitting down by the kitchen table.

"Yo' I'm ready to bounce dogz . . ." Woodz announced leaning on the kitchen window.

"You aight my nigga?" R-Dee asked. Woodz shook his head no. R-Dee understood the message loud and clear and along with Pammy went to get their coats. Woodz was feeling the breeze blowing through the window, trying to get himself together.

"Why you left?" Denise asked walking up behind Woodz. He lifted his gaze and looked into her eyes again.

"I gotta' go ma' I'm twisted you heard and might do something crazy if I stays here." Denise slowly nodded her head but showed no emotion.

"You gonna' be on the mic tonight?" She asked softly, her voice enticed Woodz even more.

"I might be . . . whats your handle anyway? Loca?" R-Dee returned from the bedrooms and tossed Woodz his coat.

"Loca? Nah only my mom calls me that . . . just call for **Hot Lips** I'll be on channel 7."

"Hot Lips? Hmm . . . I like that . . . Hot Lips, that's hot."

After Woodz and R-Dee said there good byes they slowly descended down the steps.

"My nigga I loves you and I don't have no problem with how you L.B."—Woodz knew what R-Dee was getting at so he quickly interjected.

"R-Dee be easy dogz ain't noffin' happen B . . . that's why I needed to get up outta' there nigga' before something did happen." R-Dee walked with Woodz to 109th and there the two parted ways for the night. Woodz made it upstairs and crashed into bed. He did manage to switch on his walky but he only listened and quickly fell asleep.

*　　*　　*

"YAOOOO! Ya' already know who it be! The L.B. Masters are officially in the buildin'! Holla at the hoodz own Hollywood aka Woodz ya'!" It was about 10 o'clock at night and Woodz was rolling up a nickel bag of chocolate that Gigilo had given him in school. It was another bone chilling night in Spanish Harlem and the streets were deserted, covered with snow and ice. The C.B. airwaves however were lively and full of life, just how Woodz liked it.

The crisp air blew against his face as he announced his presence on channel 1 then quietly eavesdropped on channel 10 where he found both Capone and Chula in the middle of a conversation. He sat on his bar stool and ignited the Dutch. His **Makaveli** C.D. played in his stereo as he sang along to the *Hail Mary* song.

What do we have here NOW! Nigga's wanna' ride or die . . . LALALALALALALALALALA!

"*Yo' Woodz! Pick it up nigga'!*" Capone hollered. "*Puta! That's you punk? What up!*" Chula added. Woodz smiled and took a long pull of his L'.

"*Yooo' . . . what's poppin' yo'?*" "*Hmm . . .*" He thought. Maybe this was a good time for a little pay back. "*Is that you Chula?? What up puto! What chu' doin' on my channel huuhh???*"

"*Ha your channel? I thought channel 1 was your channel?*" Chula asked wondering if Capone would be bothered by Woodz intrusion.

"*True true . . . but on some real shit, every channel is Woodz channel! Na' mean! 'Pone you betta' tell em' nigga'!*" Chula couldn't help it but laugh. "*But what up tho' puto? Where you be at and shit?*" Woodz asked her purposely disregarding Capone on the channel to siege the conversation.

"*Uhh nooo where you be at puta? You don't have time for the lil' people no more huh?*" Woodz chuckled and took a few tokes of his blunt.

"*Naahhh . . . I know I be on the move and shit but I never forget about the lil' ones ma' you know that!*"

"*Puta? You over there puffin'? Sounds like you steamin' nigga'.*" Chula assumed.

"*To da' face ya' heard!*" Woodz retorted. "*You know I still love you right puto?*" He added, chuckling off the smoke.

"Oh whatever puta . . ." Chula felt awkward about brushing Capone off like that and wondered if he was even still on the channel. He was and finally chimed into the conversation.

"Yo' Woodz what up dogz? Whats good with you?" Woodz smiled, payback was a bitch and he loved it.

"Doin' me nigga' L.B.in' like a master's suppose to, stayin' away from the bullshit and parlayin' up in the new FUN HOUSE nigga'! Basically!"

"New fun house?" Capone asked curiously. *"Word what up nigga' put me on!"*

"Put you on? Uhhh can't do it kid . . . the new fun house ain't for everybody ya' heard. Besides R-Dee doesn't want a lot of ya' to know where is at." Woodz knew that would really piss Capone off.

"R-Dee?? Nigga' you can't tell me cuz' of R-Dee!? Ha Ha . . . fuck it nigga' tell that nigga' R-Dee I said fuck him too."

"What you mean fuck R-Dee nigga'?" Woodz Countered. *"It ain't R-Dee's fault that ya' nigga's ain't stickin' to the script . . . . shit don't stop nigga' you know that."* Woodz began to get wiled up. *"I'm true to this shit nigga' fuck all the underhand games and shit . . . if you, Ace, Rabbit and that bitch ass nigga' Kenny don't wanna' fuck with us then fuck ya'! ya' go head and play ya' lil' games while the real Masters keep it moving."*

Capone had set down his walkie in the middle of Woodz ranting. He didn't want to get into no argument on the walky talky with him. *"Chula holla back at me when you done bullshittin' with these niggas . . . bullet head ass nigga' . . . you got my digits ma so holla na mean! I'm ghost!"* Woodz switched over to channel 1, pleased about how he showed up Capone. He finished his L' and plucked it out the window. Chula followed him to channel 1.

"Yaooo! Pick it up for Woody Woodz ya'! who on my motha' fuckin' channel?!"

"Hollywood nigga'! what the fuck is wrong with you?!" Shouted Chula, she wasn't feeling what went down a few moments ago between the two best friends. Woodz chuckled and hoped that she wasn't about to advocate for Capone.

"Chulita what up? Don't try to flip on me ma'. Let me handle these niggas, my niggas the way I do aight? You rollin' with me now so don't worry about what Capone or anybody say aight?" Chula sucked her teeth. She was done with Woodz attitude.

"ill nigga' you madd stink yo! You an asshole puta . . . I can't stand you right now."

"Thank you Chula! Pick it up ya'! pick it up for the asshole! Ha ha ha." Chula shut off her walky for the night, but Woodz was just getting started.

"Holleeewoood . . . you sound like your having fun tonight." Woodz smiled.

"Fresca wussup? What up girl . . . about time you holla' at your boy! Yea I'm just fuckin' around with

the fans and shit ya' heard . . . what up tho'? you gonna' let me pick you up from work this week?"

"Pick me up from work?? You wanna' pick me up now!? You hear yourself shorty?!" Fresca and Woodz laughed. She couldn't deny that he always made her laugh. Woodz regretted dissing Chula the way he did and vowed to make it up to her in the near future.

The following night R-Dee came over and he and Woodz played Nintendo 64. When he told R-Dee about shutting Capone down over the walky R-Dee couldn't stop laughing, especially about callin' him a bullet head ass nigga'. Woodz kept his walky on and his ear open for any incoming hails. He heard Hot Lipz on channel 10.

"Hot Lips pick it up . . . who you talkin' to on my channel?"

"Hollywood? Hey . . . I heard about you last night, you always in some drama huh?" Woodz cracked a smile.

"Naah don't even remind me of that ya' heard. What up with you?" Woodz wondered if R-Dee knew who Hot Lips was.

"Just hangin' with my boy, what about you? Coming over tonight?" Lucky for him R-Dee didn't know Hot Lips was Denise and he wanted to keep it that way. R-Dee asked him who he was talking to but he didn't answer him. Instead he wanted to have some fun with her and find out if she was real or not.

"Nah probably not but yo' what if I told you that I wanna' see you still? Tonight . . . can you make it happen?" R-Dee stopped the game and turned towards Woodz who was standing by the window.

"Yo' nigga' who dat! Let me holla'!" Woodz motioned for him to keep playing the game.

"Woodz . . ." Hot Lips called.

"Yea I'm here what up?" Woodz stepped out the room and into the bathroom to get away from R-Dee for a second.

"Yo Woodz you serious cuz' I'll make it happen?" Woodz didn't believe her.

"Hell yea I'm serious! Come through yo . . . you know where my twenty's at right?"

"Yea but I wont be alone . . . my boy's gonna' be with me ok?"

"Yea yea." He whispered outside of his door and walked back in the room. She sounded very eager he thought. Would she really come? He was playing with fire again and realized that he could find himself in deep drama if he didn't play his cards right.

"Yo' who's shorty? She's comin' over? Can I fuck her first? Hahaha." R-Dee asked. Woodz laughed and sat down on his bed.

"Nah I doubt she coming . . . shorty's probably bull shittin'." He said, not believing that himself.

He grabbed the walky and went to the kitchen then grabbed the garbage to throw it out in the incinerator. Hot Lips called for him just when he was about to step back inside informing him that she was on her way up. *Get the fuck outta' here* . . . Woodz said to himself. The elevator bell came alive and Hot Lips called again then emerged out of the elevator followed by her boy *Charlie*. She gave Woodz a hug and he gave Charlie a pound. Hot Lips was excited to see Woodz again and couldn't take her eyes off him. Charlie insisted on waiting for her by the elevator while they spoke near the staircase.

Hot Lips had on a black coat with a thick black scarf wrapped around her neck. Her face was reddish from the cold wind. Her eyes analyzed Woodz face. He couldn't believe that she had really shown up! He was blown away by her beauty again and for a second wished that R-Dee wasn't inside the room.

"I'm here what up? We got unfinished business don't we?" Woodz stood against the wall and just froze. His mind began racing and his body was saying to grab her, kiss her but his conscience told him the opposite. *Is you crazy? Don't play yourself Woodz! R-Dee inside!* Charlie tried to listen in to their convo. He knew Woodz reputation over the walky as a C.B. celebrity and L.B. Master but he couldn't believe that Denise might be messing around with him.

Woodz couldn't stop thinking about R-Dee coming to the door and catching him with Denise.

"Yo R-Dee's in my room."

"Soo . . . I don't care about R-Dee." She replied leaning towards his body. Woodz needed to decide what to do and quick! He finally gave in to his conscience, as much as he wanted to embrace Hot Lips and take her down, he couldn't afford having R-Dee catch him.

Before she could inch her way closer to him Woodz called for Charlie to join them. He kept his gaze on Denise's face who slowly backed away, confused. "Is he serious?!" She asked herself. Charlie slowly approached them. "Yo good lookin' for walkin' Hot Lips over here for me, I had to holla' at her about somethin' . . . take her home for me aight?"

"Aight Woodz . . . I got you." Charlie said not knowing what happened but he could tell that Denise was pissed off. She couldn't believe Woodz. She felt embarrassed and her face turned cherry red and was ready to smack flames out of Woodz. She brushed by him and walked off into the staircase regretting that she ever gave Woodz the time of day.

Woodz believed it was the best thing to do. He figured that it could never work and walked back towards his room where R-Dee was still playing the 64.

"Damn nigga'! where you go? Did that bitch Hot Lips come through?" Woodz watched Denise and Charlie scurry down 109th towards Third Avenue. "Who was she dogs? I know her?" R-Dee added.

"Yea Hot Lips came through . . . but I sent her home."

"Why nigga'? cuz' of me? Ha ha." Woodz grabbed the other controller and pressed reset to restart the game.

"Nah . . . cuz' it was Denise." He snickered causing R-Dee head to jerk.

"Denise?!" He replied forgetting all about the game. "Denise is Hot Lips?!"

"Yup . . . crazy right?" R-Dee scratched his head and gave Woodz a peculiar look.

"My nigga' don't tell me . . ." Woodz beat him to the punch.

"Relax nigga' I sent her lil' ass home, nothin' happened so be easy . . . I got a rep to keep and can't be getting' caught up with any more of these lil' crazy bitches out here."

"Good nigga' cuz that lil' bitch is a hot ass and won't bring us nothin' but trouble." R-Dee continued to run his mouth but Woodz wasn't listening. He took another look out the window towards Jefferson projects. He spotted a light turning on in Carmela's apartment. "She's home . . ." He told himself and drew the curtains shut.

Woodz watched re-run episodes of Seinfeld while listening to the walky and heard Hot Lips floating around from channel to channel. He wondered if he had made the right choice today by sending her home. He couldn't deny that he wanted her, but the circumstances weren't in his favor. "A forbidden fruit . . . word." He repeated to himself watching

Kramer and George argue about fruit on the show. Denise was that forbidden fruit he thought . . . his forbidden fruit, appealing to the eye but not ripe for the picking . . . yet.

R-Dee & Rudy 2001 New York to Philly flow

CHAPTER 14

The Celebration

The 6 Train was crowded as usual as Woodz rode back uptown returning from 100 Centre Street Criminal Court. He had to pay a $45 fine for getting caught with an open bottle of Heineken in front of Thugged Out's building around late October. Despite the crummy trip back down to court Woodz was in high spirits. His performance in school was well above his normal average solidifying him a passing year.

He also managed to meet up with Katie a few days after his out burst over the walky and got her to forgive him. He couldn't deny the strong feelings he had for her. He was considering making her his wifey, but with Nicki and Jessika in the picture now he found him self in a web of confusion.

It was a brisk January morning and he was scheduled to pick up his new program card at Park

East for the rest of the semester and judging from his overall improvement Woodz would have no more than three classes to finish up the year. The dingy 6 Train screeched into the 103rd Street station and Woodz got off. He made his way through the turnstiles and spotted Sonia entering the station with a group of her girlfriends who he knew were from Carver projects. Sonia and him managed to keep a fairly strong friendship throughout all the headaches and breakups of their past. Sonia gave him a big hug and kiss on his lips.

"Baby!! Where you comin' from and why you not in school?" Woodz chuckled, not surprised by her show of excitement to see him. He knew that she was making a show for her girls.

"Why I'm not at school? What about you loca!? I had to go down to court what's your excuse cuz' I'm on my way there now." Sonia kept an eye on her girlfriends who were waiting over by the gate to hop the train.

"I'm just chillin' me and my bitches going downtown to chill and smoke." One of the girls yelled out to Sonia to hurry up and say goodbye to her boyfriend. "I gotta' go sweetie let's get together . . . call me alright." She hugged and kissed Woodz again and he watched her run through the open gate with the other girls onto the train. He hadn't heard Sonia tell him I love you in a long time so bumping into her put a huge smile on his face.

Woodz made his way towards Park East with pep in his step. He greeted the security guards as he entered and checked in with the school's secretary Lulu. She flashed him a wide smile and questioned him about his tardiness, fumbling through a stack of program cards as Woodz explained about having to go down to court.

"Muchacho! What the hell you doing with **Heineken's** in the street! You kids I tell you . . . toma Anthony." She handed him his program card and it put an even bigger smile across his face.

"Three classes! That's it?" He asked excitedly.

"That's right sweetie all three in the afternoon . . . congratulations your on your way to graduation now take off that hat and leave me alone! All of yous!" The schedule didn't go into effect until Monday, four days away so Woodz decided to go straight home and share the news with Momma Luv and Big Tee.

Maria was there also when he arrived with the news of his eventual graduation and they congratulated him. They were proud of him and momma luv even shed tears of joy for her youngest son. Graduating High School was a feat that not too many men in their family accomplished. Woodz was a pain in the ass but she loved him to death! In light of it all Woodz felt as if a ton of weight was being lifted off his shoulders.

The weekend went smooth for him. He spent some more time with Katie and had heard over the airwaves that Foxy was throwing a birthday party so he decided to crash it and he wasn't coming alone, he brought along Jakkes who told him about a party in Jefferson he wanted to crash afterward. So the brisk January night was set.

Capone was on the corner of Lexington when he spotted both Jakkes and Woodz coming out of 1738 and Jakkes convinced Woodz to bring him along even though Capone and Woodz had not spoken for weeks. Woodz didn't care so the trio made their way towards Taft projects and ended up bumping into Ace and Jeff who decided to tag along. Foxy lived on the 13th floor of the Madison Avenue building on the corner of 114th Street. Woodz led the group towards her apartment where music could be heard playing inside.

There was a door opened down the hall with music blasting also so Jakkes and Capone approached the opened door and a slim black girl appeared.

"Party up in here what up?!" Asked Jakkes and another girl appeared from the back of the apartment . . .

"Where ya' about to go ova' there to the kiddie party?" The first girl asked Capone and Jakkes. Jakkes shot a look over at Woodz and asked the girl if they were having a party too. "Yea I guess . . . we waiting for some family and peoples to come through . . . but ya' could come through later on if ya' want . . . that shit is dead in there you'll see." Jakkes and Capone walked back over to Woodz had his ear on Foxy's door.

"Yo' nigga' lets chill with these bitches fuck this bitch nigga'! You heard her that shit is dead with lil' kids up in there my nigga'." Jakkes had the fellas laughing and Woodz was about to agree with him, but he hadn't seen Foxy in weeks and wanted to surprise her.

"Let's see what's poppin' up in here first real quick if it's trash then we out aight?" Jakkes sucked his teeth and knocked on the door with force. The door opened and a short pretty female opened the door.

"May I help you?" The music was lowered and Woodz could hear Foxy's voice in the background asking who was at the door. She spotted Woodz and covered her mouth with her hands.

"Yea I'm a friend Jenny's, Anthony . . . we here for her birthday." The female nodded her head and examined him and the fellas.

"Jenny friends huh? All of you's friends of Jenny too?" She gave the fellas a conspicuous stare. Foxy yelled for her to let them in and approached the door. She couldn't believe that Woodz was at her door on her birthday.

"What are you doing here!? Who told you? Oh my god!" She gave him a hug and led them all into the living room. There were a lot of people there already but everyone was sitting and not dancing, and they all looked real young just as the black girl down the hall had told them. Woodz was actually happy to see her and enjoyed seeing her glowing.

"I got the word over the mic so I wanted to show you some love and crash ya' heard." He replied scanning her up and down. Foxy had on tight blue jeans, pink tank top, and her long brown hair was combed straight down her back. She looked real good Woodz thought with the addition of the cherry red lipstick.

"And all these nigga's . . . I already know him, hi Capone and him I think." She said pointing at Ace who was talking to Jakkes.

"Ayo what's your name again? Jakkes asked.

"Jenny" She answered.

"Jenny what up Jakkes yo' what up? Why this shit so dead? Let's pop this shit off what up? I'll set it off. Whoever that was who opened the door tell her to come out here and I'll set it off what's good!?"

"That's cuz' these mothafucka's is frontin' and acting madd pussy!" Foxy yelled at everyone sitting and standing around the living room. "You heard him! What ya' waitin' for?!" She added, Jakkes turned and huddled with Woodz who was admiring Foxy's ass.

"Oh no no no my nigga' I can't be the only nigga' dancin' at a house party and these nigga's look like kids hell no!" Woodz shook his head at Capone who took a seat next to him. Ace and Jeff stood nearby listening and observing the female who had opened the door for them now walking their way.

"You guys want something to drink? All we got is soda no liquor so forget about that! Take the soda!"

She added walking back towards the kitchen. She was Foxy's oldest sister *Amanda* and chaperon for the night. Woodz followed her into the cluttered kitchen to fetch a drink. "Anthony right?" She asked pouring him a cup of **Coca Cola**.

"Yea." He replied.

"Wait? Is it you who Jenny be talkin' to on that fuckin' hand radio thing?" Woodz shrugged his shoulders and smiled.

"It depends . . . can I have a cup of the good stuff if I tell you?" Amanda laughed and told him to enjoy the party. Woodz sat back down as the fellas all grabbed their own cups. Capone was scoping out a girl seated by the sofa at the far end of the living room he recognized from the block. Woodz spotted her also and watched Capone as he made his way towards her.

Jakkes meanwhile tried to convince Amanda to dance with him as Foxy was putting on her new **Hot 97 C.D.**

"I know you not plannin' to sit here all night at my party!?" She asked Woodz, kneeling down in front of him and bouncing to the **Beenie Man** and **Maya** song.

"Fox I don't dance . . . didn't I tell you that? That's why I brong my boys with me so they could do the dancin' for me."

Ten minutes had passed since Wood and the gang arrived at Foxy's party and the energy of the party remained dormant, and the gang ready to leave.

"My nigga' this shit is dead B' why the fuck is we still here nigga'? look at these nigga's in here . . . half of them should be in bed for school right now Ha ha." Capone and Woodz both laughed at Jakkes. "Jenny, penny whateva' her name is dogz, she's throwin' a party with C. D's my nigga' . . . C.D.'s! a C.J.! nigga'!!" The fellas all cracked up. Woodz knew he was right.

"Aight five more minutes and we out . . . yo' Capone what up with Princess ass?" Princess was the girl Capone recognized at the other side of the living room. Jakkes knew her too and quickly interjected.

"Oh no no no no!! we don't do those my nigga'!" He shouted taking a quick look over at Princess. "That's a dirty bitch there so scratch that thought my nigga'!" Woodz could only shake his head. Jakkes was on a roll and walked over to Jenny who was talking to one of her friends and grabbed her hand to dance with her. The fellas cheered him on while her friends only looked on.

Amanda heard the cheering and helped Jenny sandwich Jakkes while they danced. Woodz hoped that it would jump start the party but Jakkes valiant effort worked to no avail. Jakkes shot Woodz a look as he rose and gave the fellas the sign . . . he'd seen enough.

"What happened? Where you going? Ya' just got here!" Foxy exclaimed realizing that Woodz and his crew were heading towards the door. She didn't want him to leave let alone the fellas. They had been the only excitement all night! She also wanted to spend time with Woodz. She held on to his arm as he led the fellas towards the door. "You leaving me?" She asked Woodz with a sad puppy face.

"Yea . . . these nigga's wanna' bounce and hit up a party in Jeff . . . what up with your peoples you got up in here? He replied not wanting to leave but he knew better.

"I know! Half the people I invited ain't show up yet . . . at least take a picture with me . . . I want a picture with you." Foxy's younger sister **Rica** snapped the picture of the bunch by the door. "Better not find out ya' went down the hall where them bitches is at." Foxy closed the door and Jakkes immediately ridiculed Woodz.

"Nigga'! I can't believe I let you drag me in there . . . how old is this bitch anyway?" Woodz shrugged his shoulders.

"Sixteen, seventeen I don't know . . . check them bitches ova' there or we out?" Capone knocked on the door but not one of the girls from earlier answered. They decided to hit the party in Jefferson and it was live! They had a few drinks and watched Jakkes steal the show on the dance floor until a fight broke out downstairs and police shut it down minutes later.

Woodz went straight upstairs when he got back to Clinton and ended up striking up a convo with Princess who was at Foxy's party over the walky.

"Why ya' break out for? That shit was dead right?" She asked Woodz who was lighting up his **Black n Mild Cream** cigar.

"Yea . . . it wasn't what I expected you heard plus nigga's wanted to go to a party in Jeff . . . shit was live too you should've came with us." Woodz spoke to Princess for about an hour before he fell asleep. He went to school on Monday loving his new schedule. After fourth period he ran around looking for Gigilo and found Nicki talkin' to one of her friends. He crept up behind her . . .

"What sup Fresca?" He whispered into her ear. She turned to give him a hug and asked him where he'd been all morning. "Oh I didn't tell you bout my new schedule? We getting' ready to graduate ma my schedule is poppin' right now! But I wouldn't mind stayin' one more year to be here with you tho' . . ." Woodz smiled.

"Yea aight nigga' you better stop bull shittin' and graduate already." The two of them were spending a lot of time talking over the airwaves lately. Woodz gave her his full attention whenever she hailed him. He stood against the wall scoping her while she spoke to someone passing by. Nicki was wearing a crispy black **Yankees** cap and two gold chains around her neck. She was always fly and Woodz loved her style!

The bell for fifth period class was about to ring so Woodz decided to share something with her before she took off.

"You know . . . being that I'm getting' ready to graduate and shit I'ma need someone to take out that night . . . you know lika' graduation date . . . basically I mean . . ." Woodz didn't get a chance to utter out what ever else he was thinking about saying because Nicki stepped in towards him and planted a nice juicy kiss on his lips. The kiss was synchronized with the bell ringing for the last period of the morning. It probably lasted only a couple of seconds but for Woodz, it seemed to slow down time and space!

"Don't be late to class Hollywood . . . sexy." She whispered tracing his lips with her fingertips then ran off to catch up with her friends by the staircase. Woodz watched her hurry off, frozen and oblivious to the guys standing outside one of the classrooms a few feet away.

"O.K Ant! We see you!" They shouted. Woodz smiled and strode to his Global Studies class, late but it was well worth it.

He got home at around 2 o'clock on the breezy and sunny afternoon and decided to take a walk to the McDonald's on 103rd on Third Avenue. He purchased his number 2 cheese burger meal and went back upstairs to eat. Later on in the night he came back downstairs to buy some batteries for his radio. He took a walk to the 99 Cent store on Third Avenue and when he was walking back he bumped into Jakkes.

"Yo' c'mon come with me to Boy's Harbor to play ball my nigga'."

"Boy's Harbor? Where on Fifth?" Woodz asked, not exactly enthusiastic about going.

"Yea nigga' c'mon I'll go with you to change or come like that fuck it." Woodz wasn't in the mood to go anywhere tonight. He was looking forward to finding Chula on the walky and maybe head over to meet with her later.

"I'm good Jakkes I don't feel like playin' no ball."

"Then fuck it don't play! There's gonna' be bitches there c'mon, let em' see your chain and shit and they'll be on your dick! Ha ha." Woodz laughed, and something in his mind told him to go but he just wanted to relax upstairs tonight.

". . . Nah I'm going upstairs my nigga'." Jakkes was upset now.

"C'mon nigga'! fuckin' midget! Nah for real Woodz c'mon . . . Ant?! Stop bull shittin'!" Woodz gave him a pound and walked away as Jakkes practically begged him to come along. "You just wanna' go upstairs and talk on that stupid radio! Play Smack Down with my brother and smoke up all of my roaches!!" Woodz looked back and chuckled at Jakkes.

"You crazy nigga'! I'll holla' at you later!"

Woodz wondered why Jakkes was so determined for him to come along with him. Upstairs he dimmed his lights to lie in bed and vibe with Chula on the walky. He was convincing her to let him come see her when he dozed off. He must've dozed off for about almost an hour until Big Tee finally woke him up.

"Anthony someone's at the door for you." Big Tee said walking away from Woodz door before he could answer.

"What!? Tito who is it?!" Big Tee didn't hear him and let in the unexpected guest. Woodz door swung open and L.J. walked into the room wearing a bright white North Face coat and was followed by *Kendu* and *Sha*.

"Why the fuck is your light off nigga'? Fuck is you doing in here . . . you better not be butt ass in here nigga'." L.J. joked adjusting the lighting. Woodz wasn't happy at all about the intrusion.

"Tee what the fuck!? Damn! Can't a nigga' relax in fuckin' peace??" Whined Woodz sitting up in bed.

"Nigga' get your lil' ass up." L.J. laughed and sat down on the burgundy swivel chair. He took off the white North Face and tossed it on the bed. Woodz rubbed his eyes and turned his attention to Kendu and Sha.

"Kendu what up? Sha fuck is you doing up in here?" Kendu and Sha were both entranced by the pictures and posters all over the room. Woodz eye balled his three guests suspiciously and assumed that they were using his home base as a refuge. "Yo' ya getting' chased by them boys or something?" L.J. sucked his teeth and pulled a Dutch cigar out of his coat pocket.

"Nah nigga' nigga's came to check you . . . what up I know you getting ready for graduation too right?

Nigga's wanna' get nice and celebrate early ya' heard!"
Kendu turned towards Woodz revealing his own Dutch
cigar also.

"Yea Ant what up my nigga'? nigga's is tryin' to
get nice what up?" Woodz and Kendu were childhood
friends and rivals. As Kendu got older he got caught up
deeper in the street life and ended up going up north.
He returned after 2 years with an attitude like if he was
the baddest motherfucker on the planet. Sha on the
other hand was a chubby 13 year old following along.

He lived on Park Avenue and Woodz normally
didn't allow outsiders like him inside his home base,
but due to them barging in unexpectedly he made an
exception. "C'mon Ant nigga's wanna' roll up." Kendu
told Woodz taking off his coat and having a seat on the
swivel chair.

L.J. also pulled out two **Steel Reserve 40** beers
from out of his coat pocket.

"Whoa whoa ya' could roll up but no puffin' or
drinkin' in here not tonight . . . I had to clean up after
ya' nigga's threw up in here last time . . . remember
that shit?!" Woodz and L.J. both laughed. He played
his **Makaveli** C.D. and Kendu rolled blunts up. Sha
was quiet just looking out the window. He didn't really
want to be there with L.J. and Kendu but decided
to tag along. He spotted Mark and Greg walking up
Lexington towards Woodz building and told L.J.

"Yo' these nigga's Mark and Gee gonna' meet us
up here or in the hallway . . . you coming out nigga'?"

215

L.J. and Kendu were ready to roll out and start the celebration. Woodz thought about Jakkes earlier.

"Fuck it we celebratin' right? I'ma get dressed real quick and meet ya' in da' hallway aight." L.J, Kendu and Sha took their show out to the hallway where they met up with Mark and Greg. Woodz got dressed and felt kind of bad that he was going back on his word to Jakkes, but he put on his gray Timbs, blue Nautica jeans, gray and yellow Old Navy sweater, even put on his gray bandana. He finally joined the others in the hallway.

L.J. was playing his new **Bad Boy** mix tape on Greg's radio and passed the 40's around so that every one could tap the bottle. Kendu lit up the L's and Mark revealed the bottle of **E&J** he brought upstairs. Woodz opened one of the 40's and posted up by the elevator. He took a heavy swig listening to the new Notorious song playing. As the drinks and L's rotated around Woodz thought about Nicki who had opened the door for him to make a move on her. Would she be the one who he would settle down with?? He couldn't wait for tomorrow.

Rabbit sat in his living room bored clicking through channels on the T.V. He muted the volume and approached his door finally hearing music being played in the hallway. He opened his door assuming that it was his brother *Will* with his boys, but when he looked in the hallway he saw Sha sitting on the floor against the wall. He stepped out into the hallway and walked towards Sha then spotted Mark.

"Rabbit! What up my nigga'? Woodz turned his head with the Dutch hanging from his lips inhaling the Chocolate Tye. He stared at Rabbit who smirked at him and greeted the fellas then him.

"What up Conejo?" He took a sip from the Erk n Jerk and smiled at Rabbit. "Haven't seen you in a minute . . . you aight?"

"Yea nigga' look at you tho' you look twisted dogs!" Woodz handed the bottle back to Gee who then offered it to Rabbit. Rabbit took a light swig and handed it back.

"What up with you and Maria? Woodz asked wiping his mouth.

"We aight . . . you know L.B. nigga'." Woodz twisted his face at him.

"That ain't your L.B. nigga' that's wifey!" Woodz laughed and so did Rabbit who asked Mark for another shot of E&J. L.J. lowered the radio down and threw out the Steel Reserve bottles down the incinerator.

"Yo a nigga' feel nice right now shit!!" He wiped his mouth and lit up a cigarette. His eyes were as red as everyone else's. The L's were all smoked up and the fellas were ready to head outside. "A nigga' need some pussy right now ya' heard!" L.J. hollered fixing his coat. "Ant you coming out nigga'?" He asked Woodz.

Woodz adjusted his black and gray Yankee fitted cap. He was smacked and figured that a little bit of air wouldn't hurt.

"Yea fuck it . . . I'ma go grab my jacket and shit . . . I'll be right back aight" He asked Rabbit what he was going to do and Rabbit decided to retrieve his coat also.

* * *

Raphael Perez was exhausted and ready to head on home. He grabbed his jacket but couldn't seem to remember where he left his wallet.

"Cono!?" He thought turning towards his wife *Antonia* who was sitting at the table sipping on coffee. "Where did I put my wallet?" He asked. She pointed towards the living room right next to the kitchen. He dragged his feet into the quiet living room and spotted it on the beige sofa.

The wallet was attached to a silver chain that he wore around his neck so that he wouldn't misplace it. He dreaded walking home all the way to Washington projects, but it has been his home since he and Antonia separated a few years back. They had three children together, two daughters, one son and a newborn grandson from their youngest daughter.

Although the two were separated and both dealing with their own health issues, they were still a family intact and loved their children. The fifty year old remained a figure in his childrens lives and did his best to be a good father. He kissed Antonia good night and exited the apartment. He had to wake up early for a welfare appointment tomorrow at seven thirty so he wanted to get home as fast as possible to go to bed.

Mr. Perez took three different kinds of medications and started to feel the effects of them as he waited for the elevator to arrive. He was pleased when it finally arrived finding it empty as well. He pressed the 1 button and leaned against the wall as it descended downstairs shaft.

The elevator stopped on the 10th floor where a crowd of teens were all hanging out and listening to music. There was smoke everywhere and the smell of Marijuana and alcohol was present.

"Hold the door." He heard L.J. tell him. L.J. was talking to Kendu while they waited for Woodz to come back. Feeling weary Mr. Perez wanted to get home now so he pressed the close button not wanting to wait any longer. The door quickly closed but L.J. rushed to stop it from closing completely. He and Kendu banged on the door until it got stuck between the tenth and ninth floor. They vowed to fuck the old man up.

Woodz strode into his room and grabbed his blue and white racing jacket that L.J. had given him. He sprayed some cologne on himself then grabbed his keys. He stepped into the bathroom splashed a little water on his face and giggled when he saw his reflection in the mirror. He was twisted. All of a sudden a strange eerie feeling fell upon him and a voice in his head told him not to go back out to the hallway. *STAY INSIDE ANT! DON'T GO OUTSIDE!* The voice warned, echoing faintly in his head.

Woodz rubbed his eyes and shook off the eerie feeling. He walked out the bathroom to rejoin the fellas back in the hallway. Rabbit and him opened their doors simultaneously and stepped out into the hallway. They both heard a commotion and someone banging against the elevator door. It was L.J. who was yelling at someone inside the elevator.

"Are you stuck?! Stupid motha' fucka'!" He yelled while Kendu and Gee tried to budge the door open.

"Who's that L? Somebody's stuck in there?" Woodz drunkenly asked, but his question seemed to fall on deaf ears because no one paid him any mind. The elevator descended one flight down so the fellas rushed down the stairs to the ninth floor but it was stuck between floors now. L.J. and Kendu continued to bang on the door yelling at whoever it was that was inside of it.

Woodz remembered that he had a Housing elevator key and reached into his pocket. "Yo! I got the key for this shit I'ma go downstairs and bring it down with my key." He wasn't sure if anybody heard him but he ran and stumbled down the ten flights of stairs trying to reach the lobby as fast as he can.

He finally reached the first floor dizzy and covered in sweat. He wobbled over to the elevator and inserted the key into the emergency keyhole but before he could turn it the elevator bell began ringing. *Oh aight they in there.* He said to himself walking over to the front door to step outside for some air.

Woodz could hear Gee's radio booming inside the elevator, laughter and then loud thumps against the elevator walls. He wondered what was going on as the strange sounds drew him back into the lobby. Woodz never expected what he saw next.

The elevator door opened and Sha, Kendu, Mark and Gee spilled out of it laughing while grabbing onto the person in the elevator. L.J. finally emerged holding someone's arm while everyone was yelling at the guy. Mr. Perez was petrified. Woodz vision was impaired and couldn't make out his face. *Oh a vic?* He assumed automatically that it was another Mexican to add on to their list.

He took a few steps towards the fellas and heard L.J. shout "Hit that nigga' Ant!" Who then shoved the man towards Woodz. Woodz first reaction was to swing and punch the man across his jaw then he shoved the man back on L.J. and watched him punch the guy also.

"Get this nigga' off me!" L.J. shouted shoving the man towards Gee and Mark. Mark knocked him down onto the floor and the four drunken fools proceeded to kick the man on the ground. Mr. Perez was knocked out from L.J.'s punch and laid lifeless on the ground.

L.J. checked his pockets then removed the chained wallet from around Mr. Perez neck as Mark, Gee and Woodz continued to stomp on him. Rabbit finally made it downstairs and couldn't believe what he was seeing.

"What the fuck is ya' nigga's doin'!? chill yo'!" He pleaded as L.J. Kendu, and Sha ran out the back door. "Yo' stop niggas!" He pleaded again grabbing Mark who stumbled against the wall then ran out the door with him. Woodz meanwhile was yelling and banging on the walls hysterically, the boy had lost his mind! He imagined himself on his favorite wrestling show and grabbed Gee's radio then pretended to smash it over Mr. Perez pummeled body. Gee finally grabbed Woodz and they both bolted out the back door.

Gee and him rushed across the street following far behind L.J. and Kendu who were turning the corner on Park Avenue. Woodz spotted a black wallet on the floor and picked it up as he and Gee caught up to Rabbit and Mark. They all hurried into the building and scrambled up to Kendu's floor. They were all out of breath and silent. Woodz caught his breath and looked through the wallet he picked up on the floor outside.

He found an photo I.D. and looked at the face of the man who they had just beaten the hell out of.

"Ayo ya' nigga's is crazy! Don't nobody say shit about this shit!" Kendu demanded leaning against the wall next to L.J.

"Yo' who the fuck was that?" Gee asked looking at Mark and everyone. They all shrugged their shoulders mean while Woodz dug through the wallet again and took a look at the man's picture. He didn't recognize the face but the name made his heart skip a beat.

Mr. Raphael Perez Sr.? Raphael Perez?? Raphael Perez!!? Oh shit! Oh shit! He repeated in his head. His face quickly turning pale and heart was beating rapidly. Woodz hoped that it was the booze doing it to him and that Raphael Perez wasn't who he thought it was. He turned towards the others who were watching him fumble through the wallet.

"Oh shit ya' . . . we fucked up . . . we fucked up yo! Ya' know who the fuck that was??" Everyone's faces were blank "That was Ray-Ray's pops yo' . . . Raphael Perez that's Ray-Ray's name! we just beat the shit outta' Ray-Ray's pops!!" He exclaimed in disbelief. Mark and Gee didn't believe it and walked towards him to see the wallet themselves.

"Oh shit . . . this nigga' ain't lying." Mark said looking over at both Kendu and L.J. who were completely silent. Rabbit took a look at the wallet also and just shook his head. They were about to panic. Woodz grabbed his head. He couldn't believe that he'd screwed up again, big time this time! *I could've stopped it . . . I should've never came out . . . Jakkes? I should've went with this nigga' yo'!* He frantically thought to himself.

223

He knelt down and covered his mouth and just stared at the wall. It wasn't making any sense to him. *Oh shit this nigga's probably dead! A old nigga' can't survive that shit . . . what the fuck did I do!?* He tried to get a hold of himself then the sound of Kendu's voice snapped him out of his zone.

"Ant nigga'! look ya' don't nobody say shit cuz' don't nobody know shit aight? Don't nobody say shit aight? Mark? Gee? Rabbit? Ant? Ant!?" Woodz jerked his head towards him and L.J. suddenly filled with a troubling thought.

"Ya' knew who it was?" He asked softly. "Ya' knew who he was!" He repeated sternly looking right at Kendu and L.J.'s eyes. Anger brewed inside of him. He wasn't inside the elevator to see who started it but was sure that someone knew who Mr. Perez was.

"You buggin' nigga' ain't nobody know shit, this nigga' could be dead! So can't none of us say shit about this shit . . . get rid of the wallet and everybody go home and lay low til' this shit dies down." Kendu wanted to make sure that the fellas were all on the same page.

He gave everyone dap and told Woodz to toss the wallet down the incinerator. Woodz mind was racing and he didn't know what to think, but he believed that they knew something. Kendu ordered Sha to go home and keep his mouth shut and went home himself. L.J. and the rest collected themselves and hopped onto the elevator to go downstairs. They quickly walked out of the building and turned on 110th street towards Lexington Avenue.

"Ya' nigga's be safe remember what this nigga' said." L.J. said disappearing down the train station steps. Mark, Rabbit, Gee and Woodz stopped by the corner Loosy store. The scene in front of Woodz building was horrific. Police cars, Fire Trucks and Ambulances surrounded the building.

"Woodz mind was still racing. Who found him? Was he dead? He thought for the worst and couldn't believe what he had done. It happened so fast. Rabbit spotted his brother Will pulling up to the corner in a M. P. V van and decided to hitch a ride with him. He told the fellas to be safe and hoped that they would be ok. The trio quickly marched up Lexington Avenue and never looked back as they turned on 111th street trooping towards Gee's projects. The celebration turned into a disaster!

CHAPTER 15

The Aftermath

They sunk their heads and sucked their teeth wishing that it was all a bad dream . . . but it was reality. As the third of three blunts was just about finished Woodz had realized that he had more to worry about then both Mark and Gee. He had to return to the building and face the fire. *This is the kinda' shit that changes nigga's lives yo'.* He thought to himself wondering if anybody had spotted them. If someone did then it was over.

He wondered who initiated the act. Who was the one that fucked their celebration up?? He sat on the floor in Gee's bathroom regretting his association with them all. Mark stood up and wiped ashes off his shirt.

"Yo' the important shit now is what this nigga' Kendu said . . . nigga's gotta' hold it down straight cheese . . . this shit's gonna' die down in a few weeks."

Gee stood up to spray his air freshener and asked if anybody was thirsty.

They each took turns using the bathroom then sat in the quiet kitchen. No one seemed to be awake in the apartment except for Gee's mom Chrissy. She walked out of her bedroom and found the trio quietly sitting at the square wooden kitchen table.

"Greg? Offer your friends somethin' to drink baby." Gee stood by Mark drinking a cup of cherry Kool-Aid.

"I did ma'." Chrissy quickly sensed that something was wrong with her son. Her motherly wit picked it up immediately! She already knew Mark, his mother Elen and her were close friends so she considered him her son. Chrissy didn't remember meeting the short Puertorican boy before. Or did she?

"Your name is Tony or Anthony right?" She asked Woodz who glanced up at her, red eyed and awkwardly. He nodded his head and forced a smile. "Boy don't be shy! I'm Chrissy, Greg tells me all the stories about ya' in Clinton! You mess wit' that skinny Spanish girl . . . that girl Melly right?" Woodz actually smirked and nodded his head again. He looked over at Gee who turned his face away grinning and gulping down the rest of his Kool-Aid.

Chrissy laughed and patted Mark on his shoulder. Greg was her oldest son. She was loved by his friends because she allowed Greg to smoke his weed, the type of mother that any teen dreamed about having! "Mark!

Baby why you so quiet? Look at you boy . . . if Elen could see you now ooh! Haha." Mark chuckled and smiled up at Chrissy.

"I'm good Chrissy . . . just high and shit basically." Chrissy still sensed that something was wrong with the boys and she expected her son to be as honest as he always was.

"Greg baby, what happened baby? Why ya' look so down? A fight? Someone got shot or beat up?" The fellas froze and shot looks at one another. Chrissy read their expressions and realized she had hit the nail on the head!

Mark gave Greg a look not to open his mouth, but Greg didn't want to hide anything from his mother . . . he trusted his mother.

"Yea Ma' somebody got hurt." Woodz jaw tighten hearing Greg open his mouth like that. *This nigga's stupid!* He thought to himself. Mark closed his eyes and slowly shook his head.

"Aight so who was it?" Chrissy asked. "One of your friends? A stranger?" She asked now serious as she stared at her son.

"A stranger ma' it was a mistake and we hopin' that shit don't get crazy."

"Greg . . ." Chrissy was quickly upset and worried now. "I told you bout getting' in trouble don't get into no bullshit out there . . . you hear me baby? That goes for ya' two too ya' better be careful and don't get ya'selves hurt out there." She gave her son a kiss and said goodnight to both Mark and Woodz. They waited until Chrissy locked her bedroom door close to ridicule Greg.

"Yo' nigga'! Is you crazy?! Why the fuck did you tell your mom's that?" Snapped Mark scratching his head and standing from his seat. Woodz looked on while as Greg placed his empty cup in the sink.

"Nigga' we good my mom's is official." Woodz hoped that Greg was right. They exited the building and made their way towards 110th Street.

"Gee where you goin' B? nigga's ain't tryin' to chill tonight." Mark said. He wanted to buy his food from *Kennedy Fried Chicken* and head upstairs. He didn't feel good about Greg telling Chrissy anything. Woodz walked quietly, nervous about going back to 109th.

"Nigga' I just wanna' find out what's good, I'm not stayin' home noid' and shit." They made their way through Taft projects on the cool night. The streets were quiet when they reached Kennedy's. Woodz stood by the doorway and spotted a small crowd in front of Thugged Out's building.

"Yo' Ray-Ray's sister's in front of the building wit' Jezzy and them . . . I don't know if she saw us." Mark peeked out holding his bag of food.

"C'mon lets walk through Park like we just walkin' and shit." He led the way as they turned towards Park Avenue. Woodz thought about Capone and wished that he could run up to his place for refuge for the rest of the night. The three of them reached the corner of 109th and Mark checked his watch.

"Yo' my nigga' I'm out . . . I'ma go bust this shit down and sleep I see ya' tomorrow . . . Gee you gonna' stay wit' Woodz?" Greg looked at Woodz who shrugged his shoulders.

"Fuck it yea." Mark gave Gee and Woodz dap and walked off towards his building. Woodz took a deep breath and slowly walked with Greg towards Lexington Avenue. The back door of the building was shut so they had no choice but to enter through the front of the building. The avenue was quiet but there was a buzz in the air that could be felt. Woodz reminded himself that no matter what he had been with Mark and Greg all night and didn't know anything.

Crossing the street from 108th Street was Jakkes, Ray-Ray and *Bibby*, a short black kid who lived on the third floor of 1738 and Ray-Ray's best friend. They spotted Woodz and Greg approaching the steps of the building and yelled out to them before they entered. Jakkes hoped that Woodz knew something about Ray-Ray's father attack. They had just questioned guys from Lexington Gardens who claimed not knowing a thing.

"Yo'! Where ya' comin' from?" Jakkes asked frantically. Woodz and Greg noticed Ray-Ray wielding a large kitchen knife in his right hand. His eyes were watery and red.

"Yo' Ray-Ray? You aight nigga'?" Greg asked glancing down at the knife and doing his best to sound as innocent as possible.

"Nah he ain't aight where ya' nigga's been at all night?" Jakkes stared right at Woodz who couldn't stop thinking about Ray-Ray's father. Greg answered.

"We've been in my crib, me, Ant and this nigga' Mark why? What the fuck is going on?" Woodz did his best not to appear nervous and watched both Bibby and Ray-Ray shoot looks at both him and Greg.

"This shit's crazy yo' . . . my nigga' nigga's robbed and beat up this nigga's pops in the building . . . fucked him up bad B we tryin' to find out who did it but NIGGA'S DON'T KNOW SHIT!!" Shouted Jakkes feeling frustrated and disturbed about the situation. Tears rolled down Ray-Ray's face while Bibby kept his stare focused on Greg.

The picture of Ray-Ray's father remained fixed in their minds. Jakkes older brother A.D. was the one who found him in the lobby lying helpless by the elevator. Jakkes stared at Woodz. He looked spaced out and shaken up. "Ant? You didn't see or hear anything on that walky talky shit my nigga'?" Woodz slowly shook his head no. His head was already spinning and heart was beating rapidly.

"Nah . . . I don't have it on me B' I'm already twisted fuckin' with these nigga's now hearin' this shit?? Ray you aight my nigga'? I'm sorry to hear this shit B'." Ray-Ray didn't respond or even look at anyone. He clutched the Ginsu kitchen knife in his hand and looked off into the distance, not believing that his father would live.

Jakkes thanked both Greg and Woodz and the two made their way into the building. There were gloves, bandages and gauze still on the lobby floor and it left Woodz feeling nauseous. He was still replaying pieces of the incident in his head and felt ashamed about how successful he and Greg played off their alibi.

They made it upstairs Woodz was immediately questioned by Big Tee and Momma Luv about his whereabouts and the incident downstairs. He denied knowing anything about it and quickly ushered Greg into the room. He sat on his bed not believing the night they had. Both let out sighs of relief and looked out the window to smoke a blunt Greg had in his pocket. After they smoked they played the 64 until the next morning.

When Greg finally went home Woodz was exhausted and tried not to think about the incident or Mr. Perez. As it stood their names were cleared by their alibi but he wondered how long it would stand. What was supposed to be a celebration had some how turned into a nightmare!

*   *   *

Woodz sat in Math class totally preoccupied with Monday night's events in his mind. He had hoped it was all a bad dream when he awoke from his deep sleep Tuesday missing a day of school but unlike Sonia's claims of being pregnant by him this had really happened! His conscience was eating him up from the moment he woke up that morning for school. All he could think about was Mr. Perez dying, how could he be able to live with that!?

"Yo' Ant what up? You aight?" Gigilo couldn't help notice that his boy was quieter than usual.

"Yea just tired yo . . . had a long night ya' heard."

"Son you know we bout to graduate! We bout to ball my nigga'!" Woodz gave Gigilo a faint smile. Graduation was the last thing on his mind. He hardly got any sleep last night so when he made it home he went straight to bed.

Everyone on Lexington Avenue was talking about the incident and Momma Luv and Big Tee were still interrogating Woodz about it. He continued to deny knowing anything about it and prayed that he would be able to get through the month. He was filled with overwhelming anger about getting himself caught up in such an ugly mess. *Why the fuck is this shit happening to me now? Fuck!!!* Just when it seemed that he was finally cleaning up his act the mess got worse!

He made it to school the next day but left after one class and went straight home. He was restless and couldn't focus. Woodz was content on spending the rest of the winter and spring upstairs if it was necessary. No matter how he tried to rid his mind off

Mr. Perez he couldn't shake the thoughts or dreams, they haunted him and brought his whole world down. He just wanted to remain in complete solitude until everything was back to normal.

Unfortunately that solitude would come to an end with a knock on the door and Jakkes walking into his room.

"What up . . ." Jakkes muttered walking straight towards the window sitting on Woodz bar stool. Woodz sat up in bed wishing that Jakkes hadn't come up. He quietly flipped through the channels on the T.V. with the remote not knowing what to say to him. Jakkes sucked his teeth and spat out the window shaking his head and finally broke his silence.

"This nigga' Ray-Ray is buggin' off this shit yo . . . his momz is sick and his fuckin' pops is twisted yo' . . . how da' fuck don't nobody know shit? Shit is crazy B' . . . I know you know somethin' Ant." A moment of silence settled in again as Woodz continued to surf through channels. He felt uneasy as Jakkes words bombarded his conscience. "I know you know somethin' Ant . . . I know you do." The words echoed all over the room and in his head. Woodz heart started beating rapidly as he battled with his conscience. *MOTHA' FUCKA"!! AHH!! I HATE THIS SHIT!!*

He wiped his mouth and thought about all the vics then Mr. Perez, and from no where the thought of all his own father who he knew little about crept into his mind. He wondered why his father abandoned him and his mother. He turned to the streets to drown his pain but only encountered more pain. *Fuck man . . . I should've went with this nigga' that night . . . why the fuck I go out with these mothafuckas . . .* The regrets piled up in his mind but there was no changing what happened.

Woodz had hit a low moment in his life. He was a failure, delinquent and full of shame. Ray-Ray had something that he didn't . . . a father, and he didn't know if he could accept having possibly taken him away from Ray-Ray. He sighed quietly and muted the T.V. He didn't know what was driving him to do what he was about to do but whatever it was had overwhelmed him.

"I should've went with you to play ball B' . . ." He muttered to Jakkes who jerked his head at him as Woodz stared at the blank T.V. He had a weird look on his face and turned towards Jakkes. He looked right at Jakkes and braced himself emotionally for what he was about to do. "I was there Jakkes . . . it was me." Jakkes fixed his face.

"Ant . . . Ant stop bullshittin' you know what happened? I knew you knew somethin'! Tell me the truth nigga' and don't say it was you cuz' you wouldn't do that my nigga' I know you nigga' who was it!?" Jakkes was frantic to know whatever it was Woodz knew. Woodz on the other hand got the feeling that Jakkes already had an idea about who was responsible. He took another deep breath and stared down at his floor.

"Me . . . Gee and these nigga's." He whispered out unable to look at Jakke's face.

"What other nigga's Ant? L.J.? Was L.J. and Kendu there too with ya'?" Jakkes knelt in front of Woodz with his hands clasped together. Woodz slowly nodded his head yes. "OHH! OH!! Mothafuckas!! I knew it!!" He exclaimed pounding his fist. Jakkes placed his hand on Woodz shoulder. "Look my nigga' you gotta' tell Ray-Ray what you just told me . . . don't worry about nuffin' I know it wasn't you who did that Ant that ain't you . . . I'll be right back aight." Jakkes turned towards the door but Woodz blocked the door with his foot.

"Nigga' is you crazy!? You want me and this nigga' to kill each other in here?!" Jakkes stared at Woodz sternly.

"Chill my nigga' trust me." Woodz stared back and moved his foot away from the door. "Fuck it." He said as Jakkes rushed out the apartment.

He knew he broke the pact that they had made in the hallway that night, but Woodz felt strangely relieved getting it off his chest. When Greg revealed a piece of it to his own mother he felt as if the pact was broken then and there. Nevertheless he felt responsible for the whole thing and wanted to face the consequences no matter how grim it was.

He believed that if it was all explained for what it was an accident then perhaps they wouldn't have much to worry about. Jakkes returned to the apartment with Ray-Ray and whisked him to the room where Woodz at on his bed resting his chin on his fists. He stared up at the two and balled up his fist tighter.

"Ant tell Ray what you told me . . . go head." Woodz opened his mouth but nothing came out. He sighed and hoped that Jakkes would break them up if Ray-Ray swung.

"I was there Ray it was me who beat up your pops dogz . . . I'm sorry Ray." Woodz kept his fist balled up as tight as he could and waited for Ray-Ray to flinch. Ray-Ray looked back at him and Jakkes who sucked his teeth and shook his head.

"Ant nigga'! Don't bullshit my nigga' tell him what you told me c'mon dogz." Woodz cleared his throat and explained what he could remember about the night. How it began as a celebration and transformed into a big accident.

"I'm sorry Ray . . . nigga's didn't plan this shit and if I would've been in that elevator that shit would've never happened." Tears of anger started forming in Woodz eyes. He couldn't conceal his emotions as much as he knew he should. Ray-Ray just stared down at the beige tiled floor.

He held back his own tears feeling furious and fighting the urge to hook off on Woodz jaw, but he promised Jakkes that he wouldn't and couldn't deny feeling a level of respect for Woodz for actually confessing to him. The little guy had manned up as for the others however, he swore that they were going to pay!

"Don't worry Ant you aight, good lookin'." Ray-Ray said turning to Jakkes who nodded his head. Jakkes gave Woodz a warm but disappointed look and walked out the room with Ray-Ray behind him.

Woodz couldn't believe that just like that it had transpired. He peeked out the window and spotted Rabbit downstairs on the corner.

"Rabbit! Rabbit!! Come up! Now!!" He hollered. Rabbit motioned that he was on his way up. Woodz went to the bathroom and splashed water on his face, he hoped that he made the right choice moments ago.

It took Rabbit almost fifteen minutes to arrive and when he did he was infuriated!

"Dogz! These nigga's just jumped me!!" Woodz closed his door.

"What? Who? Who jumped you??"

"All these nigga's! Jakkes, Ray and Bibby! I'm waitin' for the elevator and when it come they in there and grab me up . . . started swinging and kicked me on the floor . . . what the fuck yo!?" Woodz didn't understand. He clearly stated to them that Rabbit played no part in what happened, but then suddenly he understood perfectly. He had just opened a can of worms and shit was getting ready to hit the fan! Rabbit would only be the first because they weren't going to stop until each of them was dealt with.

Jakkes, Bibby and Ray-Ray walked over to Park Avenue in search for Kendu and L.J. when they spotted Sha by the back door and interrogated him, roughing him up until he confessed to everything he knew. Sha claimed his innocence and blamed it all on L.J., Woodz and Greg. When they were through with Sha they bumped into Mark walking out of his building and rushed him also.

Mark swore on his life that he didn't know anything and that who ever told them different were lying. He held his ground and immediately ran back upstairs to call Greg and L.J. The news about who was responsible quickly spread through Clinton but Woodz name was never mentioned.

Capone, Ace and the others from Clinton joined Jakkes and his partner's side in the drama. Ray-Ray wanted to get his hands on a gun so like an angry posse the group ventured to Jefferson and Washington projects in search of a hammer. They were ready to light up 109th Street so the battle lines were drawn!

Woodz remained upstairs trying to make sense of what was happening around him. He lay in bed and almost jumped out of his skin when Rabbit burst into the room unannounced.

"Yo'! Look out your window! These nigga's is fightin'!" Woodz peeked out through the royal blue curtains and his eyes bulged seeing Kendu squaring off against all three Jakkes, Ray-Ray and Bibby right outside his window! The corner was packed with people and death threats were being launched back and forth as Kendu's girlfriend Tiffany and Sha tried to hold him back. Sha ran back to warn Kendu that he was being hunted so Kendu decided to find Ray-Ray and them before they found him.

Jakke's brother A.D and others tried to restrain him and the others. They all were trying to figure out what was going on.

"Rabbit go home . . . if you could disappear nigga' aight? I'm serious." Woodz did his best to remain calm Rabbit however was paranoid! He couldn't believe how the last couple of months had unfolded. He had his own issues at home so he turned to the squad for comradeship and for a sense of family, but he only found a circle disarranged and torn apart at its core.

He was worried for Woodz who surprisingly appeared to be poised despite the carnage transpiring downstairs and wondered how Jakkes and the rest found out. He left Woodz home base feeling as if it would be the last time he would see him. L.J. was still missing in action and Mark had informed both him and Greg about their covers being blown. Greg was going to disappear with his family out of the area and L.J. would continue to lay low, Woodz however didn't know what to do.

A part of him wanted to run, but where? He still didn't want to tell Momma Luv and Big Tee the truth, but for how long could he conceal the truth from them. He remained upstairs all day and night and was even visited by Ray-Ray's sister and mom themselves later that night.

Ray-Ray had confessed to them that Woodz was a witness to the incident and was the person who told him what happened. They offered to protect him and help him disappear if he felt that he was in danger, but Woodz declined their offer. Their visit left him shaky though. He felt the pressure mounting and didn't know how long he could hold on.

CHAPTER 16

The Standoff

Detectives John Murray and Allen Dundy exited the Perez's apartment disturbed about Mr. Perez's condition. "Why the heck would anybody beat the crap outta' an old fella like that John?" Det. Dundy asked his partner of five years rubbing his forehead. They both exchanged baffled looks as they made their way down to Anthony Diaz'spartment.

Det. Murray knocked on Apt. 10 C where a heavyset brown skinned man opened the door. It was Big Tee.

"Yea may I help you?" He asked as Det. Dundy smiled and introduced his partner and himself. He informed Big Tee that they were looking for Anthony to question him about the incident that took place down in the lobby a few nights ago. Big Tee let the

Detectives inside and asked them to wait while he woke up his brother who was asleep.

Woodz was stretched out in bed but immediately awoke upon hearing the knock on the door. Having cops questioning him was not what he was hoping for. "Anthony? Anthony get up there's cops here to ask you about that shit that happened downstairs." Woodz sat up in bed cursing under his breath. "I thought you said that you didn't know anything about that?" Big Tee asked sternly, now convinced that Woodz was involved.

"I don't Tee . . ." Woodz replied grabbing and putting on his blue Nautica jeans, then slowly making his way towards the living room. His mind raced as he quickly thought of as many lies possible to deceive the two Detectives. The two tall Detectives were admiring Big Tee's fish tanks when he appeared in the doorway. Detective Murray spoke first.

"Sorry to wake you Anthony but we need to ask you a few questions about the incident that occurred on Monday night around 10 P.M." Woodz slumped on the sofa and awaited the questions as Big Tee stood near by the doorway. "According to Ms. Perez you were present that night when her husband was brutally attacked, robbed and beaten . . . is that true?" Woodz swallowed a wad of spit as Det. Dundy pulls a small note pad out of his coat pocket.

Woodz cleared his throat and chose his words carefully. He had no intention of revealing anything to the detectives. He would ride with the alibi that Ray-Ray had set for him.

"Yes . . . I was there . . ." Det. Murray dug into the beige Trench Coat pocket and pulled out several photographs. The photographs were of L.J, Kendu and Mark!

"Do you recognize any of these guys Anthony?" Det. Murray hands him the mug shots and Woodz pretended to examine the photos.

"I think I've seen them before . . . I don't know I don't really hang around here too much so, I don't know too many people from around here . . . who are they?" Det. Murray carefully analyzed Woodz.

"We were hoping that you could tell us that Anthony . . . from what the Perez family told us these seem to be her husband's attackers." Woodz stared at the mug shots and bit his lip.

"I don't know them . . . I don't hang around here too much so I don't know the guys around here." Det. Dundy scribbled away in his note pad looking around the living room.

"Do you recall seeing any of these guys on the night when Mr. Perez was brutally attacked and robbed?" Woodz realized that he had to appear oblivious as possible.

"I didn't see who beat up Mr. Perez I told them that." Both Det. Murray and Dundy were confused. They were under the impression that Woodz had witnessed first hand what had happened.

"So what or did you see?" Det. Murray asked suspiciously.

"I didn't see who beat em' up . . . I was about to come into the building and saw a bunch of guys running out the back door."

"You didn't see anybody's face or recognize any of the guys? Take a good look at the pictures Anthony." Det. Dundy was scribbling down more notes. Woodz glanced at the mug shots and handed them back to him.

"Nah . . . the only person I saw was the man laid out on the floor so I didn't even come in the building I wasn't trying to come inside!"

Det. Murray stuffed the mug shots in his pocket and rubbed his chin. He glanced down at his notes and then over at his partner who was looking over his notes.

"Do you know if any of these guys reside around here Anthony?" Murray asked.

"I dunno . . . I don't hang around here sir so if they do I don't know." The two detectives exchanged looks and were ready to leave. Det. Dundy stuck his mini note pad into his pocket and handed Woodz a small business card for him to contact them if he needed to. Woodz was relieved that the interrogation was over. The detectives exited the apartment certain that his story was fabricated.

Woodz missed another day of school but school was the last thing on his mind, the visit from the two Detectives left him paranoid. He knew that his fabricated story would only buy him so much time and time was running out. He didn't know what to do or who to turn to! The whole L.B.M squad learned of the incident but not of his participation. He remained upstairs a prisoner in his own home.

No L.B.'s or squad to bail him out, just him trying to make sense of how the situation would play out. He hadn't heard anything about L.J. or the others and blamed them for the predicament he was in. *These mothafucka's got me in this shit . . . why the fuck god? Why?* Woodz laid in bed the whole day whimpering, blaming and cursing L.J. and the rest.

At around six 0'clock an unexpected visitor showed up in his room, it was Capone. He found his best friend in darkness inside of his room slumped in bed mad at the world.

"Ant what the fuck nigga'?? Tell me this shit ain't true dogz? Ray-Ray's pops nigga'!? What the fuck was you thinkin' B'?" Capone sounded more upset than concerned. Woodz remained sulked in bed. He appreciated the visit but really wasn't in the mood to be scrutinized by Capone.

He stared at the blank T.V. as Capone stood by the bed staring at him. "C'mon nigga' get dressed and come outside for air or somethin' you can't be cooped up in here for the rest of your life B' c'mon I'm with you if anything my nigga'." Woodz didn't move a muscle. He didn't trust Capone or know why he had come up in the first place. Their friendship was on the rocks. Their glory days of being bad boyz were diminishing as the pair continued to grow apart.

Capone had dreams of becoming a rapper and Woodz was fighting against his dreams! However he realized that Capone was right. He hated being cooped up in his room. He wasn't a coward and if anything popped off then fuck it he was ready. The duo went downstairs and stood on the chilly corner of 109th. The avenue was deserted up and down Lexington. Woodz eyes were everywhere. Nobody was going to sneak up behind him.

Littlez had just visited the Perez family who also lived on her floor in 1738. At the end of summer she and her older sister moved to Wagner projects to live with their grandmother. She was also attending Park East and occasionally visited Clinton to keep up with the gossip. She couldn't believe the story that she just heard upstairs. Littlez walked down the front steps of 1738 zipping up her black North Face coat.

She spotted two lone figures on the corner and recognized them to be Capone and Woodz. Woodz name was the topic of discussion upstairs at Ray-Ray's place. Although she was pissed a part of her still cared for him and wanted to talk to him about the situation, but she was too angry and had heard enough tonight. She gave Woodz a quick brunt kiss that brushed his cheek and called him an asshole then gave Capone a kiss and walked off.

Woodz shook his head and chuckled. "I love you too Littlez." He said to himself. Ten minutes after that Woodz got tired of standing on the corner and retreated upstairs to return to his solitude. He surprisingly made it to school the following day and looked for his boy Gigilo but he was nowhere to be found. Word around school was that he had gotten locked up and that just made Woodz feel worse.

He spent most of the afternoon roaming around more than usual. He cut two of his classes in the gym and visited his teachers, watching everyone go about their business. He felt out of place, as if his days at the East were coming to an end. He left before his final period and went back home to sulk more in his solitude.

A knock on the door rattled him and he hoped that it wasn't them boys again. *Fuck! Them nigga's is back fuck* . . . He peeked through the peephole cautiously. "What the fuck??" But who he saw wasn't police, it was Jakkes and he wasn't alone . . . Ray-Ray, Bibby and his childhood friend *Coco* were all outside his door!

Woodz slid the chain on the door and cracked it open. "What up??" He asked Jakkes assuming that they were there to jump him.

"What up nigga' we came to chill with you, why you got the door chained up for?" Jakkes and Woodz both gave each other strange looks.

"Ya' came to chill with me?? Why??" Woodz kept the chain on the door. He didn't trust Jakkes or any of them.

"Yea' nigga' oh . . . Ant nigga's ain't here to do nuffin' to you nigga' we told you that you aigh't . . . so what up we chillin' out here?" Coconut and Bibby sat down on the hallway floor as Woodz finally stepped out to join them. He made sure to tie his sneakers just in case anything was said that could bring about an altercation.

He didn't know what to think. Were Jakkes and the rest showing him a sign of support? Perhaps even respect?? He stood under the doorway with the door open as his guest all sat on the waxed floor.

"Yo' Ant my nigga' what the fuck happened that night?" Bibby asked looking up at Woodz who stared down at the floor and shook his head.

"Yea Ant cuz' I cant believe this shit." Coco added rubbing his head. Woodz regretfully retold how the whole night unfolded. He didn't seem to remember everything but what he did remember was enough to fill him and the others with the grim picture and disbelief. Jakkes confessed to him that someone in Thugged Out's building had spotted them running out of the building and that the person had consoled Ray-Ray's sister about what they saw after the police and ambulances left.

"Yea my nigga' that bitch Myra peeped ya' . . . this nigga' had that bright ass *North Face* nigga' . . .

mothafucka's could see that shit from madd far." Myra was a thick pretty amazon lesbian who recognized the infamous white North Face out her window while she was smoking an L' by herself.

Woodz listened as they informed him about the hit to find L.J. and the cronies who assisted him. He couldn't believe that they had been spotted but felt it the minute they scrambled into Kendu's building. He remembered spotting Myra in front of the building with Ray-Ray's sister, Jezzy and the rest of their crowd.

"Yo' Ant let me get some soda or somethin'." Woodz looked at Coco and smiled. They had both graduated from the same elementary and Junior High School and were once best friends. Coco was the fastest kid on the block and the best in sports. Their friendship changed when Woodz created his Hakala and N.W.O. regimes. From that point on they became rivals until now it would seem.

Later in the night Big Tee and Pay were both upstairs and asking Woodz about the incident. Big Tee had the feeling that his little brother was holding back information and hope that Pedro who Woodz was more open with, could get him to come clean. Woodz stuck with the story he fed the detectives.

After the visit from Jakkes and the others Woodz was actually starting to believe that there was a chance to get through the drama. Maybe he even saved his boy L.J.'s life, but as always a knock on the door would quickly change everything.

Big Tee answered the door and hollered to Woodz who was in his room. "Who is it Tee?" He asked approaching his oldest brother. He read the look on Tee's face and prayed that it wasn't the detectives again.

"Some guy there . . . Boo? Booby or something, he said he's L.J.'s cousin I don't know." *Bupi?? Fuck!* Woodz thought to himself taking a deep breath. "Anthony what's going on? Are you in trouble?" Big Tee knew the answer to that already and hated that Woodz wouldn't tell him the truth.

"Nuffin' Tee its nuffin'." Big Tee walked away as Woodz opened the door and slowly made his way towards the elevator area. He played the wall and found *Bupi*, L.J. Kendu and Sha in front of the elevator and all with a stoic demeanor.

"Yo' Ant what the fuck is goin' on nigga'? why I'm hearin' that my name is being mentioned in that bullshit nigga'? I didn't do shit nigga' so nigga's got it twisted!" Woodz leaned against the wall and faced L.J. as he spoke.

"Yea L' your name was mentioned . . . all our names but it don't matter B' if it was or wasn't, somebody seen you that night yo' I just found out today . . . this bitch Myra saw us out her window and recognized your North face yo' . . . it was only a matter of time til' nigga's found us out." Kendu took a few steps towards Woodz who was keeping his distance. L.J. and Bupi exchanged looks and processed Woodz testimony.

251

"Listen nigga' I told ya' mothafuckas' to keep ya' mouths shut! Ant? What the fuck is you thinkin'?! This shit ain't no game nigga'! nigga's got kids and shit B'!" Kendu's voice grew angrier and thundered through the hallway. Woodz shook his head and chuckled.

"K' you think I wanted this shit to happen?! Nigga' ya' nigga's should've thought about that shit in the elevator before ya' let shit get outta' control!" Woodz took a few steps towards Kendu and balled up his fist. He and Kendu had a history of clashing so he wasn't even a bit intimidated. "Ya' nigga's let this shit happen! So ya' nigga's can't blame me! This nigga's dyin' yo' . . . my nigga' that could've been your pops in there or your uncle or some shit."

Woodz watched L.J. look at Bupi and Bupi at him. They couldn't believe what was happening.

"Look nigga' all I care about is that L.J.'s name stays outta' this shit . . ." Bupi took a few steps towards Kendu who was staring a hole through Woodz. Woodz sighed and shook his head.

"Boop' ya' don't get it? They saw all of us out the window and told this nigga's sister she recognized his coat . . . I'm trying to . . ." Kendu cut Woodz off and sounded off before he could finish.

"Lil' mothafucka'! I should've fucked you up when you came out here!" He rushed towards Woodz but Bupi grabbed his arm. Inside the apartment Big Tee and Pedro had heard enough. Big Tee ran out into the hallway wielding a metal baseball bat while Pedro held one of the kitchen knives in his hand. The two brothers stepped in between Kendu and their little brother.

"What's the problem ya'? ya' gotta' problem with my lil' brother?" Asked Big Tee and his words were fierce! Woodz was frozen and didn't know what to say or do. Bupi pulled Kendu back towards the elevator with the others.

"Ain't nuffin' fellas . . . your lil' brother's playin' a dangerous game . . . we're just tryin' to warn him talk to him." Bupi Said, last to enter the elevator.

"Don't worry we'll take care of our lil' brother aight . . . if ya' got a problem with him just make sure you see us about it." Pedro replied.

The elevator door closed and the three brothers returned inside where Woodz finally came clean in the room and told the whole story to his older brothers. Words couldn't describe how disappointed and frustrated they were with him. No matter how hard they tried to school him, guide him and encourage him to do better, he just seem to get into more trouble . . . it was impossible to reach him.

CHAPTER 17

Loyalty

Capone and Thugged Out rode the elevator up to Woodz floor hoping that he would agree to take a ride with them. Thugged Out couldn't believe that Woodz had gotten caught up in such a mess! It had been quite a while since he last stepped in Woodz room let alone his home base.

Unlike Woodz Thugged Out had committed all of his energy into hustling, working under the guidance of not only Big Cat and Black Stew but also the father of one of Capone's cousin's son. Thugged Out was slowly learning the mechanics of the game. He upgraded from weed to dope within six months and once he got his hands on his red Civic he said goodbye to school altogether and the childish rivalry that engulfed L.B.M. to devote all of his time into getting money. In the after math of his clash with Woodz that he too regretted he was able to keep Desiree as his girl and a loose tie with White Thong.

Now none of that occupied his thoughts. Woodz was in serious trouble and Capone and him hoped that their comradeship could not only help him weather the storm, but also reunify them as a unit.

"Capone nigga' this is your idea, I think this nigga's gonna' flip my nigga'." Thugged Out said. He'd seen Rabbit earlier in the day informing him that he was leaving to Puerto Rico in a matter of days! Rabbit had told him the whole story and begged him to check on Woodz. He believed that Woodz was in serious trouble and promised to return to New York.

Capone told Thugged Out to trust him and knocked on Wood door. Big Tee opened the door and was relieved to finally see familiar faces. Capone slowly made his way towards Woodz room while Thugged Out stayed with Big Tee at the door waiting to see how Woodz was going to react about seeing him upstairs.

Woodz had just finished showering and was half dressed when Capone knocked on his door. Pay followed him inside the room where Woodz sat on his bed applying lotion on his feet.

"Yo' what up dogz? You aight?" Woodz shrugged his shoulders and stared aimlessly at the T.V. He wasn't going to let Capone drag him outside again. He felt like there was nothing left for him in the streets. Pedro asked Capone about the incident.

"You wasn't there right Chris?" Capone shook his head no.

"Nah Pay I was probably in my ninth dream . . . yo' nigga' this nigga' Kenny's at the door can he come in?" Woodz jerked his head up at Capone.

"At what door!?" He retorted looking down the hallway and seeing Thugged Out standing in the doorway talking with Big Tee. "That nigga' got a lot of nerve comin' up here . . . fuck he want?"

"Ant let him in my nigga' you gotta' leave that shit in the past my nigga' Pay talk to this nigga' please." Woodz shook his head and forced a laugh. Pedro signaled for Thugged Out to come inside.

"C'mon Kenny! Hey look who's here! Kenny's here!" He shouted as Thugged Out walked with Big Tee towards the room. "Hollywood stop frontin' like you don't miss these nigga's mo'." Pedro gave Thugged Out dap when he reached the room. Thugged Out cracked a cheese smile at him. He immediately looked the room and examined the room's new look.

The paint job and furniture, pictures, posters, wall unit and the vast collection of liquor bottles neatly arranged along side of the wall unit.

Thugged Out loved it and nodded his head then fixed his gaze on his childhood friend. His smirk quickly disappeared seeing Woodz hopeless demeanor. It was nothing like the vibrant Woodz who he last saw on New Year's or at the Halloween Parade.

Woodz felt Thugged Out staring at him but he didn't raise his eyes to meet his gaze. His stubbornness and pride wouldn't allow him to forgive his best friend.

"C'mon nigga' get dressed so we could go out and chill and get up outta here." Capone said to Woodz who reclined back on his bed. Thugged Out decided to break his silence.

"I got the whip nigga' ain't nobody gonna' see you or fuck with you." Woodz finally directed his gaze at Thugged Out. He remembered the whip that scooped up Jessika and Jennifer the night he and Capone tried to show him up. He stared into Thugged Out's eyes and felt a surge of regret hit him. *It aint suppose to be like this* . . . He thought to himself while everyone in the room watched him.

What he saw in Thugged Out's eyes wasn't hate, envy or even pity, but concern, care and loyalty. He saw loyalty in his old friend's eyes and it made him feel even lower. His stupidity had torn his squad apart for good and landed him at his lowest point in his life thus far! Woodz finally agreed to go so Capone and Thugged Out led the way downstairs.

He stood atop of the staircase in front of the building as Thugged Out fetched their ride. As stubborn as Woodz was he appreciated the effort that his two best friends were making for him. He watched the red hoopty pull up in front of the building and smiled a bit to himself. *If I get through this shit everything's going back to how it was . . . word.*

He walked over to the ride with Capone and slumped into the back seat while Capone rode shotgun.

"Yo' I gotta pick my girl up real quick aight." Thugged Out told Capone. Woodz sighed to himself. Desiree was the last person he wanted to see. They drove down towards Third Avenue and came up 111th Street. Desiree was in front of the white building on the corner with her friends. She gave Thugged Out a kiss and Capone a hug. Then she noticed someone slumped in the back seat.

"Baby who's that in the back?" Thugged Out told her to just get in. She opened the door and sat looking back at who ever it was with the black hoody and black **Mets** cap covering his head. She suddenly recognized the full lips and her eyes widen. "Anthony? That's you?" Woodz peeked from under his **Mets** cap and slowly nodded at her.

"What up Dee . . ." He muttered and turned his head to stare out the window. Desiree didn't like the energy she felt from Woodz, something was wrong.

"Babe what's wrong with Anthony? Anthony you alright??" She asked.

"Nuffin' ma'." Thugged Out answered. Desiree couldn't deny that she still held feeling for the L.B. Master. She had given him her phone number after he and Nina stopped missing around but Woodz never called her. Instead, not wanting to blatantly cut Thugged Out's throat and stir up any more drama he ripped up the number.

They drove to the Boot Leg spot on 112th in Madison Avenue to purchase some booze.

"What you wanna' drink my nigga'?" Asked Capone as Thugged Out stepped out and stood by the passenger side door counting a folded stack of bills in his hand. He and Capone were ready to buy a bar out if that was what Woodz wanted! Woodz shrugged his shoulders, not enthusiastic at all about the liquor. Capone asked him again. "Ant what you want dogz?"

He motioned for Woodz to roll down his window and he did. Woodz shrugged his shoulders again tapping his finger on the other side of the door. Capone sucked his teeth and shook his head.

"Dogz! What the fuck?! Nigga's is tryin' to show you love! What do you—" Woodz sat up and cut Capone off.

"Chris! I don't give a fuck nigga'! what eva'! I didn't ask to come with ya'! get what eva' the fuck ya' want! I don't giva' fuck!!" Capone watched as Woodz rolled up the window after his outburst and managed to let out a weak laugh. He sighed and joined Thugged Out by the store's window to make their order.

Desiree stood outside the passenger side door and stuck her head through the half way rolled down window.

"Ant what's wrong? I know somethin' happened with you . . . tell me what happened." She gave Woodz a warm concerned look, wondering why he never called her.

"Nuffin' Dez nuffin' happened." He calmly replied slumping back into his seat. He closed his eyes and tried to collect his thoughts. Thugged Out and Capone returned and they drove off towards their next destination. Capone tossed Woodz a bottle of **Bacardi Dark** inside a brown paper bag on his lap. Woodz stared at the bottle for about a minute before finally opening it.

He took a long swig of the dark liquor that burned his throat and sent a sensation through his body. *Shit . . . that hit the spot!* He thought taking another swig then passing the bottle back to Capone.

"Nigga'? you don't want anymore? That's all you want??" Woodz nodded his head and sunk back into his seat. Thugged Out grabbed the bottle from Capone and took a long swig himself.

They drove to a Bar & lounge on 70th Street on Second Avenue. *Ali* was already awaiting their arrival and greeted the fellas as Desiree jumped into the front seat.

"Yo' I'ma drive my girl back to the block I'll be back." Thugged Out announced and drove off. Ali led Capone and Woodz into the gloomy Bar & Lounge towards a table at the far end of the lounge area. He ordered a few drinks for the fellas and him and made mild conversation.

Woodz mind was elsewhere during their conversation. His thoughts were stuck on the block and the incident. He didn't know what the meeting with Ali was about and really didn't care. While Ali and Capone chatted he kept his eyes glued on two nice looking white girls shooting pool in the middle of the Lounge area. Woodz wanted a closer look of the ladies so he got up from his seat and told Capone he'd be by the pool table.

Ali asked about Woodz as he and Capone watched Woodz ease his way where the girls were playing. Ali met Woodz before and knew that he and Thugged Out were close, but what he didn't know was the incident that he was involved in back in Clinton. Capone revealed the story with Ali back at the table as Woodz admired the two long hair brunettes finishing their pool game.

"They playing still?" Jack was watching the females also and waltz up behind Woodz.

"Yea . . . I think they finishin' tho' . . . shorty with the all black is bad yo'." Woodz replied.

"Feel like playin' kid?" Woodz turned towards Jack who was finishing a milky color drink. "What's your name kid?" Jack asked. Woodz glanced over to Ali and Capone's direction who were still talking, probably about him he thought.

"Woodz . . . Woodz." He answered.

"Nice to meet you Woodz my name is Jack yea I was checkin' out the chics too . . . c'mon let's play em'." Jack walked over towards the females and asked them if they wanted to play against him and Woodz. He watched as Jack spoke to the girl with the tight black dress pointing at him and smiled to him self.

To him Jack looked like a drunken undercover cop. He was a bit taller than him with a full head of blonde hair, and skinny as a skeleton. The females agreed to play them so Jack rejoined Woodz across the table. "O.K. Woodz their down to play kiddo you ready?" Jack racked the balls up for the girls as Woodz grabbed a pool stick.

"Yo' Jack I hope you got skills cuz' I'm not the best pool player yo! I watched these chics . . . they could play B'."

"Nah don't sweat it Woodz were just havin' fun right? Hey wanna' drink?" Woodz was already buzzed from the drinks he had. He nodded his head so Jack fetched two more of the mixed Bailey's drink for them.

The female in the tight black dress cracked the balls and the game was started. She and her partner easily won the first game. Woodz felt like shit losing to them, but Jack talked them into playing another game so he had a chance to redeem himself. He couldn't deny that Jack had more skills than him. He missed crucial shots and they blew the second game. The ladies scored another victory.

"Damn Jack . . . my badd yo I told you I aint play in a while . . . plus that drink got me feelin' bent yo!" They both laughed and Jack offered him another drink. Woodz accepted it and thanked him. He realized that being in the Bar & Lounge was his first night of fun in god knows how long and it felt great having fun again . . . it was a feeling that he hadn't felt in weeks. He gulped down the second drink Jack handed him.

"Jesus kid! Take it easy this stuff will creep on ya'." Woodz thanked him again for the drinks and apologized about losing the games then wobbled his way back to the table where Ali and Capone were still seated.

"Damn nigga' you aight? You look twisted Woodz sit down nigga'." Capone said as Woodz began rambling about how he blew the two games against the females. Ali and Capone could only laugh watching Wood erupt in laughter.

They were ready to leave so Ali led the duo towards the door out the Bar & Lounge. Woodz felt the drinks hit him as he walked towards the door and the second the cold air outside hit him it was like a typhoon! The sound of everything around him and people walking by him made him extremely dizzy. He felt like if he was about to collapse!

Suddenly a black cab pulled up in front of the Bar & Lounge and Thugged Out emerged out of the back seat. He was holding the same bottle of Bacardi Dark empty now and yelling at the top of his lungs. Then just when he began to walk towards them he slipped on the icy floor and landed flat on his back! Woodz burst out laughing at Thugged Out who cursed aloud then started laughing out hysterically too!

Ali and Capone were speechless and stared at both Thugged Out and Woodz bewildered. Ali finally helped Thugged Out up from the icy ground, as Capone looked on. It was the fist time in a long time since both Woodz and him shared such a bizarre moment. Capone sat in the back of the cab with the too fools as they continue to laugh and slap fives. The cab driver turned around to see why they were they laughing so much.

"They're drunk." Ali and Capone both told the African cabbie. They arrived back on the block in front of Woodz building. Woodz spilled out of the cab still laughing ludicrously.

"Yo' this nigga's crazy! Hahaha!" He shouted.

"Nah nigga'! YOU CRAZY!! Hahaha!" Thugged Out replied almost slipping on the slippery sidewalk again. All Capone could do was snicker, quietly enjoying the moment. Woodz thanked them for the ride and made his way up the stairs into the building. Jakkes was on the corner and spotted him walking up the stairs as he walked towards Capone and Thugged Out.

Woodz head was spinning and the laughter had ceased as reality hit him, and the remembrance of the incident came crashing back to his mind. Thugged Out gave Capone and Jakkes pounds and walked with Ali towards 110th. Capone and Jakkes followed Woodz inside the building.

"Hold up nigga'!" Hollered Jakkes as Woodz wobbled his way towards the elevator.

"I'm good yo' . . . I'ma go upstairs and lay my ass down." He said giggling again.

"Nah nah lets chill on Jakkes floor for a minute." Said Capone as the elevator ascended upstairs. Jakkes couldn't help but snicker at the sight of Woodz leaning on the wall of the elevator, looking like a straight wino!

"Yo'? Why we'll stoppin' on seven?" Woodz asked drunkenly.

"C'mon nigga' chill for a minute you twisted B'." Jakkes followed Capone out the elevator but Woodz wasn't budging. "Woodz c'mon nigga'." Capone asked becoming frustrated again.

Woodz finally stepped out into the hallway. His legs felt rubbery, he was tipsy and couldn't stand anymore so he collapse on the floor in front of the elevator. Capone and Jakkes both sat at the far end of the hallway besides each other facing him.

They watched Woodz laying face flat on the floor, expressing their disappointment in him. Woodz could barely hear their voices his head sung. He closed his eyes and heard voices saw images and colors . . . his head was spinning out of control. What felt like hours later was merely only a few minutes as the sound of Jakkes mother's voice woke him up.

He couldn't make out what she was saying but he finally rose to his feet then pressed the elevator button.

"Ant where you going nigga'? Be easy dogz . . ." Jakkes plea fell on deaf ears. Woodz could barely stand and ignored him as the elevator opened. He looked directly at Capone and Jakkes and read what seemed to be looks of disgust across their faces.

"I'm out yo' . . ." Woodz muttered stepping into the elevator. "Fuck ya' nigga's too." He weakly added as the door closed. He made it home and went straight towards the room where he collapsed in bed. The bed felt so good he thought to himself quickly blacking out.

CHAPTER 18

Say Good Bye To Hollywood

Across the street from 1738 in 1760 an old man looked out from his third floor window and shook his head in disbelief as he watched Woodz head appear then vomiting out his window. Woodz awoke feeling sick as a dog and whatever he tried to drink wouldn't settle in his stomach. Instead, it was regurgitated everywhere! The pounding hangover didn't help much either, his head felt like it was ready to explode.

After twenty minutes or so he finally got his stomach to settle down and lay back in bed. He felt like crap and despite the show of comradeship from Capone and Thugged Out, he still felt alone and against all odds. The squad was missing in action, he hadn't spoken over the mic in days and none of the girls tried to contact him. Woodz had never felt so depressed and he wondered if Mark and the others were suffering like him also.

Later on in the day Jakkes came by to see him and delivered unpleasant news.

"Yo' they got Mark at his crib last night, I just found out upstairs at this nigga's crib." Woodz just stared at Jakkes. He lay back in bed frozen . . . he couldn't believe it. "Yo' you should go upstairs and talk to Antonia my nigga'." Jakkes added as Woodz switched on his T.V.

"Antonia? For what so they can kill my ass up there?" Woodz replied putting his sweat pants on. "Nah nigga' they wont happy to see my ass."

"Ant my nigga' . . . on some real shit they don't wanna' call pepa on you but if you just sit around and act like its noffin' . . ." Jakkes paused, not daring to finish his statement. He sighed and shrugged his shoulders looking at the T.V. "I think you should go up there and holla' my nigga' I'm out yo' I'ma be in my crib don't go up there without me if you do aight?" Jakkes left Woodz in the room in deep thought. "This nigga's locked up?? Oh shit this shit ain't good man . . ." He feared the worst and something told him that the worse was inevitable.

Night fell at around 5:30. The chilly weather froze up the left over snow on the ground outside. Woodz remained upstairs through the entire day contemplating his fate. With Mark now in police custody behind the incident he knew that it wouldn't be long until they came for him. *I gotta' go upstairs and talk to these people . . . what the fuck I'ma tell em'???* He walked over to his window and laid his head against the cold glass window.

His C.B. stood a few inches away from him. He wondered if anybody was trying to contact him so he picked it up and switched it on. He listened to the multiple voices filling the airwaves. *Damn I'ma miss this shit.* He thought, feeling as if it would be one of the last times he uses the hand radio apparatus. Before he made his curtain call he placed his thick gray towel under the door and went into his stash to finish a clipped L' Pedro had left him.

Woodz lit the clip and took a deep toke of the bud. "Pick it up for Hollywood ya'." It wasn't his usual vibrant introduction but after a few seconds someone responded.

"Yo' Hollywood that's you Woodz? Fuck you been at my nigga'??" Woodz smiled and blew a cloud of smoke out his mouth.

"Yo' who this?" He asked opening his window to pluck ashes out.

"Never who that nigga' this is Buddha nigga'! yo' I heard you was at Foxy's party yo'." Buddha lived on 115th Street on Park Avenue, a young goofy looking fat kid who was infatuated with Foxy and idolized Woodz. Woodz chuckled. It felt good hearing a friendly voice over the mic, even if it was Buddha's silly voice.

"Buddha what up mothafucka'! I've been in the cut you heard . . . yea I was up in the party, why you wasn't there?" He took another pull from the L', it had about three pulls left.

"Hell no nigga' I heard that shit was trrakky!" They both laughed.

"Fuck outta' here nigga'! she probably ain't invite yo' fat ass! That's why!" The sound of other voices laughing on the channel could be heard and Woodz loved it. He was about to surf through the channels one last time when a very familiar voice called out to him.

"Holleeeewoood . . . white chocolate . . ." It was Fresca.

"Ahh shit . . ." Woodz thought to himself plucking the roach out the window. He wiped his mouth. *Damn this is gonna' be hard yo'.* He thought, hating that his walky talky reign had to end with Nicki. *"Hollywood? You not going to pick it up?"* She asked.

"Carifresca . . . wuzzup sexy? How you?" He answered smoothly.

"Me? Nigga' where the fuck you been at? I haven't seen you at school, you ain't been on the mic . . . whats up with you lil' man?" Woodz stared up at the stars in the sky. The whole sky seemed to shine even brighter at the moment. He spoke in a deep low voice.

"I'm here you heard." He paused for a second feeling the bud taking its effect on him. *"Yo' you heard about some shit that happened over here a few days ago?"*

"Yea I heard something about it, why?" Woodz stared down at the C.B. radio . . . he was going to really miss it.

"Uhmm . . . I was kinda' part of it you heard, so I might be in some trouble . . . and going away for a while . . . you copy?" Fresca sat up in bed and looked over towards Woodz building across the street from her window and shook her head.

"Stop playin' nigga' I hope you didn't help do that shit? Damn nigga'."

"Yea." Woodz replied softly.

"Damn nigga! What's wrong wit' ya' nigga's over there?! I heard that nigga's in the hospital fucked up Hollywood . . . ya' better hope he don't die." The entire channel had become silent as Fresca's voice angrily filled the airwaves. *"Ya' nigga's is stupid yo'."* She added. Woodz could only listen. He knew that there were others listening as well.

It was all good just a week ago . . . He thought. When he was walking Nicki to the train station on her way to work, then days later when she called him from her job . . . and of course the kiss at school. *Shit ain't fair!* He shouted out loud spitting out the window. Nicki couldn't believe how Woodz had crept into her heart and that now it seemed as if he was being snatched right out of it.

"Damn nigga' that's fucked up . . . I dunno' what to say to you." Woodz didn't know what to say either, hearing the pain and shame in Nicki's voice. He knew

that she was slowly falling for him, but now none of that mattered. He spat out the window again and slowly shook his head.

"Make sure you graduate sexy . . . and Littlez too . . . keep doing what ya' doing. You're an intelligent girl you heard and I'm glad that I met you, and that I finally got my kiss! Wooo!" Fresca and him both laughed in fact so did everybody on the channel who were eaves dropping on their conversation. They didn't get the full gist of what they were discussing but it sounded as if Hollywood was in trouble and was saying goodbye.

"Yo' Fresca and do me a favor, let everyone know that it was an accident when people start finding out about it and shit . . . that shit should've never happened." Fresca nodded her head but didn't know what to think.

"Damn nigga'! This is crazy! I can't believe you Hollywood . . . oooh I could smack the shit outta' you right now for real." She was upset and sad, knowing that she would miss him if he really disappeared. *"I know you lyin' nigga' . . . you better be lying."*

"Nah ha ha I feel you tho' . . . I'ma be aight and we'll see each other again . . . just make sure that you don't get too caught up with this walky talky shit, and don't let nobody fool you sayin' they Hollywood aight? That goes for all of ya'. Ya' all be good out there . . . damn I'ma miss ya'!" Some one replied for Woodz to hold his head and they would miss him too.

"Nah nigga'." Fresca replied. *"This is it for me . . . I'm done with this shit now."* Woodz realized it was time to say goodbye, say goodbye to Hollywood.

"Fresca be good alright??"

"Yea Anthony oops, I mean Hollywood, sorry!" Fresca smirked and didn't believe that she was actually wiping a tear from her cheek.

"This is Hollywood signing off ya' be easy, peace." He shut off the C.B radio and placed it down by the corner of the window ledge. Woodz proceeded to clean up his room and arranged his tapes and C. D.s. He also returned the window gates back into the windows and suddenly realized that he would probably never see his room, window or walky talky again.

Last but not least he hung his beloved gold chain on the knob of his dresser drawer and looked around one last time, and just when he was about to exit the room he stopped in front of his bed and knelt down on his knees to pray. "God . . . I know that I always call you when I'm in trouble and I'm asking you to forgive me for that! I really need some protection cuz' I don't know what's about to happen to me . . . all I know is that I might not be comin' back to this room, I don't even know if you real or not! Ha but if you are then I need your protection for real . . . and please take care of Tee and Mami for me . . . take care of me and all of us . . . Amen."

Woodz crossed himself and shut the light off. He closed his door and opened his mother's door then peeked in the room. She was asleep so he tip toed into the room and stared at her. "I'm sorry mami . . . I love you." He whispered and blew a kiss at her then exited the room. Momma Luv must've felt his presence because she quickly got up and called his name but he was gone.

Big Tee was in the living room watching T.V. when Woodz sat down next to him. He wanted to tell his older brother about everything and what he was getting ready to do, but he was too ashamed. He slapped Tee's knee and left the apartment dressed only in a white T-shirt, gray sweat pants and his gray Timbs.

He went down to Jakke's floor and sat on the floor of his hallway. There he thought about the last couple of weeks and how his whole world came crashing down all around him. After about ten minutes he was tired of waiting for Jakkes and couldn't believe what he was about to do. Incredibly he wasn't afraid and walked upstairs to Ray-Ray's apartment by himself.

He knocked on Ray-Ray's apartment door and the voices he heard inside all fell silent as someone looked out through the peephole. One of Ray-Ray's female cousins opened the door and called out for Antonia who appeared at the door and stared a hole through Woodz.

"You know we were comin' to get you right?" She said crossing her arms.

"I'm here." Was Woodz only reply as he stepped into the apartment and walked into the living room.

He had been inside the apartment before and had met Ray-Ray's father on that one day. Now here he was about to turn himself in to the police for possibly killing him.

Woodz walked towards the window and sat down on the floor and faced the living room. He listened to Antonia mention calling the cops but he didn't flinch or think about fleeing. Woodz just sat there quietly, what was there to say? He thought. A knock on the door rattled him but it was only Jakkes who had just come from Woodz apartment looking for him.

"Where he at?" Jakkes asked Antonia and she informed him that Woodz was in the living room. Jakkes stepped in the living room and found Woodz sitting against the radiator. "Yo I just came from your house nigga' did you talk to Antonia?" Woodz looked up at him and shook his head.

"For what? What do you want me to tell em'? ain't noffin' to say B."

"Ant my nigga' they in there callin' the cops nigga'! And you sittin' out here waitin'! My nigga what's wrong with you?! Go talk to them!" Jakkes pleaded.

"Ain't noffin' to say Jacob . . . I'm here." The cops arrived minutes later and Antonia directed them towards the living room where Woodz was seated. Everyone was quiet as a beautiful Puertorican female officer slapped the cuffs on Woodz and read him his rights. Jakkes continued to plea for Antonia to stop them from taking Woodz.

"Jacob what do you want me to do!? He hasn't said anything!" She replied.

"Nigga' say something! Ant?! Fuck yo'! This shit ain't right!" Yelled Jakkes as Woodz was led out towards the door. He looked everyone in the eye with a look of deep regret and remorse.

"There's nothing to say J . . . I'm sorry ya'." He was taken by the officers into the elevator and out the building on the chilly night. Jakkes followed them downstairs and painfully watched as Woodz was placed in the back seat of the squad car.

"Yo! I love you nigga'! Don't worry we got you! I'ma go tell Tee!" He hollered. Woodz looked back at the building as the car pulled away from the icy covered curb and held back the tears, quietly saying goodbye to the block, L.B.M. and good bye to Hollywood.

CHAPTER 19

Bad Cop Good Cop

Woodz had never been inside of the 123rd Street prescient. Wearing only a white T-shirt, gray sweat pants and boots in 20 degree weather, he was escorted into the prescient immediately catching the attention of other officers floating around.

"Jesus Christ guys! You didn't even let the kid get dressed!" Joked one officer walking behind the huge long wooden desk cluttered with paperwork and other officers working. Woodz was instructed to stand in front of the desk while his paperwork was organized. After about ten minutes he was finally led into the back area into a holding cell which someone was already occupying.

The cell was about 4x4 feet wide with a hard stainless steel bench bolted to the wall.

"Damn shorty you aight??" Woodz cell mate asked as he took a seat on the bench. He sighed and shook his head, never looking directly at his cell mate *Just.* Justin Ramirez aka Just had been chased out of the 119th Street park between Second and First Avenue by officers on foot patrol. He and his crew were smoking blunts and enjoying the night when the cops crashed their party.

He couldn't believe that the officers made a big fuss about them smoking, and out of five of the guys who scattered he was the unlucky one who was captured. Now the sight of Woodz scrawny body being tossed in the cell with him made him a believer, no one young or old were safe from police.

Woodz sat quietly on the uncomfortable bench beside Just, still high and stumped. He sat there listening to Just ramble on about being arrested for a blunt. Just offered Woodz a cigarette but he didn't accept it. He wanted Just to shut the hell up and leave him alone!

About ten minutes later an officer advised Just he was being moved. The news was not only relieving to him but also to Woodz, who didn't want to be bothered by anybody.

"They call me Just fam what they call you?" Asked Just standing to stretch his legs.

"Woodz...they call me Woodz." He muttered.

"Whats good Woodz. I dont know your situation but whatever it is hold your head baby boy aight...

278

and don't let these pigs break you in here aight my nigga'?" Woodz glanced up at the tanned, bald head Puertorican kid and nodded his head.

He was alone now in the cramped cell, where time seemed to slowly pass. He stared over at the officer's desk covered with paperwork, folders and crime stoppers posters. His mind was racing and he wanted to scream at the top of his lungs! Moments later the Caucasian officer walked into the room and approached the cell.

"Anthony Diaz?" Woodz nodded his head. "Your family is out there, they brought a jacket for you do you want it?" Woodz answered yes and the officer stepped out the holding area again.

He tried to see out the cell but the double doors blocked his view. He felt ashamed as he always did when he was stuck in a precinct, knowing that he was responsible for being there in the first place. The officer returned and handed him the black Colombia Rain Jacket through the bars. He was told that Big Tee, Momma Luv and Jakkes were out there but he wouldn't be able to see any of them. He knew they were furious with him and prayed that things would unfold in his favor.

After what felt like hours of being inside the cell Woodz was finally taken to an interrogation area. He had never been in such an area but seen plenty of them on T.V. *I hope this shit don't take forever man...I wanna get the fuck outta here.* He thought to himself being seated and cuffed to a chair. In all of his previous arrest he was always released on either R&R or with Community Service, so he expected no different this time around. Little did he know his ignorance would be challenged like never before.

Woodz sat face to face with the same two detectives who paid him that morning visit days ago. Det. Dundy offered him a soda and cigarettes but he refused, hardening his gaze and watching the clock up on the wall. The detectives sat facing him while they shuffled through paperwork, preparing to institute an age old technique of interrogation called Bad Cop / Good Cop.

"Okay Anthony..." Det. Dundy/good cop began. "You okay? How you feelin'?" Woodz slowly nodded his head, curious to know what all the paperwork and folders contained. "Look Anthony, this is a very serious crime so it would be helpful if you cooperated with us, this way this can all be processed quickly and you'll be back home with your family...isn't that what you want? Tell us what happened and we'll make sure that the judge takes it easy on you."

Woodz kept his demeanor stone cold, not even budging, hoping the detectives would become restless and let him go. Detective Murray took over.

"Alright Mr Diaz, I'ma show you some things that may help convince you to cooperate and realize the seriousness of this case...because I don't think you see the whole picture." Det. Murray puffed on his cigarette while he sorted through the paperwork. "According to this, on February second at around 9 p.m. you were smoking blunts and drinking 40 ounces with L.J. Mark, Greg and Rabbit in the hallway, in building 1738 with your crew...an old man then refused to hold the elevator for all of yous, you all entered the elevator then you proceeded to beat the old man up and rob him. Then you smashed your **Panasonic** radio over his head knocking him out unconscious...is that true or not?" Woodz felt his heart begin to beat rapidly. *How the fuck*!? He did his best to look unaffected by the accusations.

The Detectives stared at Woodz, waiting to spot any unusual body language.

"Listen Anthony...if your convicted you face a maximum term of 25 five years in prison...25 YEARS! And god forbid that Mr. Perez dies in that hospital because you know what that means right?? life Anthony LIFE! No parole...think about that." Woodz could feel the trickles of sweat slowly rolling down from his head and back.

The picture that Detective Murray was painting was grim but what was more disturbing to him was the in-depth account of the incident. He was certain that Ray-Ray's family exposed certain things to them, but what they were sharing with him could have only come from one of the fellas admission.

Woodz was kept in the dreadful interrogation room for about ten minutes so far but kept his poise and cool and more importantly, his mouth shut! Making the two detectives very frustrated. Their bad cop good cop technique wasn't working, but they weren't done yet. They could sense that the mention of serving life in prison hit a nerve in him, all they needed now was the back breaker !

Woodz glanced up at the black circular clock hung up on the wall again. *Damn! 15 minutes? It feels like I've been in here forever! What da' fuck!?* He thought frantically watching Detective's Murray and Dundy sort out more paperwork. He didn't know what they were up to but he had a feeling that it wasn't good.

"Listen Anthony-" Det Dundy sat up in his seat, holding paperwork in his hands. "From the that we've gathered thus far, we have you marked as the ring leader, in some sort of gang initiation. Bloods, Crips, possibly even Latin Kings...you were one of the oldest, it took place in not only your building you reside in but on your floor as well. We don't know what took place that night however you do so it is imperative that you work with us." Det. Murray quickly chimed in.

"We can't show you these statements that we've already collected, but you do see them right?" Woodz stared at the sheets of paper held by Det. Murray, not believing that someone had wrote a statement already! "Anthony, if your trying to protect your friends... realize that your wasting your time, your friends have already given you up." Det. Dundy watched as Woodz facial expression tensed up, their plan was working.

Woodz couldn't take his eyes off the statements. *Ya mothafuckas!* He yelled in his head becoming with the outrageous claims of the detectives. Det. Murray lit up another cigarette and reached over to grab a folder.

"Mr. Diaz, do you remember how Mr. Perez looked before you and your buddies fled the scene? Hm? Before you left him dying on the floor?" *Oh shit* He thought nervously, hoping that they weren't going to show him what he thought that were about to show him. Det. Dundy continued. "We wanna' show you the damage you and your pals did to Mr. Perez? Who might never wake up from out of his coma...did you know that?"

Woodz didn't know that he was in a coma and wondered if it was a lie. "Does he look familiar to you Anthony?" The folder contained gruesome images of Mr. Perez just as Woodz knew. His whole face was swollen and he looked dead already. "A broken jaw, fractured cheek bone, broken rib..." Det. Dundy read the list of his injuries. Woodz quickly looked away from the pictures, they were making his stomach turn in knots!

His mind began drifting off back to the incident. He didn't remember everything clearly, except for punching and grabbing the radio away from Gee. *This nigga' gotta be dead yo!* He sadly thought. Detective Murray's voice snapped him out of his zone.

"This man is dying Anthony!" He shouted at Woodz. "Do you see what you've done!? You've destroyed this innocent man's life and his family! And if he dies...life in prison for you Anthony...LIFE!" Det. Murray's face was red as an apple from yelling at Woodz but he saw that Woodz was shaken now, their strategy was working.

Woodz hung his head and tried to hold back the tears. His mind was racing out of control with thoughts of his father, mother and the incident all flooding his head like an avalanche. The thought of possibly killing Ray-Ray's father was becoming overwhelming at the moment. The detectives had the whole story wrong, maybe he could be the one to clarify it for them he thought. It wasn't any initiation, it was an accident!

"This is bullshit yo...this wasn't no initiation it was an accident!" Woodz shouted finally breaking his silence. The two detectives had finally made him crack. They were beginning to worry that he was going to hold water but Woodz inexperience in the game would be his downfall. The detectives waited patiently for him to speak again as Woodz tried to collect his thoughts.

"Anthony take your time and relax." Det. Murray said softly while Det. Dundy pushed a pen and piece of paper in front of him. Woodz head was spinning. He just wanted this whole ordeal to be over. "Would you rather have us write it down or do you want to write it yourself?"

Woodz didn't know what to do. Everything was happening too fast! All he could think about was

Ray-Ray's father being dead and having to do life in jail. The two detectives watched as he nervously grabbed the pen with tears rolling down his tired face, frantically scribbling down his statement on the blank piece of paper. He thought it was the right thing to do, he didn't remember everything that had happened but knew that whatever was written on those statements were wrong.

It wasn't any gang initiation, he wasn't inside the elevator and it was all a big accident! Woodz jotted down what he could remember...L.J. And the rest coming to pick him up, the celebration, someone inside the elevator, hitting the man then later finding out that it wasn't no ordinary drunk Mexican, but Ray-Ray's father! The decision to write a statement was a crucial error on Woodz part. Silence is gold in the situation he was in, but in thinking that the blame was being placed on him already in written statements, he believed that it was his only choice.

It would be a hard lesson for him to learn, everything you say or write can be used against you in the court of law! The two detectives read his statement and were speechless. Woodz scrawling on the pages of white paper didn't sound like a fabricated story or even an attempt to shift the blame on someone else, it was more of an over emotional admission. They gathered up their paperwork and returned Woodz back into the holding cell.

Woodz decided to take the Dr. Pepper and New Port cigarettes they offered him, sitting back on the cold stainless steel bench. He guzzled down the soda and puffed on the new Port trying to make sense of what had just transpired moments ago. He laid his back across the narrow uncomfortable bench, hoping that when he awoke it would all be another bad dream.

Three hours passed and Woodz was finally transferred over to the 21st. Precinct on the west side. He was kept there for about three hours before he and a load of other detainees were hauled downtown to Central Booking inside a long N.Y.P.D. Armored transport van. It was a ride that he was unfortunately accustomed to. An always long, crowded and bumpy ride that only got worse when it was time to be processed and stuffed in the holding pens downtown.

Cell therapy was designed to emotionally drain the energy out of you, before you finally got to see a judge, which could be between 1 to 3 days. The cells were huge and jammed with people making it feel like a sardine can. Woodz hated the sight and smell of the cells. The faces which filled up the cells were always sorry, bitter and repulsive to watch. Hustlers, pimps, crack heads, bail jumpers, pick pocket kids, stick up boys...the list went on.

He quietly sat on the corner of a narrow wooden bench staring at a raggedy dressed old white guy curled up next to the urine filled toilet, shaking his head. *How the fuck duz' this shit happen to me again? Fuckin' fuckin' shit man...* He spent three hungry nights being bounced from cell to cell, signing forms and forcing down stale bologna sand wishes.

He was finally processed to the final holding cell designed to prepare the detainees so that they can meet their court appointed attorney, then to go in front of the judge. The cell was filthy, smelly and covered with bodies of guys who were waiting to be called out into court. Woodz didn't use the phone once and did his best to avoid the cold hard floors.

After what felt days his lawyer called out his name from a barred window that divided the holding cell from the lawyer's pen.

"Hello, Anthony right?" Cordially asked the blonde young looking lawyer. "Anthony Diaz right? My name is Patrick Furman and I've been appointed by court to represent you, do you understand and speak English or do you need an interpreter?" Woodz tiredly nodded his head grabbing on to the bars. Mr. Furman shuffled through his case folder until coming across the police report.

His facial expression became dead serious as he read over Woodz charges and the description of the offense. "This is a very serious case and charge Anthony...although it's your first felony and you have a good school and family history, the judge is going to try and set a very high bail . . . I will do my best to have him lower the bail as much as possible do you understand or have any questions? Are you ok?"

Woodz hopelessly stared at Patrick, not fully processing everything he had just explained to him. The words *bail* and *as much as possible* set bells off in his head but he was too weak and drained emotionally to fully comprehend what was being said.

"Nah...i just wanna' go home." His only reply. Mr. Furman nodded his head and closed his briefcase then instructed Woodz to get ready to be called soon. When he was finally summoned into court, he was escorted by a tall black court officer towards a bench area inside.

There was a hearing for a middle aged black male accused of Petty Larceny in progress. He was remanded, given bail for about 500 dollars then taken back into the holding area. Woodz scanned the crowded courtroom and managed a faint smile, spotting Big Tee, Jakkes, Pedro and Capone. His name was finally called followed by a series of docket numbers.

"In the matter of People vs Diaz charged for four counts of Assault in the 1st degree, how does the defendant plea?" The middle aged Asian judge announced. His voice thundered through the court room.

"Not guilty your honor." replied Woodz lawyer, waiting for the judge to place a bail on his client.

"Counselor due to the seriousness of these charges, bail has been set at 50,000 dollars . . . I have been informed that you wish to plea on your clients behalf and have the bail reduced?" Woodz felt his heart sink inside of his stomach. *50g's?? This nigga' think I'm John fuckin' Gotti!?* He turned his head slightly to see Jakkes and the rest, they couldn't believe it either.

"Yes your honor. My client is a first time offender, has no criminal record and is currently going to school...quite frankly his family who are present at the moment do not have the luxury or can even fathom paying such a hefty bail at this time." Woodz lawyer sounded sincere and not like one of those asshole lawyers. He liked his lawyer.

"Very well..." The judge continued, sorting out paperwork piled on his desk. "Bail will be set at 10,000 dollars, if your client is unable to pay this amount he will be held and processed to our holding facility, next case!"

"10,000? That's it?!" Woodz couldn't believe it. He expected the bail to be reduced lower. He was escorted back towards the wooden bench and sat down, slowly realizing that he wasn't going home like he thought.

"I'm sorry Anthony, take my card and call me if anything, I'll see you soon." Mr Furman handed him his card and walked off to speak to Big Tee and Pedro. Woodz looked over at their direction and got their attention.

"Yo! Sell all my shit! Holla at Guidi, get a bails bond! Get me the fuck outta' here!" He shouted at Pedro and Jakkes who got as close as they could to him. They encouraged him to stay strong and promised that they would do their best to get him out.

The tall court officer motioned for Woodz to return back inside so just like that, his freedom was gone. He trudged back into the holding pen completely fatigued, finally realizing his reality. *Oh shit...I'm not going home yo...*He took a seat on the metal bench and stared at everyone around him. *Where the fuck is they taking me then??*

Ten minutes later he was moved downstairs to another holding area located on the other side of the building. *Where the fuck is they taking me to?* He wondered holding on to the cell bars, watching a white kid do pushups on the floor. He waited for the kid to finish his last set of 25 and asked him where they were being taken.

"The island kid yup, Rikers Island." He answered circling the huge cell, then hitting the floor again to do another 25. *Rikers Island?? Get the fuck outta' here* Woodz pressed his head against the bars and sighed deeply. *Shit, maybe I should do some push ups too... pheeww, this can't be real...it can't.*

The bus ride was bumpy and uncomfortable. Woodz was cuffed with another young Spanish kid who coldly stared up ahead of the bus not saying a word.

"Damn man, I'm beginning to really miss Harlem yo." Woodz muttered staring out at Elmhurst Queens through the window.

"Where you at in the world son?" The kid asked.

"East side 110th Street." Woodz replied. The kid nodded his head and looked out the window.

"I'm on 107th in Columbus." They both nodded their heads. Woodz recalled passing through there a few times with Thugged Out and the rest. "There it is." The kid announced to him, pointing out the window towards a cluster of tall and short buildings in the distance. As the bus crossed over a long bridge surrounded by the East River, Woodz stared at the body of water in awe as the sight painfully reminded him of the peaceful and beautiful pier on the F.D.R Drive. He then fixed his stare at the structures in silence.

All the buildings looked like old hospitals.

"This is gonna' be a long fuckin' day B." he said to the kid who nodded his head and sucked his teeth. The bus drove and made a series of turns, then drove through huge gates until finally reaching the infamous facility known as, C-74.

CHAPTER 20

C-74, Adolescents at war!

If anybody ever told you that they weren't scared the first time goin' up in the 4 building . . . they were full of shit! This in-take area is a fuckin' zoo! About six to eight cell's big and small, designed to hold mothafuckas' according to what borough you were going to court at. The cells are almost full to the tee with mostly black and Spanish kids and white boy's coming back from court screamin' like a bunch of fuckin' caged animals. I can't lie, this shit is insane.

I get crammed into the smaller cells across from the larger ones with three other nigga's. The kid I was handcuffed to on the bus, and two Morenos who looked bugged the fuck out. One of them was callin' out to the C. O.s for about ten minutes.

"Fuck yo'! I gotta' take a piss B! yo C.O.! porter!" My lil' ass ain't saying shit. I'm just listenin' to homeboy cry out for the police who are all at their desk chillin' not payin' anyone no fuckin' mind. But what or who the fuck is porter? I ask fam and he tells me.

The porters are the inmates who work for the C. O.s. That sweep and mop the floors, serve food, carry property back and forth. They remind me of floor monitor's that we had back in school. Special ass kissin' mothafuckas' who the police treat better than everyone else. They could eat, smoke, wear whatever gear they want, and got first dibs on our property while we being processed in and outta' the area.

"Yo' C.O.! how long is you nigga's gonna' have mothafuckas' up in here! I gotta' use the bathroom!! Yo' C.O!!"

I wanted to tell this nigga' to shut the fuck up! Watchin' him call out for the police cuz' they were like five feet away and just ignorin' the mothafucka'! I know that he was annoying the shit out of them! Cuz' he was annoying the shit out of us in the cell, and nigga's is already stressed the fuck out in here! Well . . . I know I am.

While fam holla'd at the top of his lungs I still can't believe that my stupid ass is up in C-74. I always heard Mobb Deep, N.O.R.E. and Biggie talk about shit, but to actually be in here feel's crazy! The look and smell of the place is like dead and just reminds me of a zoo. Word. I can't stop thinkin' that I'm up in a zoo, seeing all of the guy's up in these cages.

One of the porters finally gets pissed off with the kid yellin' in our cell and diddy bops his way towards our cell.

"What da' fuck is you yellin' for nigga'! The porter had on some baggy ass blue jeans, white tee, and a pair of fucked up black and red Jordans.

"Son I gotta' take a piss! Tell police to let me go to the bathroom!" The porter shook his head and told one of the C. O.s that the kid is about to piss himself. A big fat black C.O. cracks the gate and tells us it was our one and only bathroom run, so my lil' ass goes too.

After we all lock back in the cell the kid starts callin' the porter again. I could see the porter fuckin' him up as soon as he came out the cell!

"Porter! Real quick!" He flags down the porter again who's smokin' a loosy.

"My nigga' . . . you killin' me wit' the screamin' shit, what up now?! And stop callin' me porter! Murda', my name *Murda'*."

"Yo' my nigga' . . . nigga's could use a cigarette up in here . . . word . . ."

Murda' looks at all of us in the cell and smirks. He takes a long pull of his loosy and gives it to him, surprising the shit out of us!

"Here . . . make sure them nigga's smoke too aight? Cuz' I ain't comin' back ova' here . . . we got court returns outside bout' to come inside . . . so these nigga's is gonna' be on their bullshit." Everybody takes a few pulls from the C.I., I wasn't going to smoke but fuck it! My lil' ass needs to smoke!

After like three hours of being in that lil' fuckin' cell we finally got taken ova' to the processing area. We hand over all our personal belongings, keys, jewelry, pictures, and footwear. The property was all bagged and tagged up. We took I.D. pictures and got a speech from the processing officer.

"Always keep your I. D.s on you. These mothafuckas' is your credit cards, licenses, your money, your life! Don't ever leave the shit behind!" Is what the fat black cop tells all of us.

Why is it that most of these C.O mothafuckas' be fat, ugly motha' fuckas'?! And act like fuckin' killas' tho'!? Anyways, he calls each of us and gives us a pin number for the phones, runnin' the same speech about not losing, or forgettin' it and lettin' anybody steal it cuz' they'll use our numbers and eat up our calls. I use my birthday 3-23-82 for my pin number.

I don't care about my raggedy ass Timbs, a nigga' would have to be stupid for wantin' these fucked up shits! But then I see the banana color slippers they gave us, Oh hell no!

"Yo' What the fuck is these yo'?!" I asked the rest of the fellas. An old timer who was with us laughed at my question.

"Patakis . . . yea kid, the AIR Jordans and Uptowns in here. They could be whateva' you want them to be." The rest of the fellas laughed along with him, while I held up the Bruce Lee looking' slippers in my hand. "Patakis huh?" Fuck it, I slips the shits on my sore feet.

We finally get our ten minute phone call and I was thirsty to holla at the familia man! But I'm not callin' home base. Hell no! I'm not tryin' to hear momma luv cryin' ova' the phone. So I call Pedro.

"Hello?" He answered after the second ring.

"Yo' Pay it's me." I got the big smile across my face.

"Yo' nigga! Ant? Where da' fuck are you? You aight!?" I could tell that Pay's happy as hell to hear my voice . . . shit it feels like years since I last spoke to my big twin!

"I'm on the island B . . . Riker mothafuckin' Island you heard? In C-74, goin' through the intake shit . . . yo this shit is crazy Pay." I felt tears starting to fill up in my eyes. Don't cry nigga'! I tell myself.

"Ant man . . . I don't know where to start or what to say. I love you my brother and I hate the fact that you're in there, but I heard what you did, turning yourself in . . . and I respect you for that Mo', serious . . ." The tears start gushin' down my eyes yo! So much that I had to turn my body away from the police and bury my head to hide my face! I couldn't let nigga's see me cryin' lika' lil' bitch! Plus I had to show him that I was strong, so I tried to suck it up.

"Yo Pay *Sniff*, I'm sorry nigga' I know I fucked up and let you and the family down yo. I know ya probably wanna' kill me right now sniff, that shit wasn't suppose to happen, and I couldn't take it no more B' . . ."

"My brother listen . . . that ain't important right now . . ."

I heard the C.O. yell out five minutes to me, letting me know that my time was running out. Pedro continued. "The only thing that's important right now is that you stay strong kid, feel me? We love you and we tryin' to come up wit' the bail for you, and get you outta' there . . . we gonna' get through this shit together you hear me Ant?" I couldn't hold back the tears no more those shits were like a water fall down my face

"Yo *sniff* . . . *sniff* give my love to mami and everybody aight? I gotta' go, love you Pay."

"I love you too mo' hold your head." I hang the phone up and wipe my face lookin' down at the floor when I get back into the cell. I sit in the back of the cell trying to get a hold of myself. I realize that I'm on my own and it's crushing me . . . it's fuckin' me up!

We all used the phone and then porters brings us feed up trays and nigga's is starvin'! Instead of dinner, dinner was called chow, and when I got a look at what chow was I almost threw up!

"What da' fuck is this shit?!" Me and another kid both ask. The slop on the trays is wet noodles with chunks of beef, and huge pieces of carrots all mixed together . . . shit looked like straight up slop! I watch nigga's bust that shit down and I was starvin' too so

I eat as much as I could. After chow we're issued toiletries, a mattress, pillow, bed set, and a green drinking cup with a bar of soap and toothbrush in it.

We gotta' carry all of that shit to where ever it is we going to be sleeping tonight. We had to be stripped searched and this shit was humiliating! Faggot ass police tellin' us to strip, lift our nuts and bend over so that they can look at our assholes? If that ain't faggot shit then what the fuck is!? I can't believe this stripping shit.

They made us strip back in the bookings but nothing like this. We all line up waiting for the police to escort us to our Housing Units when I see somebody from the block, it's motha' fuckin' Pudge!

Pudge is a fat Moreno who chilled wit' Marc and them and started his own lil' clique called **11-0 Mafia**. Some homie shit I'm supposed to be down with too. He's returning from court and can't believe seein' me in here wit' Patakis on my feet! I nod my head at him, tired as hell!

"Yo'! Hold your head ya' heard!" He shouts to me. I nod my head again and forced a weak smile, he shook his head no and gave me a serious look. "Yo' serious nigga'! Hold your head!!"

A stocky Spanish C.O. leads us down a long gloomy hallway. There's about twelve of us and as we came up to a Housing Unit one or two names were called then we kept it movin' down the hall. My heart's fuckin' poundin'! word! I don't know shit about what

3-Main, 5-Lower, or 6-Upper is, but I'm prayin' that what eva' one they drop me off in won't be a fucked up House.

The C.O. leads about five of us down the long narrow hallway and down a staircase until we reach metal detectors and a C.O.'s post next to a door. I hear him say something about the Sprungs while he signs a burgundy book then leads us outside. The Sprungs were three domes, sprung 1, and Sprung 2 and 3. We followed him in the freezing night towards Sprung 3, the reception sprung.

We finally reach the officer's post called the bubble and dropped our stuff on the floor, tired as hell. There's two sides of the Sprung the North and the South side. While the police organize our paperwork, I think about Mark and wonder if I'll bump into him in the Sprungs. One of the C. O.s is a thick red bone chic damn she's badd!! The guys already up in the houses are crowded up scoping us out while the C. O.s designate us to a housing unit.

They buggin' me out cuz' they were all looking down at our feet what the fuck is they looking at? The Patakis? Four of us are placed in the South side so we drag our shit towards some empty beds around the same area. All eyes were on us. I guess it's normal for the new guys to get grilled. I drop my shit on the bunk and look around the joint, the shit looks lika' shelter!

There's about fifty beds side by side wit' nigga's chillin' listenin' to lil' Walk man's, eatin' snacks, laughing, jokin' and shit . . . just chillin'! I look ova' to where the police got a lil' desk set up in front of the house and see a familiar face from the corner of my eye . . . it's Mark's bum ass! Our eyes meet and we give each other a light head nod.

He don't rush ova' to greet me but I don't care tho'. I spot the bathroom and walk ova' there and that's when he decides to walk towards me. The nigga' gives me a weak pound and hug.

"Damn nigga' why you actin' so scare to come holla at me B'? What up?" I ask as we walk up some steps into the bathroom.

"Nah nigga' it's almost count time and these nigga's be on some shit . . . what up tho'?" I feel some funny vibe's comin' from him but a part of me could understand . . . I think. He's tight at me he gotta' be.

He offers me some cookies and shit and I said hell yea! I was starvin'! Neither of us say anything about the case and why? We got all day tomorrow to kick it about that.

"Yo how is this shit in here B'?" I ask looking around the whole dorm, shit looks like some group home shit.

"Yo' it's time for the count I'll try to come to your bed aight." We rush back to our beds as the female police calls out for everyone to play their beds for the count. We stand by our bed while she and another officer counts everyone. She got a crazy fat ass yo, damn! She calls quiet time and shuts off the lights.

I stay my ass on my bed but Mark sneaks ova' and blesses me with cookies and chips that he said his momz brought him on a visit. For the rest of the night I vibe with the guys who I came in with. It was like we had an unwritten bond with each other. I also get to finally learn their names. *Dub* was the one I was cuffed wit' on the bus, a freckled face, light skinned Puertorican kid and *Archer* the crazy Moreno from Brooklyn callin' for the porters earlier.

Archer and I click from the jump and stay up to three in the morning just vibin' and sharin' stories, wonderin' what our first day in the Sprungs will be like. I feel like I'm in a new world and finally being in a bed feels better than a motha' fucka'! I was expecting to see people rippin' each other heads off the minute I stepped in here but it was noffin' like that.

Everybody's laid back it kinda' makes me feel like I'm back on the block for a minute . . . word. I wake up the next morning earlier than a motha' fucka'. Brush my teeth with some real toothpaste that Mark gave me, and a bullshit toothbrush they gave us at intake. I watch everything and everybody.

The walk to the Mess Hall feels crazy! Like some real boot camp shit. We have to march through the freezing weather and quietly down the long fuckin' hallway or Corridor like the police call it, with our cups and in bed number order. The Mess hall is a big noisy fake ass cafeteria, C. O.s standing everywhere and breakfast is bullshit! We get some Cornflakes, milk, lil' juices and an apple . . . talk about a breakfast of champions!

One thing that I can't complain about tho' is the female C. O.s, these bitches are gorgeous! Where the fuck is they at back home? Morenas, Spanish and even some pretty white girls too and they be actin' like freaks too? It's L.B paradise yo'!

Back in the Sprung Archer, Dub and I get the run down about the Sprungs, the bitches and the building in all. Sprung 3 is reception, Sprung 2 is the program house where everyone is tryin' to go and Sprung 1 is where the bloods run shit like the building . . . gladiator school!

Mark tells us about the female C. O.s' getting' busted fuckin' with nigga's, something called jugglin' food and clothes for cigarettes and weed, then how no one wants to be in the building. So there's a lot of snitchin' and ass kissin' goin' on in the Sprungs. Not to mention a lot of frontin'! Mark hooks me up with some Dial soaps so I jumps into the shower . . . damn a nigga' is stinkin'! We vibe a lil' and he tells me about when pepa got em' at his crib, Elen visiting him a few days before and that he's tryin' to get to Sprung 2 also.

He got cool wit' a few nigga's already so we don't really be around each other too much. I know what it is tho' so I can't sweat it. I can't sweat it I have to get on my feet and get my own shit cuz' I'm not askin' him or anybody else for shit no more. I finally called home base and spoke to Big Tee and Momma' Luv' to let em' know that I'm aight. Momma' luv' cried ten minutes of that fifteen minute call . . . damn she made it hard for a motha' fucka' to be strong! Big Tee promised he would be on the next visit over the weekend to bring me food, socks, draws, shirts and other shit.

Archer sees me lying in bed after the call and comes over to check on me.

"Woodz what up? You aight?" Hell no I wasn't alright! I'm stressed the fuck out!

"Yea I'm good Arch, just tryin' to get use to this shit . . . I hope my people's come up wit' the bail B'." The days pass quickly in the Sprung. To pass time nigga's play chess, spades, checkers, watch T.V. all day in the T.V. room call the day room, or just lay in bed all day and night. I'm thirsty to get a Walkman from commissary, that's where we copp our food and shit. Last I heard Rocafella' was beefin' wit' The L.O.X. and Nas too!

Every night it's like new faces came into Sprung 3. Black, Spanish, tall, short, fat, skinny, all types of nigga's! Last night some big fat Spanish kid tried to punk a short Spanish kid for his coat. I didn't know fat boys name but shorty's name is Chino from the Bronx I think. *Chino* is a lil' tough mothafucka'! He wasn't comin' off his NORTHFACE Snorkel fat boy had fucked wit' the wrong lil' nigga'! Chino duffed fat boy out and was moved into the building. Mark got moved over to Sprung 1 today leavin' me dolo up in here . . . or I thought.

Layin' in the cut all this time was another kid who I knew from the block, *O-Man* from Schoenberg Projects. O-Man and me weren't that cool but we knew each other. He had a reputation of being a lil' chubby grimy mothafucka'! But up in here we clicked like we were best friends yo . . . word. He got knocked for havin' some cracks on him noffin' serious, he was gone on his next court date. I liked O-Man and miss his company, especially after Archer got sent to Sprung 1 too.

Big Tee and Pedro come to see me on Saturday and oh shit! It never neva' felt so good to see my brothers yo word! They bugged out seein' me with my hair dumb long and curly but were glad that I was aight and that me and Mark is cool too. I rock a gray jumpsuit on the visit floor and had to be stripped searched afterward.

These strip searches are a motha' fucka' but it's worth seein' the family. They bought me the nice package too, except for footwear. I gotta' wait for the next package for that so I gotta' rock my Patakis for another week. But I don't give a fuck, a nigga' got food and clothes now!

My last day in Sprung 3 another familiar face walks in through the doors, it's Kendu. I had signed the papers to go to the program Sprung so I'm not gonna' let this nigga' fuck it up for me. Kendu shoots me crazy looks but never says anything. He chills wit' his homies then finally asks about Mark and Gee. I tell em' that Mark had just left and I don't know about Gee. He tells me that he'll be out soon and he was . . . the next day. I meet up wit' Mark in crazy ass Sprung 1 and tell him about Kendu's one day appearance and like me he got the feeling that something's fishy about it.

Chino BX! Never doubt the fight in any man.

CHAPTER 21

My ADIDAS!

After surviving two days in wild ass Sprung 1 I finally make it ova' to Sprung 2 and got problems as soon as I step in the piece. Big Tee and Pay came through wit' another visit and bless me wit' some more goodies but also my new kicks, A fresh pair of Shell Top Adidas! Maria had copped them for me and so I waste no time throwin' on the white and black classics on me feet . . . no more Patakis baby!

I drag my bed and shit into Sprung 2 waiting for the police to assign me to either the north or south side when the crowd of nigga's stand by analyzin' nigga's feets and shit. A skinny crack head lookin' black kid goes crazy when he sees my shells! Ah fuck. I drag my shit ova' to a bed all the way near the window and day room. Mark is on the North side but I got my boy Archer on the south so I'm good.

I just dump shit on the top of my bed and watch the kid run around lettin' nigga's know that he wants my kicks. Man I'm gonna' fuck dis' skinny nigga' up if he plays himself! Sprung 2 looks a lot more cleaner than the other Sprungs and I hope they had hot water in the showers cuz' the showers up in Sprung 3 were colder than motha' fucka'! I can't tell you how the showers in Sprung 1 was I ain't gonna' lie, I didn't leave the bed once there! Hey, call me what you want but I ain't stupid!

I've only been in C-74 for a hot four weeks still new to this shit. If there's one thing that I've picked up from being around these grimy mothafuckas' is to watch everyone and everything! After the count we have to remain on our bunks for quiet time, so there's no real movement allowed but we could still talk. Yo I watch that cross eyed mothafucka' like a cat watchin' mice and shit. He was talkin' to the porter in the house, a short chubby Spanish lookin' kid who everyone calls *Penguin*. I finally start unpackin' my shit and here he came easing his way towards my bed with a broom in hand.

"Ayo son . . . what up they call me Penguin check it out right . . . you see the kid ova' there?" He looks towards the other side of the dorm where the kid is at sitting on top of his bed noddin' his head at me and pointing towards the bathroom.

"Yea" I say not giving a fuck and went back to foldin' my shirts up.

"Aight . . . that's *Krossova* he wants five minutes in the bathroom." Of course I know what five minutes is but I decide to play dumb.

"Five minutes? For what? What the fuck is five minutes?" Penguin lowers his gaze down to my crispy black on white shells.

"For those . . . so look five minutes one on one . . . and whoeva' walks out with da' shells is good." I slide my bin under my bed and flash a fuck you smile to the bird, who the fuck he thinks I am a fuckin' sesame street baby or somethin'!

"Go tell Kross to come get the sneakers if he want em' that bad . . . I'll be right here waitin' so we could get our five minutes aight?" I know Penguin isn't gonna' like that.

"Nah son it doesn't work that way . . . that's gonna' make it hot out here . . . and nigga's ain't tyrin' to get bagged and go to the buildin'." I don't know who Penguin think he is, but this nigga' must be a lame!

"Look fam, I just got here but I'm not a dumb nigga' . . . I know what's gonna' happen if I go in there for a one on one, nigga's is goin' to jump me so I'm not goin' in there . . . tell fam to come get the shits if he really want them' or leave me the fuck alone cuz' I got enough problems to fuckin' deal wit' aight?" Penguin pretends to sweep up some dirt around the beds in the area and chuckle to himself, I think he liked the stand I took.

I signal to Kross to come ova' but the kid shakes his head no, this nigga' looks younga' than me god damn! He looks like he wants to cry when Penguin tells em' what I said. The other guys around him, big mothafucka's too all laugh at him and lay in bed callin' him a bitch and shit. Oh this nigga' must be may taggin' and shit . . . or got a battery in his back! May taggin' is what they called nigga's who do other peoples' laundry.

I picked up all the jail talk up in here like crazy. *A bird* and lame is someone not liked or respected, a bitch basically. *May tag, son* is someone you fuck wit' and eat wit', peoples. *The town* is home. Getting *washed up* is like sayin' getting' fucked up. *A brick* is a pack of cigarettes and a *new yorker* is a cigarette. Speakin' of smokin', I saw some crazy shit ova' in Sprung 3. Mothafuckas' using bible paper to roll up trees and cigarette tobacco, some shit called *blue thunder*, nigga's stickin' dimes and nicks' up their asses on the visit to take back to the house to sell and smoke! Oh shit these nigga's is loose!

I guess that Kriss Kross didn't want the kicks cuz' his skinny ass neva' came ova' to get em'. He's still throwin' a fit about me not wantin' to play the bathroom but I finally do go to take a piss and the nigga' don't come in! Penguin did tho' and he tells me the real deal about Kross. Just like I thought, the nigga' is soft and being bullied so he was tryin' to make a name for himself. So the other nigga's put a battery in his back, meaning they gassed em' up, to step to me for my kicks but he punked out.

Penguin liked my style from that point on and tells me if Kross or anybody else tries to play me to let em' know. I don't trust that mothafucka', he reminds me of Thugged Out a lil' . . . real shady and shit but I'm glad to had got passed that. I get cool with the nigga's around me quick after that, they all know about me callin' his bluff. A Spanish kid next to me name *Milk 501* from Brooklyn, and a Moreno next to him name *Mega*. I shared some of my chips and shit with them while we gigged on Kross' pussy ass.

They break down the deal in Sprung 2 to me. On Monday all the new guys who don't have no G.E.D or Diplomas would be taken to school to be tested for either Pr-G.E.D, G.E.D or A.B.E, that's basically special Ed. Our first day of program would start in the afternoon. The program is directed by four counselors, the two who worked on our side were women, an old lady name *Mrs. Williams* and *Sarah*, a kinda' young lookin' white chic.

They cool and sit wit' all of us one on one to give us interviews and find out about our cases and shit. Everyone is forced to participate in the program even if you have a fuck the world attitude. Supposedly they wrote letters to the court if you had good participation, so you know my lil' ass needs all the help I could get!

I didn't know what to expect my first day wit' the shit that happened wit' Kross. We all sit in a big circle and certain guys were given responsibilities durin' group. Someone opens the group up, somebody reads current events, sports and then another introduces all the new people in the group. Archer and some other kid introduced themselves, then it was my turn.

"I'm from Harlem . . . and uh, ya could call me Anthony, Ant, or Tone . . . it don't matter to me." I hear a few nigga's laughin' sayin' Anthony?? like if they neva' called a mothafucka' by his name before. I don't know why I didn't say Woodz' . . . I don't know, I guess lately I ain't been feelin' like Woodz' . . . so fuck it. The meeting lasts an hour, mostly about drugs, violence and being wit' our families. We end the group in prayer and that's that, back to the bullshit!

After the meeting a few guys approach me and Archer by my bed. Ah shit.

"Ayo son where in Harlem you from?" This nigga' here is a big black mothafucka'! wit' a shiny ass fro too, what the fuck he want!?

"110th on Lex ave. why?" He looks ova' to his man next to him another big kid wit' one of those Muslim hats on his head.

"Nah I'm sayin' son, you from the street right? So why da' fuck would we wanna' call you by your government for? What they called you in the hood nigga'? That's what I wanna' call you na mean?" I stare up at the giant in front of me and gotta' admit, he has a point. I don't know why I acted so scurr and shit durin' group . . . I don't know maybe the shit wit' Kross is still fuckin' wit me.

"They call me *Trajedy* and this my right hand son *Hav*'. Son if you think we give a fuck about that shit wit' Kross nah my nigga' we ain't tryin' to press you or nuffin' . . . yous' a lil' nigga' na' mean, we'll be playin' ourselves if we fucked wit' you." Archer gives me a look like if everything is cool I hope so, cuz' these nigga's could mop the floor wit' my lil' ass! I guess these nigga's is feelin' me or something' . . . maybe I got Kross to thank for that.

"They call me Woodz Traj' Hav' what up . . . my bad if it looked like I was buggin' during group and shit I'm still tryin' to get used to this shit you heard?" I give both of the big homies a pound then lay in my bed. Damn I'm missin' the fuckin' block yo' . . . Kross and me don't cross paths after that but he ends up being moved to the buildin' anyway.

I go to the school and gotta' take a placement test. Man . . . I put anything on that shit! I'm not tryin' to settle for no fuckin' G.E.D, I want my Park East Diploma! The days pass and pass and I start adapting to my new world. I'm throwin' up a few times a day tho' I guess that's from being homesick. Nigga's in the house start actin' crazy after a week or two. The homies is tryin' to let their balls hang so any Crips or Day room dummies, guys that watch T.V all day and night, them nigga's who they don't like, they wash they asses up!

I just mind my business, me, Milk, and Mega who was down wit' them but played the cut a lot. He's jugglin' food and shit, getting' his lil' hustle on so he don't giva' fuck about any birds in the house unless they owe him money. Milk 501 is a so-called B-Boy always talkin' graffiti shit and being part of the **Rock Steady Crew**. Crazy ass nigga' could spit tho'. He's here for gettin' bagged on the train wit' some Ecstasy pills so he won't be here too long.

My first court day finally come but the hearing is adjourned for another date. It was a court day for Mark too but they kept us in different cells. A whole bunch of us were kept in a cell for like five hours waiting to be taken downstairs to the buses. The buzz around New York is the case with Puffy and Shyne, they being charged for shootin' up a club. Caught up in the mix wit' them is Jennifer Lopez aka J-Lo Puffy's chic, who they say helped these nigga's get rid of the gun and lied to pepa about it.

A Puertorican kid name *Storm* was moved into a cell next door from us for cussin' out a C.O. Storm is a sneaky mothafucka' who got moved out the Sprungs after havin' a fight wit' another Puertorican kid in our house. I peeped him eye balling my shells when I came back from court and listen quietly while he's tellin' his man in the cell wit' me about my joints. Damn I'm startin' to regret havin' these fuckin' kicks!

"Oye manito . . . ayi tiene los tenis mio . . . los Adidas blanca . . ." This nigga' is dumb enough to think that I don't know Spanish! I just play the wall and watch son who Storm's hollerin' at. He not that big and shit just a lil' taller than me, skinny and quiet too. He must bee a King too cuz' Storm is King and it's why he got washed up! I watch homeboy glance down at my kicks and tell Storm that he see em'. He tells Storm that he would let em' know and eases his way towards me. I got my lil' fist ready too, as soon as he tries boy . . .

"Oye shorty, what up? Let me ask you a question . . . where you from?" I glanced around the cell and notice that everybody is in their own lil' world . . . fuck!

"The Barrio . . . 110th on Lex and Park." Son twists his face when I answer him.

"110TH on Park Avenue? Hmm . . . you know my cousin *Jun-Jun* from ova' there?" Jun-Jun? Why does that name sound so familiar?

"Jun-Jun? He be on Park Ave?" I think about it for a second and then it hits me. "Oh you talkin' bout' Junior? ***Bad-Boy*** wit' the tattoos on his back?" I suck my teeth and laugh but still keep my knuckles tight! "That's my son B' my L.B. family ya' heard . . . hell yea' I know crazy ass Junior! You be ova' there too?" Homeboy didn't need to hear no more. He tells me to give him a sec' and walks back towards the corner of the cell that separates the other cell next to us to holla at Storm.

"Oye . . . that's a no go manito . . . ese' chamacito familia . . . you heard?"

I don't hear Storms reply but I could see his face and know that he ain't happy . . . fuck you Storm! Bad boy's cousin got called for the buses. He didn't tell me about Storm plottin' on my kicks but I don't care. I just make sure that I give Storm a straight up fuck you look not only for him but for all the bitch ass nigga's who be violatin' nigga's in these cells for fuckin' sneakers and shit.

Jumping mothafuckas' cuz' they too pussy to yap em' themselves . . . most of the time at least. I hear about some heads who do dolo but whateva'! With all the bullshit we gotta' go through wit' court and police, mothafuckas' still wanna' violate each other! Why?! Nigga's don't make sense sometimes yo . . .

The bus ride back is stressful like hell. Riding through the city stuck in a fuckin' Riker's bus handcuffed not knowin' if you would survive, or eva' see the streets again . . . Every second it feels lika' fuckin' nightmare . . . word.

CHAPTER 22

Change of power

"These nigga's is tryin' to give motha' fuckas' 12 . . . 12 fuckin' years B'!" The other end of the line sounds like it went dead for a minute when I tell Pedro that. He can't believe the bomb that I dropped on him.

"Mo' chill out aight', you not goin' to do no twelve years . . . aight? Think positive my brother, alright?" Shit, easy for him to say he ain't the one wakin' up to mothafuckin' strip searches at five in the mornin', or seein' nigga's get blasted or just beat da' fuck up! And just think my fuckin' birthday is just days away and here I am stressed the fuck out on the island.

Just back from court where some fake Judge Judy lookin' bitch and some Jackie Chan Chinese lookin' fuckin' D.A was talkin' about givin' me and these nigga's ten and twelve years! This shit can't be happening' man . . . hell nah!

I even got a new lawyer but this nigga' ain't actin' like no lawyer. Pay hired him to represent me after that first hearin'. Shit I would've stayed wit' that white boy if I knew this fake ass Ron Harper lookin' motha fucka' was gonna' act lika' bitch in front of the judge. After our last court date this nigga' Gee walked up in Sprung 2 lookin' raggedy than a mothafucka'!

It was fucked up seein' his ass in here but actually felt good seein' him period. Me and Mark knew that he would spill in eventually. He was hollerin' at nigga's in the town and the word was that Gee and this nigga' L.J. were being hunted down. Jakkes and them is on some real man huntin' shit. The only nigga' that holla'd at me so far was Capone. He wrote me a Kite and Big Tee and Pay told me that Thugged Out wanna' to come visit me. I don't care . . . nah, let me stop frontin' I miss my nigga' Thugged Out! All these nigga's! I wanna' to holla at a few heads like Nicki, Flaca, and Melly.

Melly went to Job Corp right before the summer but she wasn't alone. Clari and a girl name Smiley from park Ave went with her too.

They all ended up in Job Corp to get their G.E.D.s. They couldn't cut it in regular school and how could they? They were a bunch of Buddha heads, alchies, and played the ave all day and night! Nigga's from the block teased em' but we was happy and proud that they were handlin' their business. That's one thing I give Melly and Clari they weren't dumb bitches, they smart as hell just too fuckin' hard headed damn!

Mark had Clari comin' to see him wit' his momz and showed me some kites that she wrote em' while we went to the Law Library to get info about our cases to get help cuz' nigga's is lost! We brang Gee along wit' us and each of us hooked up wit' different law clerks who school us about our charge and what we gotta' do to avoid getting mad time.

They made nigga's feel confident lika' mothafucka' in the library but when we heard that crazy bitch talk about givin' us ten to twelve years! Ah man . . . all that library shit went out the window.

Pedro and Thugged Out come to see me for my birthday, nigga's can't believe that I'm lettin' my hair grow mad long in here. I told them that nigga's be getting' their hair braided but by homos and I'm not lettin' no faggot touch my hair. I'm plannin' to cut my shit but I'ma let it grow for now. The visit goes too fast so I couldn't even ask Thugged Out about the squad and the L.B's, where the fuck were these bitches at! He promises to holla' at Chulita and them and to be back next week.

Damn I miss my squad but now I'm startin' to think that these nigga's is turnin' their backs on me! By my birthday we were all locked up, me, Mark, Gee, and also L.J. He get's caught goin' to play ball wit' Kendu after Jakkes, Ray-Ray and them told police about where he was at. It's some foul as shit, these nigga's think that they bringin' justice and shit. A part of me feel's fucked up and yea responsible about us bein' up in here but at least nigga's is alive and not shot, stabbed or some other crazy shit. Cuz' these nigga's out there is startin' to get on some bullshit on the block.

L.J doesn't land up in the 4 building. The word is that he's in C-73 or somethin'. Gee and Mark is chillin' on the North side. They suicide porters who could hang out all night to make sure that nobody kills themselves during the night. The police is feelin' them and they holdin' it down. Me, Arch and some other nigga's is chillin' on our side. We got New Yorkers, food, walk mans and some nigga's even got bud . . . but I'm not smokin'. Nigga's even sing me happy birthday during group . . . ha ha . . . ah man this shit is stressin' me out . . . Jerylin where are you when I really need you!?

I decide to write my lil' sister Flaca a kite. I miss the shit outta' her, Amari, Nolo' and Perucho! Flaca is the one out of all the lil' sisters who we said will be the prettiest and successful when she gets older. I don't know if she's gonna' holla back but fuck it. Shit, Melly might wanna' holla if she see that Flaca got a letter from me . . . I'll holla at Melly why not?

Being that I fucked around wit' that placement test I took in the school they throw me in a A.B.E class! Damn these nigga's in this class are a bunch of dumb mothafuckas'! The teacher's is sweethearts tho' and they quick to pick up that I don't belong in here. My behavior and grades ain't A.B.E material so they don't understand how I got stuck in this stupid nigga' class if I'm not actin' like these stupid nigga's. My grades is official, even tho' I be buggin' out wit' these nigga's from time to time.

We violate the teachers sometimes just for fun and shit. We got a Cuban lady for our Spanish teacher . . . oh my god! This bitch is beautiful!! Lovely Lady I love you mama but you ain't got shit on this lady here baby! *Ms. Colon* . . . she got the long dark hair, smooth pretty India face, titties and ass is crazy . . . ah man, I'm in love! She's a shorty too . . . and is feelin' how I be helpin' these clown ass nigga's wit' their work and shit.

I gotta' give these nigga's some credit, they be too busy fantasizin' off this bitch to act like clowns! One of the Sergeants workin' the school buildin' is supposedly fuckin' her too but we don't giva' fuck, nigga's is tryin' to bag Ms. Colon! Our science teacher is official too some tall light skin Spanish nigga'. Son is smooth lika' baby's ass too! Wearin' fresh suits and shit to work. Waves in his hair, crispy hair line . . . *Mr. Padilla.*

Mr. P like we call him. Really tries to teach nigga's grown man shit. It's like he actually cares about us and nigga's be feelin' his energy. Shit up in the house is cool I guess. We not getting searched like crazy no more and I got some mail back from my nena Flaca, even Melly. Fresca never holla'd back and that fucked me up. I sent her some deep official kites, drawings and all that . . . but I guess it's that out of sight, out of mind shit I'm always hearin' about.

Yesterday Ms. Williams tells me that since I turned nineteen I was officially considered an adult and might get moved to the adult facility. I ask everybody about the adult facilities and nigga's tell me that they proper! You could smoke, work and be up in population chillin'! Shit, nigga's got me feelin' like I would be a lucky mothafucka' if I do get moved.

Thugged Out comes to see me by himself just like he promised. Nigga' even brong my package from home . . . I'm feelin' that you heard.

"What's good my nigga'?" We slap fives and he's about to throw up the L.B shake but I keep it simple.

"Chill my nigga' nigga's get slugged for throwin' up gang signs and shit . . . yo? What's good wit' this shirt B'?!" This nigga' got on a white long sleeved shirt that has our names on the sleeves! L.B.M across the middle, Hollywood on the left and Thugged Out on the right . . . the shit is official!

"Shit is hot right? Yea nigga' you know how we do, L.B. Masters for life my nigga'." I give K a pound and tell em' about the case and what's happenin' up in here. This nigga' is actin' like he knows about this Riker's shit and jokes wit' C. O's on the V.I. floor like if they already know him! He starts tellin' me about what's happenin' on the block since I've been gone and some of this shit's blowin' my head off!

Rabbit comes back from P.R and got scooped up by pepa then let go, so people is sayin' he tellin' on me and the others and got pressed about it. That's not all tho' this nigga' got Maria pregnant!

"Maria's pregnant?! By Rabbit! Get the fuck outta' here! This nigga' put a seed in Maria's' ass? She already got a daughter from . . . whateva' that nigga's name is."

"My nigga' she's due any day now! I'm tellin' you dogz nigga's is buggin' out there!" We both peep some chics comin' inside the V.I. floor, two bad lookin' Morenas damn!

"Yo' what up wit' Nicki and Katie? I thought you was gonna' holla at them for me and give em' my numbers and shit?"

"My nigga' I gave these bitches your numbers I even gave it to Littlez too . . . I've seen lil' Katie but that lil' bitch is doin' her . . . oh you know that this nigga' Capone was fuckin' around wit' Melly right?"

"WHAT!?" I burst out laughin' hearing' what he just said. Capone was fuckin' wit' Melly!? "And what happened? Yo' don't tell me he was tryin' to wife her up too?"

"That nigga' was toungin' the bitch down! But they don't fuck around no more . . . I heard you wrote lil' Nat' she wrote you back?" I shake my head, still laughin' about Capone. I look across the V.I. floor at a baby cryin' a few tables away then at the C.O. endin' peoples visits nearby, I know he's comin' to us soon.

You gotta' be a porter or a nigga' who makes noise to rock on the V.I. floor for madd long. Police love nigga's who are wild and shit.

"Yo we got a new L.B. initiate . . . Maria's' baby pops, this nigga' Jose."

"Jose that's his name! How the fuck did ya' get that bird ass nigga' around?" We wanted to pound Jose out a while back but being that he was Maria's man and shit, nigga's didn't touch em'.

"He's ready to be L.B. my nigga' but Rabbit wanna' fuck him up . . . but we can't do noffin' yet anyway."

"Why not?" I ask suspiciously watchin' the C.O. come closer to our table.

"Nigga' we need your vote . . . you Hollywood dogz . . . you know your vote gotta' count." I stare at Thugged Out for a second not knowin' how to respond to what he just said. Shit is crazy, these nigga's still consider me the head Master . . . damn . . . this nigga' fucked me up wit' that.

"Kenny, ya don't need my vote nigga'." He gives me a confused look.

"Dogz just cuz' you in here don't mean shit . . . your vote count for everything . . . we L.B. my nigga' this shit don't stop." The sound of that crazy judge bitch voice fills my head and it makes me realize that my L.B. Master reign might be over.

"My nigga' . . . these mothafuckas' is tryin' to give me and these nigga's like 10 years for this shit . . . I don't think we gonna' get that much time but I might not be out there for a minute, so ya' gonna' have to hold down the squad wit' out me."

"10 years!? Nigga' that nigga' ain't dead! Ya' ain't kill the nigga', I think he's out the hospital already . . . hell yea! My nigga' you stupid?! The nigga's out the hospital already. They can't give you mad time, this is your first case dogz . . . don't even believe that shit." I wanna' believe my best friend so much but a part of me feels otherwise.

"Listen . . . I'm givin' you the power to handle all L.B. business for now on . . . new L.B's whateva' . . . I'm passin' you the torch nigga'. I'm up in here K so I can't worry about L.B. business anymore . . . I gotta' concentrate on this shit in here to survive my nigga' . . . na' mean? I love ya nigga's and miss ya' like crazy! But I have to make it outta' this shit B' . . . so until I do you got the juice B' . . . hold it down ya heard?"

Kenny can't believe that I gave up my position like that but what else am I suppose to do? Nigga's is in here gettin' blasted, violated, jumped . . . I'm not tryin' to end up like these nigga's in here.

Me, Mark and Gee go back to the law library to holla at these jailhouse lawyers and so that we could politic a lil'. We on opposite sides in the Sprung but can't cross visit like that. I tell em' about what Thugged Out had told me bout the block and Mr. Perez being out the hospital.

"So this nigga's aight' then right?" Asks Gee munching' on some Vienna Finger cookies that they sold in Commissary.

"This nigga' saw him but not up close . . . but he's out the hospital so he ain't dead . . . as long as he ain't dead ya heard."

"My momz' said she seen em' wit' one of those shits on his neck . . . like when your neck is broke and shit." Says Mark who's busy tradin' off cookies for New Yorkers. Seein' him and the old timers makin' their moves is like being on the block hustling'!

"Yo' man there's one thing that still fucks wit' me . . . what the fuck happened in that elevator B'? Ya' nigga's still ain't tell me what happened or who started it . . . I know somebody had to set it off cuz' we just don't fuck anybody up especially if they from our building." Mark and Gee exchange looks then glance around the room.

"On some real shit . . ." Gee says biting off half of a Vienna Finger. "Them nigga's was tight that he didn't hold the door so someone slapped his hat off . . . he went to pick it up and shit and gave nigga's a look like he was about to say something, someone pushed him and this nigga' Kendu was tryin' to scare em' . . . nigga's was laughin' and shit . . . then that's when you came and this nigga' L' pushed him to you . . ."

I grab a cookie and bust the shit down while I listen to this nigga' beat around the bush. He's still holdin' back!

"Man listen . . ." Mark says stuffin' loosies inside his sock. "Nigga's were twisted so nigga's don't remember everything but that shit don't matter, this nigga' aight and we need to get the fuck outta' here . . . oh they about to call go back yo'." Our next court date was about three weeks away and I'm stressin' lika' mothafucka'!

I get back from library and put away my snacks and clothes from the package and find a book stuffed in the large brown paper bag. I unload the package into my blue bin and hold the hard cover book in my hands. The book's title is *Down These Mean Streets* by **Piri Thomas**. My sister Maria's man *Ivan* sent me the book to read, crazy cuz' the last book I probably read was in school. We had to read *Of Mice And Men* in English class. Being that I need something to keep my mind off the streets and case I start reading the joint . . . and yo this shit is official!

It's about a Puertorican kid growin' up in Spanish Harlem back when the Italians were still runnin' the hood then Blacks and Hispanics were startin' to take over. I'm up in the book all fuckin' day and night. Damn I neva' knew readin' could be so official, especially when the story is on some real life shit and about the hood. On the real, it's makin' me wanna' write a book about the hood too!

This morning I get packed up and told that I'm being moved over to O.B.C.C. aka Oh Boy. They packed me up after commissary and during group.

I felt my heart skip a beat when this chic told me to pack up. I was comfortable ass hell up in here plus I'm cool wit' mad nigga's too. Gee and Mark give me their I.D. numbers so I could fly em' kites.

I'm gonna' miss these nigga's but I tell em' that I would see em' in court. I get stripped searched and put up in the holding cells wit' two old timers for like two hours. We carry our property tied up in our quilts, get handcuffed and hop on a van. A nigga' name *Happy Land* told me that Oh Boy is sweet, so I'm not shook. I even see Chinos' lil' ass in the buildin' again and got his name and numbers too. Then I see one of the twins from Taft! My nigga' Tyrell! The van pulls away from the 4 buildin' and we on our way to ***O.B.C.C.***

CHAPTER 23

O.B.C.C.

The ride over to **Oh Boy** only takes a couple of minutes. The facility is near the river wit' a high ass ugly gray lookin' buildin' called **The Bing.** The windows of The Bing are all gated and I remember Pay' tellin' me that you could see the shit from the roof of his building in Sound View. The building looks lika' maze inside, quiet and empty lika' motha fucka'!

"Where's everybody at?" I ask the brown skinned C.O. chic escortin' me through the corridors. Ooh . . . she had a pretty ass face!

"It's count time so everything is locked down." She shuffles my paperwork in her lil' brown hands and leads me towards a staircase. Damn I hope we get where ever we were goin' quick! Cuz' this shit is heavy ass hell! "Here we are Diaz 7 lower . . . c'mon." She was buzzed into the unit and holds the door for me so I carry my property into the house. The day room is right by the door and also a phone. The C. O.s' bubble is long and in between 7-lower and another house on the other side.

I put down my heavy ass property and watch my pretty ass escort walk over to a small desk where another pretty black C.O. chic is sittin' at. Damn! There's bad chics everywhere on the fuckin' island! My escort calls me over so I grab my shit and give my name and I.D. number to the C.O. sittin' at the desk. My escort walks pass me and exits out the door leavin' me standin' frozen by this other C.O. chic at her desk.

"Diaz? What's wrong?" This chic asks givin' me a puzzled look.

"I'm waiting' for you to tell me what bed is mine." I'm not scared but I know what happens to nigga's when they do shit wit' out C.O.'s tellin' you to do it especially these bitches, they quick to spazz on mothafucka's.

"Where you just come from Diaz?" She asks smilin' at me. She has a wide forehead like Maya but a pretty ass fuckin' smile! Just to tall for me.

"C-74." She nods her head, lookin' like she understands why I'm not makin' a move.

"Okay Diaz, you could go pick any bed you want. There should be three or four beds empty OK? I'm *Ms. B* the steady here, my house is laid back and this isn't C-74 aight? Why did they move you anyway a fight?"

I feel a lil' uncomfortable talkin' to this bitch, I don't want nigga's to think that I'm a bubble boy and shit, but I answer Miss brown sugar.

"Nah, I turned nineteen a couple of weeks ago."

"Alright . . . well happy birthday and believe me your in a better place now." I thank beautiful and walk straight towards the farthest bed towards the back of the house. I make it to a bed against the wall and drop my load onto the steel bunk, bed number eight. She was right about the joint being laid back cuz' there's nigga's sleepin', readin' and up in the day room watchin' T.V. It definitely don't feel like any of the Sprungs. I sit on top of the metal bunk and analyze the house. I feel good about making it out of the 4 building in one piece, where nigga's is getting' washed up left and right. Maybe my son Happy land was right, and I could fall back ova' here and just chill.

There's some young lookin' nigga's in here but mostly old timers. Nigga's looked my way and just kept it movin'. I know my curly fro is lookin' crazy! My shit is still woofin' but I'm plannin' to cut it this week. I don't want no homo touchin' my shit' or the wrong jail house barber choppin' my shit off cuz' these nigga's is butchers in the Barber shops. I pull out a Beef Stick from my property and munch on it. Ah fuck . . . some big ass black mothafucka' is headin' straight towards my bed, probably my new neighbor.

"What up lil' bro? Where you comin' from?" He sits down on the bed next to mine.

"The 4 building." I answer chewin' on the spicy Beef Stick.

"Let me guess you was throwin' down over there?"

"Nah . . . I turned nineteen a couple weeks ago so I'm too old to be in the four, I ain't mad tho' that shit is crazy ova' there." I chuckle and so does my new neighbor. He don't look lika' bad guy so far. I offer him a Beef Stick and the big guy gladly accepts.

"Good lookin' shorts . . . what they call you lil' homie?"

"My name is Ant but everybody calls me Woodz."

"Ant? What short for Anthony?" I nod my head yea and open a bag of Potato Stix from commissary, these shits are bangin'!

"Okay, I'm big Ant you heard but everybody just calls me by my last name, *Powell*." I think I made a good impression on Big Ant, maybe he feels my swag already. I can't lie, I don't think that I'm like the rest of the young nigga's in here . . . I don't know, I kinda' feel like I'm on some different level shit . . . word. "So what's a young brotha' like you doin' up in here B', you look lika' innocent lil' nigga' to be in here, word . . . you should be in school or somethin'." I gotta' laugh hearin' Big Ant say that and even he had to chuckle at it.

I like this old timer, he was lika' big gentle mothafucka' . . . like Malcolm! Damn my nigga' Malcolm . . . I miss you big homie! I think twice about his question real quick tho'. I don't like to talk about the case wit' anybody. The last thing I need is nigga's all in my business.

"Gang Assault . . . me and my boys got twisted one night and beat the shit outta' some guy from around the way . . . dumb shit word. Now we all locked the fuck up."

"Damn . . . anybody tellin'?" Big Ant asks me, takin' a sip of some coffee that he had in his green cup. I make sure that I choose my words carefully. I suck my teeth and crumble up the bag of Potato Stix.

"Man . . . nigga's let the police get us wit' that bad cop good cop shit and got us tellin' on each other . . . it's like four of us and we all fell for the shit." Powell slowly shakes his head and lies back on his bed. He gives me a look like if he feels sorry for me but I didn't need mothafuckas' feelin' sorry for me, I need nigga's to help me get the fuck outta' here!

"Where you from Woodz? Yo what's that short for Hollywood?" I nod my head and we both chuckle.

"East Harlem, 110th on Lex."

"Word? That's where you at? I'm on 135th. On Madison kid."

"Oh Mad Ave.? okay!" Powell and me speak some more while I start makin' up my bed. I ask em' about O.B.C.C, 7-Lower and the C.O. chic up front. I tell him that she's was my future wife she just didn't know it yet! He cracks up and gives me the run down on the place. Another old timer walks ova' our direction hollerin' out Powell's name

"Yo' he's from the East side too Woodz." Powell says slappin' his man a loud five. "Yo' Tye this is Woodz my new lil' man . . . we ova' here kickin' it about Harlem bustin' down Beef Sticks and shit . . . damn I love those shits! You got more of those shits Woodz?" I laugh and toss em' another Beef Stick and offer one to Tye who says hell yea and thanks me.

"What up kid, *Tye*, you from the world? he sits on the corner of Powell's bed and we rap about Harlem.

I get used to Oh Boy real quick and one of the Spanish dudes even gives me my own phone slot time. The phone is probably the biggest reason that nigga's beefin' up in here, one phone for the ricans, the blacks and the other for the homies, some real crazy shit for real. I don't waste no time callin' the crib and tellin' Big Tee and Momma' Luv' where I'm at and that I'm OK. I got madd books and I wanna' to read em' all!

Tye takes me out to the yard and got me to start workin' out wit' him. They got pull-up bars, dip-bars and a lil' section for weight liftin'. The yard is kinda' big and right next to The Bing. The shit hovers ova' the whole yard and you could hear nigga's screamin' out they windows. I watch nigga's play ball, spin the yard and wonder if I'm eva' gonna' see the block again.

I go down to the school area to take another one of those placement tests and just like I did back in the four building, I put whateva' on that shit! I'm not settlin' for no fuckin' G.E.D. I know that I can still get my joint from Park East. I just don't know how I'ma do it . . . The principal of the school is an aight lookin' older brawd. She looks Colombian or some shit and I swear to god that she's givin' me the eye B', word to my motha'!

It's the end of April and my next court day. I put on my blue jeans, a gray, white and red long sleeve shirt with my new black Reebok Classics, even in jail a nigga' still tries to keep shit Hollywood style ya' heard. I try to mix it up for court tho', sometimes I throw on button ups wit' some slacks. My lawyer told me to keep dressin' proper cuz' it would make a good impression on the judge. Shit hard to tell, bitch wanna' give me twelve fuckin' years! Maybe I should just go butt ass and shit . . . what you wear don't mean shit!

I had gave that nigga' Penguin my Shell Toes as a going home present. He was sweatin' my shits from the moment I stepped into Sprung 2 and didn't have shit to go home in, so I gave em' the Shells fuck it. Along wit' the books that I was startin' to read Tye gives me a pocket size bible to have. I bring it wit' me to court and read through it from time to time. I like the **New Testament** where Jesus is supposedly doin' his thing, shinin' wit' nigga's hatin' on him and plottin' to kill em'. I don't really understand the bible like that, most of it sounds bugged the fuck out, but Tye's teachin' me a lil' something.

Big Tee told me ova' the phone that we all had the same court day so I keep an eye out for Mark and these nigga's. I wanna' see L.J.'s crazy ass but I don't wanna' fight em' any of them, I wanna' get the fuck out! When our bus pulls into the intake area of the court building we all get paired off and handcuffed. A short Spanish C.O reads out our names then escorts us up to the holdin' cells.

This fuckin' cell therapy is killin' my ass. It makes the days drag, drag and drag . . . you can't even tell what day or time it is. Every fuckin' day feels the same! Fuck! We march up to like the second floor or somethin' and I see both Mark and Gee together in one of the cells. Nigga's look stressed the fuck out. After like two hours of waiting I was brong up to the cell right next to Part 62. Mark and Gee were brong up like ten minutes afterward.

"Damn nigga' bout time you cut that fuckin' fro!" I smile at Gee and give him and Mark dap. We sit and don't say too much so I pull out my bible and turn to the book of John. Mark walks towards me and asks to see it.

"I got the same shit, this is all the um New Testament. My momz' gave me one of these shits . . . let me find out my nigga' you getting on some religious shit?" I don't answer him, just shrug my shoulders and go back to my reading.

We finally get to see L.J. when he's led up the stairs by a tall black C.O. and tossed in the cell wit' us. We make eye contact but that's it. I sit a few feet away from them and L.J wastes no time voicing his thoughts.

"Yo' listen, I don't know if any of ya' nigga's know about this law shit but I know a lil' bit . . . these nigga's is gonna' try to scare us to take the high plea but pleas always go down as long as nigga's don't take it. Ya' can't copp out on some real shit." We all listen to L.J. who looks more fatter since the last time I seen em'. He got on a white T-shirt, black jeans and a pair of black uptowns. Both Gee and Mark shoot looks at each other and nod their heads. I know what they were thinking. The law clerks in the four building told us the same shit so this nigga' L.J. isn't bullshittin'.

"So you sayin' we should take it to trial? Cuz' yo' I ain't tryin' to go to trial B' straight cheese." Mark says standin' up to stretch his legs. "Nigga's in the law library told us the same shit L' so you know what you talkin' about . . . nigga's just wanna' go home B ya heard?" Gee nods his head and looks ova' at me. I'm sittin' up on the stainless steel bench holdin' my head wit' my left hand.

"Nah we definitely not tryin' to take it to trial na mean, that'll be stupid . . . nigga's fucked that up already wit' the statements and what eva' happened fuck it . . . right now tho' we gotta' focus on this shit cuz' this bitch is crazy you hear me? This shit ain't for me and I hope ya' feel the same way." I'm not sayin' shit I'm just listening. I'm tryin' to copp out or noffin' and if that means go to trial then fuck it.

A court officer calls Mark, Gee, and me out into court and my fuckin' heart starts to beat faster than a mothafucka'. I follow them inside the quiet courtroom. We stand behind a long wooden desk. I peep some of our family members in the audience, their whispers and grasps could be heard. I wanna' to turn around so bad to say what up but the two brolic court officer's faces makes a nigga' think twice about that.

Judge Wright looked like she could be in her fifties and from what I hear in the bullpens this bitch got a fucked up reputation. She's known for slayin' mothafuckas' in her court, givin' out football numbers for time. I could imagine what she thinks about us after readin' about the case and shit, she probably wants us hanged.

There's three lawyers present for us. **Gerald Hall** is my lawyer. A black bald head guy nigga' even rocks a earring in his ear, ol' fake pretty boy ass nigga'! He looks like Ron Harper from the Lakers. Gee got some chubby white lady and Mark got some old white guy. Why the fuck did I have the only black lawyer?! Don't these nigga's know that white lawyers ain't really tryin' to help us? They stand in front of the judge and start proposing' programs and shit for us instead of incarceration.

I heard somethin' like **Youthful Offender**, **Alternatives To Incarceration** what eva' all that meant. It don't look like the fake Judge Judy lookin' bitch is goin' for it. She motions for all three attorneys to approach her desk, removes her glasses and speaks quietly to each three. Not too quiet tho' cuz' I could hear her. I don't know about these nigga's but I hear her loud and clear.

"Listen . . . I'm not interested in granting them anything! This is a horrible crime and I'm not letting them get away with this . . ." The lawyers look at each other and Mark's lawyer rubs the bridge of his nose. Me, Mark and Gee shoot looks at each other too, we must've all heard her and thought the same thing . . . is this bitch for real!?

She continues to state off the record that the prior offer from the D.A. isn't going to change. 10 years for Luis and Anderson and 12 for both Diaz and Shaw. We get escorted back to the holdin' cell where L.J. is sittin' wit' his head buried in his hands.

"Yo' nigga's ain't goin' home man . . . this bitch is wildin' son!" I stare at Mark who sucks his teeth and continues to whine. The court officer motions for L.J. to step into court and he disappears inside. I sit back down not knowin' how to react, this bitch is really tryin' to slay us!

"Is this bitch crazy? Yo' she buggin' B' . . . ah man." Gee sits quietly like me, runnin' his fingers through his nappy braids while Mark is goin' up top. One by one the C.O moves us out the cell and back to the holdin' cells we belonged.

Everybody who came from the same facility is kept together. The ride back for me is fucked up. I tried to read my lil' bible but I was ready to launch that shit somewhere. I took a hot shower then called home base after I got back to 7-lower. I couldn't tell momma luv' how much time these mothafuckas' were tryin' to give me. I don't believe that they will . . . they can't!

For the next few weeks I try my best to not think about twelve years. I fly kites to Flaca, Melly and from what I can tell me and Melly is clickin' again. Now I gotta' get her ass up to a visit. She's sendin' me some real official flicks too. There's one small one wit' her rockin' some baby blue lingerie, her back and face facin' the camera pokin' her ass out . . . and ooh! That ass lookin' juicy! I ain't gonna' lie, a nigga' got money to the flicks . . . meaning beat off . . . ha ha. Hey, fuck do you expect in here? I've seen nigga's beat off to newspaper articles, Source magazines and even in their beds when a female police works the house . . . nigga's is crazy!

Summer school starts in May and I'm placed in a Pre G.E.D class, but after a few days the teachers had to upgrade me to G.E.D cuz' my grades is off the charts! Shit is crazy, why the fuck back in The East was math so hard then in here I'm knockin' this shit out? These teachers are sweethearts too. There's a lil' Chinese lookin' lady name *Ms. C* and a skinny white chic wit' long blonde hair name *Ms. C* too. A dark skin Dominican chic name *Ms. V* who taught A.B.E and wooo! mami is gorgeous! These nigga's in class be frontin' just so that they can be around her.

There's a fat Santa Claus lookin' math teacher name *Mr. Ski*, a funny bald head English teacher name

Mr. P, *Mr. Ruiz* a slim Puertorican dude from the B.X and then . . . um um um! And then there was *Ms. Coles* and I'm tellin' ya . . . she gotta' be the baddest chic I've eva' seen in my life! I think I'm in love . . . HOLLA!

Behind The Wall with Jo-Jo The Bully & my dude Angel with the familia

CHAPTER 24

The Copp Out

Ms. Coles is a lil' taller than me, maybe like thirty something' she won't tell us her age. White, maybe Jewish, Italian? Nah I don't think she's Italian . . . Nah, I think she's Jewish. I would ask her but I don't want her to think a nigga's tryin' to be thirsty like the rest of these nigga's in here. She rocks short curly brown hair, open toe sandals showin' off her cute lil feet and her toes are always painted. She also got toe rings. Silver rings on her toes to go wit' the other rings on her ears and fingers . . . this chic is classy wit' it! To top it off oh man, she got a body that a nigga' would die for! Where this white chic get a body like this?!

I always sit in back of all the classes to listen to the teachers and to watch these bugged out nigga's, but when they call on me to participate I always speak, but try not to sound too much like a silly nigga' especially if Ms. Cole's around, I make sure I'm on point when she's up in the classroom. Instead of standin' in front of class she always sits by us and teaches her English class like that. Hmm, maybe she knows nigga' is eyein' them big ass titties and fatty she got.

Every time she sits next to me tho' I play it mad smooth. I stare right into her dark brown eyes and be fantasinzin' being all up in her . . . word. I know a nigga's locked up and shit but I think I could bag this bitch . . . who knows? L.B.C up in O.B.C.C.!?

When I'm not in school I'm back in the house either playin' cards wit' Tye on the phone or readin' one of Powell's books until it's time for me to go to my midnight cleanup program in the Bing. One of the fellas in the house put in a good word for me and got me a job.

Big Tee came on the visit the day after court and brong me another package. In the package is another book from Ivan called *Bodega Dreams* by **Luis Quinones**. This joint is about Spanish Harlem too, official. Powell has crazy books and I've probably read like nine of them already. Books by **Jackie Collins**, **Dean Koontz**, mad **Donnell Goines** books like *Black Girl Lost, Whoreson,* and *Street Pimps*. Powell told me that **John Grisham** was his favorite author. A Time To Kill, The Firm, all of his books had mad action and shit.

Tye got some books on the low too, mostly black author books. He lets me read some shit called The

Coldest Winter Ever by *Sista' Soulja* and oh shit this shit is the best book eva'! The bitch in the story is named Winter proper too. Shorty's pops is in the drug game and she gets caught up in it. I can't lie I fell in love wit' the book, basically books in general!

My vocabulary is steppin' up on the low to fuckin' wit' all these books. I realized it when Flaca said somethin' about it ova' the phone when I finally called her. She was happy as hell to hear my voice, and I was glad to hear hers too. I holla'd at mad nigga's ova' the phone, Papo, Hut, Buddha', Monolo and of course Melly.

Everybody swears they miss me, but they wasn't sendin' me kites tho'! I guess it's that out of sight out of mind bullshit. When I finally holla at Capone he got Jakkes in his crib. These nigga's go crazy when they hear my voice.

"Ant!? That's you my nigga'!? Oh shit my nigga' what's good?! "I could hear Jakkes in the background tryin' to wrestle the jack away from Pone'

"Yo' Ant! Hollywood my nigga'! I love you my nigga'! For real dogz, no bullshit I fuckin' love you and miss you nigga' . . . you aight'?" I sit on the floor holdin' the jack wit' my right hand starin' at nigga's in the house go in and outta' of the bathroom.

"Yea Jakkes I'm aight you heard . . . I miss ya too my nigga'. What ya doin'?"

"We up here in bullet head's crib chillin' my nigga' chillin' . . . hold up Ant." Bullet head is what Jakkes calls Capone cuz' of his long head. Ah man, that shit is hilarious when he calls him that. Capone hates it tho'. He always fires back by callin' his momz Jerry Springer cuz' she looks just like em'. These nigga's go back and forth wit' it.

"Yo Hollywood? Hollywood my nigga'! This nigga' Rabbit just came in yo' . . ." Jakkes starts whisperin'. "Yo this nigga' Kenny fucked Rabbit up you heard? Don't tell em' I told you aight'?" The mention of Rabbit's name refreshes my memory about him supposedly snitchin' nigga's out. Jakkes tells him I'm on the phone so he grabs it. It's our first communication wit' each other since the incident.

"Rabbit what up? You aight?"

"Diablo sosio shit is crazy out here, I still can not believe you in there dogz." Powell walks by me and slaps me a five.

"Yea kid . . . I'm aight tho', make sure you be easy on the block son, I'm hearin' a lot of crazy shit about ya'. Yo' what's up wit R-Dee, where the fuck he at?"

"Man fuck that nigga' Woodz, my nigga', these nigga's ain't been the same since you left dogz . . . my nigga' nuffin' is the same . . . me and this nigga' Kenny had a fight."

"A fight!?" I play it off like Jakkes asked me to. "Yo put Capone back on." Rabbit passes Pone' back the phone but I hear Pone' say that he's gonna' put me on speaker phone.

"Hollywood?" I stand up to stretch my legs knowin' that my 15 minute # 1 call is almost ova.

"Yea . . . yo' when was you gonna' tell me that these nigga's had a fight?" I hear Jakkes teasin' Rabbit about gettin' fucked up.

"Dogz shit out here is bananas since you've been in there . . . we wanna' go see you but we ain't got out I. D.s." Damn how the fuck nobody got their I. D.s out there?

"Aight, well see if ya' could get them shits cuz' I wanna' see ya' nigga's B . . . word I miss ya' you heard?" The three of them all scream L.B. and Hollywood together . . . what a bunch of fools.

"Dogz when you comin' out?" Asks Capone and I stay shut for a minute not wantin' to tell em' about the possibility of gettin' slayed wit' 12 joints.

"I can't call it yet my nigga', I gotta' go back to court and see what these mothafucka's say and shit ya' heard."

The computerized phone operator announces that I have 60 seconds left in the call. "Yo' try to get your I. D.s man all of ya' . . . I'll call back soon, I love ya' and miss ya' don't worry about me a nigga's chillin' and being easy aight." They all shout I love you, miss you and Jakkes shouts that he wants me home, fuck Mark and L.J. 30 *seconds*. "Jakkes you crazy, I'll holla soon aight?" They all shout L.B and the line cuts off. It's my third call of the day so I don't get on again. The bill is taken from our accounts, but I always have money cuz' Big Tee and Momma Luv' be hittin' me off wit' cash through the mail. I go back to my bed and lay down thinkin' about the block, the case, feelin' like if I'm neva' gonna' see any of them again.

7-Lower is one of the best houses to be in. Every house gets weekly searches and the searches be real fucked up. **The Turtles** or **E.S.U.** runs up in the joint like at five in the morin' yellin' and screamin', scarin' the shit out of mothafuckas'. I hate the mothafuckin' searches. They make you strip in front of other nigga's, flip our property all over the place then make us stand right behind each other wit' our dicks damn near in a mothafuckas' ass.

They treat us like fuckin' animals and then when nigga's refuse to strip and shit, they hem your ass up and fuck you up outside where the cameras can't catch it . . . fuckin' pussies. I get along wit' most of them, mostly the females but on some real shit all ya C. O.s is pussies! Ya' gang up on nigga's but be scare to square off one on one.

These nigga's is foul, not all of them but most of them. 7-Lower is like an honor house and a lot of bullshit don't happen up here, so we don't get a lot of searches. We probably had like two since I got here two month's ago. Other than that shit is laid back just like Ms. B told me the day I got here.

The house is half Black and Spanish, not only Boriquas and Dominicans but Mexicans, Colombians and Peruvians too. The Mexicans in here are all young nigga's and it fucks me up cuz' on the ave we was quick to violate these nigga's for nuffin'. And now in here, I realize that these nigga's is cool and really look out for each other. I get along wit' basically everyone, I'm the youngest in here and nigga's don't fuck wit me'.

The C.O chics like me too, they stay flirtin' and askin' me to do solids for them. One chic Ms. D, an old white chic short like Chulas' ass, made me her personal porter inside the bubble wit' her. She old but damn Ms. D got a fat ass! Every time I'm near her I think about Chula back home. I haven't written or called her yet but I'm plannin' to.

The N.B.A Finals arrive and we all watchin' it in the day room, hype about *Iverson* and the *Sixers* goin' against the **Lakers** and nigga's want to see the Lakers get cracked! I want A.I. to get this ring lika' motha' fucka' but I don't think they could fuck wit' the Lakers, the *Lakers* got Shaq man! Who's gonna' hold *Shaq Diesel*?

I parley wit' Tye, Powell and a nigga' name *Harv* from Brooklyn. A funny ass chubby bald headed Boriqua nigga' who always jokes around and keeps us laughin'. My next court day is days away and I'm pissed the fuck off about the news I got ova' the phone. Gee and Mark both fuckin' Copped out . . . they copped out to 10 fuckin' years! TEN FUCKIN' YEARS?! What the fuck is wrong wit' these nigga's!

I couldn't believe it when Pay and Big Tee told me ova' the phone. I wanted to fuckin' cry yo . . . word.

I told Tye and Powell about it and they tellin' me that now all the pressure is gonna' be on L.J. and me to copp out next. *"Don't take it A, don't take it . . ."* is what they and just about everyone keeps tellin' me. I can't lie, I'm scared about what's gonna' happen this Thursday when I go down to court.

So I don't think about it and focus on better shit. Powell got accepted to a program so he's about to bounce soon! I convinced my principle in school to contact Park East and find out bout' my graduation situation and one of the secretaries confirmed that all I needed was two credits and two tests and this chic says I can obtain it right now! With my performance here so far I had the two credits in the bag. All I need now is the tests . . . so let's do it baby!

"Yo' A you got snacks ova' there?" Harv' asks snappin' me outta' my zone. I tell em' yea and hurry ova' to my bed and grab a bunch of Doritos, Blueberry muffins and Beef Sticks. That's all we could buy in commissary fuckin' junk food but we make all kind of meals wit' the snacks. Burritos with the Doritos and Beef Sticks make official sand wishes. I return to the table and lay out the snacks on the blue day room table.

"Okay my nigga'! That's what the fuck I'm talkin' about! Yo Tye I like this nigga' A yo." Tye nods his head and wastes no time bustin' down two bags of Doritos, smokin' his New Yorker.

"That's my son B' ya' heard! East side kidddd that's how we do!" He's cheerin' for L.A, while we all rooted for Philly. I sit back in my chair and light up my own loosy. It's crazy how we just smoke inside the house, we didn't have to hide it or sneak to smoke, nigga's just smoked.

"Yo' Tye look at this nigga' smokin' his Kools Cigarette all cool and shit . . . Ha ha . . . yous' a smooth lil' nigga' A . . . matter fact I got the butter name for you son check it out . . ." Tye and me shoot looks at one another shakin' our heads. Harv' is a young nigga' stuck in an old body . . . ol' Fat Joe in the face ass nigga'!

"I got it! Check it out . . . A . . . Class, **A-Class**! Wooo! Don't lie that's butter right? Tye? Tell me that ain't slick son for this nigga'?" Tye chuckles and looks ova' at me.

"A-Class . . . A-Class?? Hm, I like that son that's butter you heard? Yea Son! C'mon Shaq! Grab the fuckin' ball man!!" Tye focused back on the game, the Sixers were crackin' L. A's ass! Holla! I looked ova' at Harv' and told em' he was crazy.

"Don't front A you know you like that my nigga', A-Class B' that's your new name for now on aight." I smile and puffed on my Kools Loosy repeatin' the name in my head. *A-class . . . A Class . . . A-Class.* Hmm that is shit is fly yo . . . I like that.

* * *

I'm nervous as a motha' fucka' for this court day. Wit' these nigga's havin' copped out already me and L.J. back is on the wall. Our cases been kept separate the whole time, but now they probably gonna' combine out shit . . . fuck! The one thing I always love about the bus ride is seeing the city again. The buildings, streets, people, I miss every bit of it and I'm dyin' to be a part of it again.

I hate this locked up shit! I can't sleep at nite, my dreams fuck wit' me, the food is garbage and bitches, I need pussy! I'm tired of the Tele and Boom Boom room fuck! Then these C.O. bitches be teasin' mothafuckas'! I can't get one bitch to see me, these nigga's is procrastinating on bringin' me an L.B. What the fuck?! I need to get the fuck outta' here but thanks to these stupid motha' fuckas' it might be ova' now.

I finally get to part 62 after like five fuckin' hours of squattin' against the dingy walls in these fuckin' cells. A brolic lookin' Spanish C.O stands ova' by another Court Part right across from 62. I read my lil' Bible specifically Psalm 23, it's a Psalm that Tye is always readin' when he's stressin' or tryin' to comfort someone in the house. *The lord is my shepherd; I shall not want . . . yea, though I walk through the valley of the shadow of death, I will fear no evil . . .* Verse 4 is my favorite line and it always makes me feel confident and shit.

I tried going to services for a minute but a foul nigga' like me don't belong in no church. I'm goin' to hell for the shit I've done all these years . . . god ain't gonna' want my grimy ass. Plus I always fall asleep in service word! Hearin' these people preachin' and preachin' . . . that shit makes a mothafucka' sleepy ass hell! I still pray and read it tho'. The door opens and my pretty boy lawyer appears at the cell in front of me.

"How you doin' Anthony?" I nod my head and stand face to face with him. "Look Anthony, I've been doin' all I can to convince both the D.A. and Judge to come down on the offer, but they are not budging. They are still offering the twelve years and now with the plea agreement reached with your co-defendants, it's going to be a lot more harder to convince them to come down in the offer." Hall grabs on to the bars and stares at me, is this nigga' serious?

"Mr. Hall I'm not takin' no motha' fuckin' twelve years. Fuck what these idiots did I ain't takin' shit so fuck it . . . let's go to trial then." Hall sighs and the court officer lets him know that the judge is ready.

"Anthony, if you go to trail you will face the maximum time . . . I don't see the logic in taking it to trial . . . get ready 'cause your coming in . . . oh your family is out there too, um your brother I believe." I suck my teeth and curse these motha' fuckas' and I curse life for puttin' me in this fuckin' predicament. Hopefully all the god stuff does me some good, cuz' I need it!

The court is empty wit' the exemption of the Judge, stenographer, two court officers, the D.A. and my brother Pay'. Nobody is in the stands to rep. No Friends or family except for mothafuckin' Pedro?! Where the fuck is everybody at?! The Court Clerk signals to the Judge Judy bitch that she's ready so Judge Judy signals for the D.A to set it off.

"For the people, *Eddie Stevens*." The D.A. isn't the Chinese lookin' guy, another white mothafucka'. I think I heard him say A.D.A or somethin'. My lawyer stands to my right and introduces himself as my representative. Fake Judge Judy shuffles some papers on her desk and removes her glasses from her wrinkled face.

"Mr. Hall I am aware that your client requests to speak to his brother who is present here."

"Yes your honor." Oh shit . . . this nigga' didn't tell me about that.

"Mr. Diaz, it has to be a very brief visit. There can be no contact between you two . . . you are to sit in the chair right behind you and your brother will remain seated in the first row . . . do you understand?" I nod my head but I'm confused. Why the fuck is she lettin' me talk to Pay'? "Okay you have five minutes." I sit in the wooden seat behind me and give Pay' a weak ass smile.

"Listen Ant, they talkin' bout' goin' to trial and shit . . . I know you don't want that . . ."

"Pay' man . . . I can't do all that time yo!" I try to hold back the tears but the shits just come out like a waterfall and shit . . . I miss my brother yo . . . The only father figure I had in my life. Not to say that I don't love Big Tee and Guidi, but Pay' is my fuckin' hero! Who took me movies, parties, smoked wit' me . . . the nigga' made me feel special when eva' I was stressin' up in home base. I'm tryin' to stay strong like he told me, keep my head up and shit . . . but this shit is fuckin' hard!

"Yo' outta' twelve years you do about ten . . . you already got lika' year in already, that means only nine years bro' . . . you'll still be young nigga' and your life won't be ova' . . . it sounds fucked up mo' but we want you home as soon as possible." The tears keep runnin' down my face, I'm sobbin' lika' real bitch. This nigga's tryin' to convince me to Copp out like these nigga's did! I look ova' to the door, I wanna' make a run for it . . . away from this mothafuckin' court and these mothafuckas' tryin' to fuck my life up foreva'. The fellas back in the house told me not to Copp out no matter what . . . and now this nigga' wants me to Copp out . . . fuck yo!

I jump back into the other seat and face this old evil bitch. Look at my face you evil bitch! I hope I fuckin' haunt you at nite. She begins to speak again but it looked like if seein' me cry fucked her up a lil bit.

"Now . . . this case is for, I guess for you to really advise me whether or not your client is going to trail Monday, which in time we will proceed Jury selection . . . or if he is going to take the offer. The offer today is that if Mr. Diaz admits his participation and guilt in Gang Assault of the fifty year old man in this building, in the elevator, and your client having been one of the individuals that is alleged to have hit the man with a radio, resulting in the mans' broken neck, and being on a respirator for several weeks . . . and almost dying . . . if he admits to some of these activities in references to the assault charges, court would impose a sentence of twelve years. If your client does not wish to take the plea today, the case will go over to Monday, at which time the people will be ready to try the case . . . is that correct?"

The A.D.A says somethin' about askin' for a short adjournment on Monday, confusin' this bitch. She says that she understood that Monday was the day to have a speedy trial. "We need to prepare this witness if he comes in to testify, or if the District Attorney needs to do that . . . or if your client is going to take the plea." She was talkin' to Hall straight up, glancin' at me. I wondered who was the witness she referred to, Kendu? Sha? Rabbit?? It doesn't matter I guess.

My mind feels like if I'm stuck in a fuckin' livin' nightmare, this can't be happening. She says somethin' about goin' to trial, facin' twenty five years and tells Hall to talk to me. Hall asks me to consider takin' the plea, how I'll be makin' the right choice . . . is this nigga' smokin'?! Judge Wright could see that I wasn't goin' for it. "I should tell you too . . . the other defendants have already plead guilty." I wanna' scream on this bitch. BITCH! I don't give a fuck about these stupid nigga's! That's on them . . . suck my dick!

I think she was growin' restless and that's what I need, this nigga' tho' was actin' like I was doin' somethin' wrong! Shakin' is head and lookin' down at me . . . nigga'! You could suck my dick too faggot! "Would you like to go in the back and talk some more?" She asks Hall.

"I would appreciate that." Hall signals for me to head towards the door back to the cell. He starts explainin' the dangers of goin' to trial and I'm fuckin' tired of hearin' about trial and twenty five years . . . I know this shit already nigga'!

I screams on this nigga' to either get the plea dropped down or bounce if he wasn't going to rep me at trial. We both walk back in and I looked ova' at Pedro who looked tired than a mothafucka'. My heart beatin' lika' drum, this is the moment of truth!

"Mr. Hall, you had more time to speak to you client." My feet are startin' to hurt lika' motha' fucka' standin' here so long! I look up at Hall, he starts talking again.

"I have spoken to my client not only today but on other occasions, given him all of the information that I have with respect to the case . . . all I know about the case, including the investigations that my own office has done, have been made available to my client . . ."

This nigga' sounds like he's tryin to win an Oscar or somethin'! He clears his throat and continues. "It has been my recommendations that he take the offer, or take the plea or twelve years offered by both court counsel . . . and my client does not wish to avail to that."

While this nigga's babblin' I'm prayin' that this bitch changed her mind and reduces the twelve down to five, eight, shit at least ten like these nigga's! Instead she drills me about the crime. How Mr. Perez was attacked on the elevator brutally . . . how we're friends of his family, how supposedly I got angry when he didn't hold the elevator lady! I don't know what happened! Didn't ya' read my statement? God damn!

She shuffles through her paperwork and all of a sudden I feel drained, like all my energy just got sucked out of my fuckin' body. My head hurts and I feel dizzy, what the fuck? I feel like I did when them two pigs were showin' me the flicks of Mr. Perez and the statements . . . what the fuck is wrong wit' me?!

The Judge and Hall keep talkin' but I don't hear or understand shit they're sayin' . . . all I hear is trial, trial, trial. He says shit about me expressin' remorse, my statement, goin' to school and learnin' my lesson the hardest way imaginable . . . I'm tired of all this . . . I wanna' go home already. I wanna' see my room again, look out my window, talk on my walky, play wit' the dog, the cat . . . mami . . . I wanna' see my momz! I can't take this shit anymore!!

"Your honor, if I may make a brief record . . ." Now the gay lookin' A.D.A. nigga' starts talkin', why don't everyone shut the fuck up and let me leave!! "I don't want to have to bring the victim and the family members down here for trial . . . but they are prepared to do that . . . just as the victims daughter came in for the Grand Jury . . . It was a very painful process for her, but she did it."

This nigga's voice is cold hearted. He kept his stare at Judge Wright and never looked my way once . . . fuckin' fag. Wright starts blastin' me again about the case, the coma, radio, hospital, and trial, trial, TRIAL! I feel my heart and spirit just die . . . my whole world goes crashin' down in flames. These people ain't gonna' let me leave until I submit . . . and give up hope . . . and I think they got me . . . I'm sorry ya, mami, Ray-Ray, I'm sorry dogz.

I utter out I'll take it to Hall and he jerks his head down at me. He can't believe that they had finally broken me, and neither could I.

"You taking the plea?" He asks me hovering over me lika' anxious car sales man thirsty to sale you a fucked up hoopty. I nod my head and stare straight at the stenographer who's typin' everythin' said in court. Her hands move faster than a mothafucka' and she neva' looks down at the paper once! Judge Wright calls Hall. "Your Honor, I have been authorized by my client to withdraw his previously enter plea of not guilty, and enter a plea of guilty to the crime of Gang Assault in the first Degree, in the full satisfaction of indictment number . . ."

I don't hear the numbers, I just stare at this judge bitch feelin' like my life is ova'. The bitch looks happy that I finally copped out, I'm surprised that fuckin' balloons ain't fallen out the ceiling. She asks me if I understand everythin' that just happened and what she's sayin'. I nod my head up and down but I don't know shit. I don't understand their fancy court language, or symbol of a fuckin' lady wit' her eyes blindfolded on the wall . . . I don't know shit. If I did I wouldn't be here now lettin' them destroy my life.

I look back at Pay' who gives me a lite nod, his eyes red from cryin' too. They finally escort me out the courtroom after what felt like hours of being torn down. The tears flow down my cheeks in the cell as I stand against the bars askin' god why? Why me god? The nigga's not dead god . . . I'm sorry god. This nigga' Hall walks outta' the court room and finds me starin' up at the ceiling waitin' for the shit to fall on me. He reaches into his pocket and pulls out two brown cigarettes. He offers me one and I take it, then throw it right at his fuckin' black face. "Fuck you Hall . . . and fuck your brown cigarette."

He grinds his teeth and picks up the cigarette from the floor. He puts it on the gate and signs

"Anthony, I'm sorry that I wasn't able to help you . . ." I listen to this nigga' as he puffs on his skinny brown cigarette, it smells sweet. He goes into some speech about becomin' a man, Judge Wright being a bitch and still being young when I'm released. The tall black C.O comes to take me downstairs once he's finish I grab the brown cigarette and smokes it in the holdin' cell downstairs. We ain't suppose to smoke but I don't giva' fuck if they catch me.

The bus ride back to Oh Boy is long, quiet, and stressful. Everythin' feels like if it's comin' to an end for me. My boy Powell is leavin' Monday, being that I copped out I won't be able to work In The Bing anymore and my date to be sentence is on September eleventh, 9-11 . . . ain't that a bitch?

CHAPTER 25

The Bing

"Hello?" The phone rang twice Katie finally answers it. Damn it feels good to hear her voice. I had Big Tee dig in my silver case where all my numbers is at to get Chulita's digits. I squatted down against the wall holdin' Sidney Sheldon's Tell me your dreams books.

"What up puto?" I finally answer.

"Who's this?"

"Who else in the world is gonna' call you puto ma'!"

"OH MY GOD! PUTA! What's up nigga'!! Oh shit where the fuck you at? I was just askin' Thugged Out about you yesterday! I miss you nigga'!" I cracked a mean smile hearin' my Chulita get all excited and shit . . . damn I miss holdin' her lil' ass.

"I miss you too girl what up? How you doin'?"

"How I'm doin'? Nigga' how you doin'!? Where are you?"

"I'm on Rikers Island, in some shit called O.B.C.C. Didn't this nigga' Kenny give you my address to write me?"

"Nah nigga', that nigga' been runnin' around lika' chicken wit' no head . . . I've been tryin' to get your address from him and Capone, I don't see your boy Rabbit no more . . . but they've been playin' games." This don't make sense, why the fuck would these nigga's be holdin' my info like that? I kick it with Chula for like an hour, all my free calls. She couldn't believe it when she heard about what happened and was waitin' for me to holla at her.

Supposedly someone ova' the C.B is jockin' my swag already and goin' by the name Hollywood! But everybody could tell it's not me so the impostor doesn't get love from anyone! Thirsty ass mothafucka'! I gave her my info and she promised to write A.S.A.P. Nobody in the house was happy to hear about me coppin' out to the twelve beans, a lot of the guys are mad at me but what the fuck was I suppose to do? I didn't have no chance from the beginning all of the shit is my fault anyways so fuck it . . . I might as well take whateva' comes my way.

Powell left on Monday and I was happy and sad to see em' leave. Powell is my big homie! He gave me the address to the program and I promised to write him. Tye and me still hold it down tho', minus Harv' who gave me my new handle A-Class. He got bailed out and wished us the best. I told em' that I would think about keepin' the name he gave me, he told me I betta' and got his fat ass out of here as quickly as possible.

Tye started jugglin' smokes and commissary and asked me to help em' keep the books. I agreed to fuck it, I might as well help my boy out before they ship me outta' here. He talked to some skinny black mothafucka' in the house name *Silky* who works in the Law Library to help me get my plea back. Silky said that it is possible through a couple of motions but didn't promise me jack shit.

Summer school is comin' to a close soon and Ms. Coles announced to us that it would be her final summer workin' at O.B.C.C. The fellas are heart broken. All the teachers are sweethearts and showed us mad love but Ms. Cole was it! She is beautiful, has class and her smile erased any pain or stress we felt at any time. I'm scheduled to take two tests that I need a math test and a writing test. Mr. Ski began tutoring me for the math test everyday during and after school. He really wants me to pass it and I love the fat Santa Claus lookin' guy for it.

Mr. Parada is preparing me for the writing test. We always make fun of his name Parada because its parade in English. He encourages me to write write write! Asked me if I read books and who is my favorite author. I told em' I didn't start readin' until I came in here but since I started I've been hooked.

"That's nothing to feel bad about Anthony, your an excellent reader and the more you keep reading and writing your mind is gonna' grow grow grow!" Mr. Parade is a funny mothafucka'. He's a short chubby old white dude goin' bald but loves tellin' stories to make us laugh. We have fun learning from him. He told me to think about writin' a book about whateva'! My life, a girl, a dog, just write write write!

Since I copped out my classification got raised so they dropped me from the mid-night clean-up crew. Damn I miss the crew! We got our supplies at around twelve then got escorted by a black stocky C.O name *Camby*. Camby has a long ass scar across his left cheek and from what I heard, one of the nigga's in the Bing gave it to him. They say he was an asshole back then. Now he was cool wit' nigga's . . . go figure.

The Bing is in the Annex part of O.B.C.C. where nigga's wit' high classify cases is kept. The Annex is made of two sides like the Sprungs, the North and South. There's five floors but the Bing is only on three floors. I am the youngest out of the crew, six of us in total. Me, a chubby down south nigga' name **Biggs,** a dark skin half Puertorican Jamaican kid wit' dread locks name *Angel*, and another kid wit' dreads wit' a funny ass name, **Osiris**. He's **God-Body** I think, cuz' he always hollarin' at nigga's by sayin' Peace God! And spoke funny sayin' shit like what's the science and Why equals self, whateva' that shit mean. There's mad nigga's who understand it.

There is also an old timer name *Derrick*, real quiet and always carryin' a lil' bible like the one I got. I got cool wit' the crew quick. Biggs has the most time on the crew. He got almost two years on the island fightin' a drug case. Angel is a two time Felon goin' to court for Assault and drug charges. Osiris is from New Jersey, in the drug game but got locked up after a three hours high speed chase from Jersey into New York! His case made the news too. Derrick had some conspiracy shit against him. He's crazy quiet so we don't really know the details of his case.

In the Bing we swept the floors, mopped, buffed floors and picked up all the garbage from the floor. We not allowed to socialize wit' nigga's in the cells, pass contraband like books, cigarettes, lighters, food, noffin'! My first day of cleanin' is bananas. There two long ass tiers wit like 100 fuckin' cells stretchin' down em'.

The bubble is by the door and the C. O.s' talked crazy to the nigga's in the cells, but so did they. They curse out the police, try to lure in the females to their cells, call them bitches, hoes, spat at them, throw piss and shit on them, burned the cells, flooded it, throw garbage out on the tier . . . these nigga's is like animals!

You get put in the Bing for catchin' a ticket in population. It has to be a Tier 2 or 3 for fighting' being out of place getting caught wit' contraband, drugs, a weapon and you could stay anywhere from days to weeks, even months to years in the Bing . . . damn! They even have lil' cages outside of the house where they put nigga's in when they attack police or can't be kept in the cells . . . damn they really treat nigga's like dogs.

It took me a while to get used to the noises, the garbage, the screamin', water and fires. Shit is a mad house! Nigga's started callin' me Pikachu from the Pokemon cartoon. I got cool wit' nigga's quick and when the coast is clear, I passed them shit. I started brigin' smokes, dynamite/lighters or matches . . . whateva' nigga's needed. Biggs is a beast tho' he smuggles mad cigarettes, fire, food, and had enough time to clean up wit' out Camby or the other C. O.s' catchin' him.

We not allowed to bring nuffin' in for the dudes locked in there but we didn't give a fuck, nigga's is in a struggle for real! Plus they always had weed, stamps and soap. Practically everything! So we don't have to go to the store, we just hustled and juggled. We probably had ten minutes to clean each floor. Camby wanted us done wit' all the floors in half an hour!

After we'd get done we eat, get patted down and then Camby would take us to the Officer's Mess hall called the K.K to get hit off wit' egg sandwiches, packs of sugar, coffee, sodas, we got hit off. Biggs locks on 5-Upper and sells everything! He don't eat sweets, chicken or red meat, just fish so he got nigga's me do our thing too, but this

coppin' everythin' off him. Biggs knows how to get money.

Angel, Osiris and me do our thing too, but this nigga' Biggs is a beast wit' it! He always calls me his road dog and crimey cuz' we look out for each other when we're makin' our moves, nigga's loved us in the Bing. I went out to the yard this morning to meet up wit' the crew by the pull-up bars. They were tryin' to find out about me cuz' I didn't show up for work in two days. I walked towards them and gave all of them dap.

"Junior! Where the hell you been at? I needed my road dawg wit'me last nite!" I smile at Biggs and throw playful punches at Angel. He was like the big brother I neva' had. He was mad protective of me and had some ill lookin' eyes . . . if looks could kill, bodies!

"Nene what up? You alright?" I wanna' spin the yard so the three of us walk and smoked our cigarettes. I tell em' about faggot ass Hall, the evil Judge bitch and coppin' out lika' bitch cuz' of the pressure from Pay and everything.

"Damn nene, I was hopin' that you wouldn't copp out!" Angel took off his white T-Shirt, it's hotta' than a mothafucka' out here! He got a Taz tattoo on his right arm and always talks about his wife and ten kids that he has . . . this nigga' has ten fuckin' kids already! He's not even thirty five yet! God damn!

"So what? You goin' to put motion in to get your plea back then?" Biggs asked tossin' his cigarette on the floor. He can't take the heat no more so we walk towards the wall where there's shade.

"Yea I'ma try, a nigga' name silky in my house is helpin' me wit' it . . . he said I could put in a . . . inconsistent? Nah that's not it."

"Insufficient Counsel . . . yea you could do that. They'll give you a new lawyer if you get the plea back." We looked across the yard. I see Osiris by the benches talkin' to some guys I seen around. They all in a circle and each of them is speaking one at a time.

"You told mami already?" Angel asked. I nod my head yes. I didn't tell her but she know already, Pay' and them had to had told her. I asked about work.

"Oh son . . . you missed it! HarHarHar!" Biggs has the crazy old man laugh. He had a funny lookin' gap in his teeth too but said that all of his kids have it, it's in the genes. "This nigga' Jojo on the fourth floor right, they bringing' him back from court so they got em' in that lil' room where we get searched at and the nigga' knocks out one of the police mothafuckas' like BOOM! Yo that shit was crazy."

He was talkin' about **Jojo the bully** from Brooklyn. A big light skinned nigga' who claimed to be the best rapper on the island. He was a big young mothafucka' mad cool and playful, until you get on his bad side. The C.O. he knocked out is an asshole who always tries to violate nigga's in that lil' room. It was only a matter of time until someone put him in his fuckin' place.

"Oh and your man Milk be cryin' about seein' you." Damn my son Milk 501! Milk got his ass in the Bing after catchin' two dirty dick/urine tickets. The nigga' is a pothead, I always brong em' smokes and lil' snacks. Biggs don't fuck wit' em' so Milk will have to hold his head until he get out.

After a couple of fights in our house, we get hit wit' back to back searches. The house was flippin', nigga's that been here for a minute is leavin'. Some got bailed out, transferred, or went up north. 9-11 is a few week's away so to kill the time I do push ups, keep readin', spend time at the law library dolo or wit' Silky gettin' my motions ready.

He kept it straight up wit' me and said that my chances is slim, but not impossible. Chula wrote me just like she promised. Capone and these nigga's still haven't come through. Big Tee and Pay come every week bring me underwear, money and their support.

Melly and me still write each other. I call her every other day. Flaca is turnin' sixteen this week so I sent her some nice cards that a nigga' name Face made in the house. I always tried to give Nat something for her birthdays. For one of her birthdays I brought her a pair of white Uptowns, then the next year I copped her a cute gold chain wit' her name on it. She's my lil' sister, I would buy her the moon if I could.

Melly got jealous when I copped Flaca the chain but I know she was feelin' what I did for her lil' sister. There's so many of them that their momz can't buy all of them shit they want. Amary is actin' crazy runnin' away, smokin' her day and nights away wit' her friends and so is Manolo and Perucho. Big Tee told me on the V.I. that two girls had knocked on the door for me a few days ago. He didn't ask their names just told them that I wasn't around.

"Tee! You didn't tell em' where I'm at? Damn you could've gave em' my numbers."

"I didn't know what to do they left mad fast before I could say somethin' else, sorry dogz." I lay in bed all night wonderin' who the girls were, flash and a friend? Jessika and Jennifer? Maybe even Jenny and one of her girls . . . damn I wanna' go home!! Melly is makin' me feel like if she wants to get back together. She tells me she still in love wit' me, writes me twice or three times a week, and I been droppin' some deep shit in my letters to her to her.

I got my hands on Pac's **Rose That Grew From Concrete**, his book of poetry, damn this nigga' Pac was the truth! I fell in love wit' the poems and wrote my favorite ones to Melly and some to Chula too. I even brong the book down to school to show Mr. Parade and Ms. Coles. They both love it. Ms. Coles tried to get me to spit one to her and I did. And um! I think I got this chic B'!

Summer school finally came to an end so everybody sadly said good byes to one another. By the time the teachers return for the first day of school most of us might be gone . . . shit I know I will. I had passed the tests that I needed but there was no word from Park East about me gettin' a diploma. The principle told me that she working on it then asked me about my case. I told her about me coppin' out and her face turned grim.

"Let's see what happens alright? Be good and take care of yourself." She shook my hand and I walked outta' her office. I sit in one of the classes where all these nigga's is swarmin' Ms. Coles like flies on shit damn! I sit on the desk next to her and watch these nigga's say the lamest shit, all tryin' to get her info or giver her theirs. She listens to them and flash her beautiful smile at us, damn that smile makes my dick hard . . . hey? I'ma man ain't I? Ms. Coles ain't stupid, she know why all these nigga's is hangin' down here so long, when normally nigga's be out before the go back is called.

I glance around the classroom. The posters, desks and drawings that people drew that have been taped to the walls of the room. I know that I won't see this class again for regular semester. By then I'll probably be somewhere faraway. I spot a drawing of a rabbit with a man face. The man's face is sad but his body is that of a blue rabbit. I grab a piece of paper and ask Ms. Coles for her blue pen in her hand.

She hands me the pen and smiles. Some nigga' is beatin' her in the head about how he's gonna' miss the school . . . the nigga's frontin' all he wants is your address Ms. Coles! I laugh to myself and start drawin' the far rabbit man across the room, damn my eyes is official. I peep her from the corner of my eye tryin' to see what I'm drawin'.

I hide the paper from her view and smile at her. It takes me like sixty seconds to finish it. Damn . . . it came out better than I thought. I write . . . *To Ms. Coles, Have a great summer, Thank you for everything . . . I'm hopping to see you again Anthony . . ."* It's corny I know but it's the only thing I could think of. I slide her the pen and paper and watch her smile light up the room again.

"Thank you Anthony, did you just come up with this?" The clowns around her break their necks to see what I drew. A couple of them suck their teeth and ask what the fuck is it? I give Ms. Coles my good ol' smile and point towards the drawin' of the shit across the room . . . yea ma' my skillz is up you heard! She sees it and realizes that I drew it by lookin' at it, on some real professional shit. Her face lights up and looks down st the drawin' again. "Wow Anthony . . . that's amazing!" The clowns hawkin' her finally figure out that I drew it off the wall and they give me a crazy look.

A couple of them nod their heads respectin' my skills. I tell her she can keep it and thank her again and just ease my way outta' the classroom . . . take notes nigga's! I could feel her watchin' me as I bounce. But I don't leave, I bump into Mr. Ski and Parade sittin' outside the class so I chill wit' em' for a few minutes before I go back.

Anthony 'A-Class' Quinones

One by one the clowns in the class bounce probably mad that they couldn't win Ms. Coles info it's now or neva' for me. She'll walk by me any minute so I hope my bunny man did the trick! It's almost time for the 3:45 count so she needs to hurry up! She finally walks outta' the class with the last of the clowns still hangin' off her shit, damn nigga's let her breathe!

"Give me your Din number before you leave." She tells me. Oh shit . . . I look up and smile as she walks towards the office area in the back . . . Woodz you mothafucka'!! She whispered it in my ear when she breezed by me. Her voice was so soft and sexy . . . plus she blessed me wit' a whiff of her perfume . . . um! I scrambles to find a pen and piece of paper and snatch a pen outta' Mr. Ski's pocket, then grab a piece of paper off the floor to jot down my name and number feelin' mad nervous and shit, it's like being in Prep again!

She returns from the back and grabs the paper outta' my hand, puts it in her bag then smiles at me.

"You'll have my P.O box when I write you, take care of yourself okay?" I look up at Ms. Coles in awe. Damn . . . this is the last time that I may see this beautiful women in front of me . . . fuck!

"I will Ms. Coles, thank you . . . oh, I gotta' go!" I give hugs to Mr. P and Ski and hurry back to the house before I get caught late for the count. Yea Thugged Out! I'm still true to this!!

CHAPTER 26
9/11

It's a beautiful fuckin' Tuesday mornin' and here I am sittin' up in this funky ass Riker's bus shackled lika' mothafuckin' slave! On my way to get sentenced to 12 fuckin' years for my first eva' felony charge . . . god fuckin' damn! I stare out the window wit' my thoughts on the block, my L.B squad, bitches and my fuckin' life . . . hell of a life it is.

I've been doing my best to survive on that mothafuckin' island but this shit ain't easy! I don't fuck wit' a lot of dudes, read whateva' book I get my hands on, listen to HOT 97 and KISS F.M. all fuckin' day, fly kites to these bitches and to home base. My phone Jones is serious, the BOOM BOOM room is open 24 hours a day and my locker and bin ain't Neva' empty . . . but I hate this shit.

I hate wakin' up and lookin' at these bum mothafuckas' around me. I hate hearin' the faggot C.O.'s talkin' tough, jumpin' on nigga's then runnin' up in the house to flip our property. I hate hearin' momma luv cry ova' the phone, the look Big Tee gives me every time our visit is ova' . . . I hate being locked up yo . . . the other night I got outta' bed like at three in the mornin' covered wit' sweat after havin' some crazy fuckin' dream wit' demons and shit word.

Some of the demons were Mexicans and it had me shook lika' mothafucka'! I sat up in bed shakin', prayin' that I was dreamin' all of this shit, but I wasn't. Then mothafuckas' tears started runnin' down my eyes and I couldn't control myself, nigga's probably seen me too but I don't giva' fuck. Nigga's cry all the time in here, that's part of doing time. So if anybody tells you that they don't cry in here then they're full of shit!

This shit ain't no dream, but it's a livin' nightmare. I blew graduation, lost Chula, Nicki, Foxy and even tho' me and Melly is vibin' hard right now, I know this bitch don't wanna' be wit' me. She doesn't know about the 12 years yet, once she finds out tho' I know she's gonna' bounce on me . . . it's what people do when nigga's get locked up.

Now I know how my nigga' J.T. felt after he got knocked and I didn't look out for him like he expected me to. I wrote em' a couple of times and accepted some of his calls, but a nigga' didn't try to see him, send em' loot, flicks, nuffin'! Instead I let the drama up in home base and on the block make me forget about my nigga' J.T. Hooker.

The nigga' who put me on to the game, even tho' I didn't last long in it. J.T. bigged me up to Big Cat and hooked me up anytime I needed smoke. Now I'm the one sittin' on this hard ass bus seat shackled feelin' what he went through . . . my bad J.T.! I'm sorry that I wasn't a better friend to you, I didn't know son . . . but now I do.

It don't matter tho', this evil Judge Judy lookin' bitch is about to slay my ass and send me up north for like foreva'! My only chance to stop it is them motions that me and Silk sent out last week to her, Hall and the D.A. nigga'. If that doesn't work I guess I can kiss the game goodbye like my son Jada said. Despite all my fuckin' drama it is a fuckin' beautiful day.

The sky is clear blue, sun's shinin' and the skyline looks official from the B.Q.E headin' towards money makin' Manhattan. Pay's been workin' at the Twin Towers for a couple of weeks doin' some Janitor shit. He says the place is butter and the money is sweet. Pay always thinks that he's the boss every time he gets an official gig. He had the official gig workin' at Yankee Stadium a couple of years ago, but fucked it up somehow word! He Neva' finished high school, but always keeps official jobs.

The bus drove into Manhattan speedin' thorough streets and hittin' corners and shit. We drive up the block where all the old Chinese people be doing yoga shit, stretchin' and shit and I know that 100 Centre street building is right around the corner. I like seeing the old Chinese people doing they stretches, that shit looks mad peaceful, and they be mad deep early in the morn doing it too.

A whole bunch of us get processed like always then dumped into cells to wait like a hundred hours before our names are called for court. This shit is fuckin' depressin', I gotta' wait hours to be sentenced to fuckin' 12 years in jail! All the cells look and smell the same and make a nigga' feel like hangin' up somewhere. It's like these shits take your energy outta' you . . . mothafuckin' cell therapy.

A few of us go up to like the third floor and I don't see L.J. anywhere or anybody I know. I don't even know if he copped out or not. By now he should've found out that I did and I know he gotta' be tight! I get dropped in a cell wit' some loud mothafuckas' talkin' shit about their Judges and getting' bailed out . . . dope head lookin' motha' fuckas'.

I plant my ass on the bench bolted against the wall and look up towards a nice size window facin' a park area behind the building. I could see one of the Twin Towers, I think it's Tower 1 and not the one Pay works in. I pull out my mini bible and skim through pages. I really don't feel like readin' this shit, for what? This bible and god shit ain't helpin' me. I've been prayin' lika' mothafucka', goin' to church to be saved and I still can't get a mothafuckin' break!

Everyday I watch crackheads and sick mothafuckas' get bailed out or just let out period. Everyday Mothafuckas' like this old nigga' talkin' shit about his judge and C.O.'s

"All these mothafuckas'! nigga's ain't tryin' to let a mothafucka' go! I'ma bail out this bitch and these nigga's ain't gonna' see my black ass again . . . know what I'm sayin'?" He has another stupid nigga' next to him noddin' his head, a real fuckin' yes man. "Fuck these cracker mothafuckas'! Know what I'm sayin'? This is it for me . . . these nigga's won't catch me no more after this!" I wish this old nigga' would just shut the fuck up!

The older guy next to him starts babblin' now too. He ain't older then the old timer but he's older than me. I don't know what time it is but its Tuesday I know that, and we just go t here, but it feels like if I've been in this cells for hours! The too loud mouths finally quiet down and I start to think about Melly, Chula, the block man . . . ***BOOOOOOOM!!!!!***

"OH SHIT WHAT THE FUCK!" C.O! C.O!" What the fuck was that man!? A loud fuckin' explosion rocked the whole building makin' all of us in the cell duck down and take cover. The loud old timer was buggin' tho!" "C.O! C.O!" He's screamin' at the top of his lungs. "Anybody hurt in here? What the fuck was that? Where the fuck is these fuckin' C.O.'s?"

He starts hollerin' for the C.O.'s again while the rest of us glanced around at one another, trying to figure out what the fuck was the explosion. Then I see it.

"Oh shit, yo look!" I point out the window towards the Twin Towers, one of them shits is on fire!

"Holy shit man! That shit is flamin'! C.O.!!" The old timer yelled on the gate for a C.O. while the rest of us started out towards the smoke covering the building. That shit is smokin'!

A C.O. finally runs pass out cell but didn't stop. Another Spanish C.O. followed the first one yellin' into his walky talkie. The old timer tried to get one of them to stop and tell us what was going on.

"God damn! These nigga's need to let us know what the fuck is happenin'! I ain't tryin' to die in this bitch . . . I'm supposed to be gettin' bailed out man! C.O.! C.O.!" I stand on the bench starin' out the window my fuckin' mind is blank. Is nigga's attackin' New York again? Oh shit . . . Pedro . . . ah man! My fuckin' brother's in them fuckin' buildings Yo'! Fuck! A chubby Spanish C.O finally comes to our gate.

"Is everyone alright?!" We all say yea and ask what's goin' on. "Listen we gonna' need all of you to stay calm and report if anybody's hurt . . . we don't know what's happenin' . . . all we know is that one of the Twin Towers just got hit by a fuckin' plane man, a plane just crashed into the building . . . we probably gonna' get you guys outta' here as quick as possible."

The C.O runs off being followed by two other officers. I stay on the bench frozen not knowin' what to think! The guys were all lookin' out the window towards the black smoke coming outta' the burning building a few blocks away. The smoke quickly filled up the clear blue sky. This shit was crazy!

"Yo! Them Arab nigga's is probably bombin' these white mothafuckas' again like back in 92 yo . . . shit is about to go down fuck it! Bomb all this shit!" The old guy and his yes man were the only ones runnin' their mouths, the rest of us were stuck lookin' at the black smoke, seein people runnin' and screamin' downstairs. "America be thinkin' they can't be touched! But now these nigga's got shit poppin' off! Wooo!"

I wanna' tell these fools to shit the fuck up! But maybe this nigga' is right and nobody else was debatin' or saying anything. This nigga' buggin' tho' their people running for their lives outside and people is dyin' ova' in that building! A heavy set black C.O. was walkin' by checkin' all the cells and stopped in front of our cell.

"Yo' C.O. what the fuck is going on out there?" Another guy in the cell asked him.

"I don't even know man . . ." He says catching his breath, covered in sweat. "A fuckin' exploration in one of those towers man . . . maybe terrorist, we might be under attack again." The C.O. walked away screamin' into his black walky talkie. The guys in the cell were all quiet now, even the two loud mouths. We all stare out the window at the building surrounded by smoke. Oh shit . . . Pedro, this nigga' Pay ova' there . . .

My fuckin' heart starts beatin' like crazy. I walk back and forth in the cell wantin' to tell somebody about Pay but what the fuck would they know? These nigga's don't know me and probably don't giva' fuck about me anyway. I sit down and tried to relax my nerves . . . ***Boooooom!!!*** AH FUCK! Another fuckin' explosion shakin' the whole fuckin' building! There's mad screams outside and people runnin' around crazy. We all took cover in the cell. I squat down by the toilet stall and wall, what the fuck is goin' on?!!

"Yo'!! We unda' attack yo'! Oh shit! This shit is crazy!" Yells the old heads yes man. He started cryin' about being bailed out, I'm not even thinkin' about my case fuck that! Shit if anything, this shit might actually help me out. Maybe this old Judge bitch won't be able to continue our case. The short Spanish C.O. came back to the cell lookin' scared lika' mothafucka'!

"Guys listen . . . we're evacuating the building, we gonna' get you guys out of here in ten minutes . . . is anybody hurt?"

"C.O what was the second explosion? That shit shook the whole buildin' yo and there's more smoke comin' from the buildin'." I stay my ass on the bench not believin' this shit is happening. Pay man . . . I hope you ain't in that building.

"There was another Plane . . ." Says the C.O wiping sweat from his forehead. "Another plane flew into the other tower, a fuckin' plane . . . both towers have been hit . . . it's a fuckin' mess out there." Another plane? Two planes?! Everyone is quiet now. Nigga's scratched their heads tryin' to make sense of this shit. It's like being in the middle of a war, but trapped in a motha' fuckin' cell! Fuck!

"Fuck yo . . ." A slim tall black guy says standing. He was one of the quietest guys in here. "My aunt works there . . ."

"My mans wife works there . . ." Another guy said. It's like everyone realized that this shit was serious! Nigga's started naming family and friends who they knew there. My mind is only on Pay', my fuckin' brother is somewhere ova' there . . . or maybe he was here at court like last time?

Outside there's mad screams, sirens and smoke everywhere. The streets is lika' war zone. People are runnin', cops were runnin' around, and we stuck in this mothafuckin' court buildin' . . . Damn, what if this building got hit next?? We all hear a loud ass rumble and I was ready to grab on to the toilet if I had to! But noffin' happened to this building, it's the tower that we could see from out windows . . . it's collapsing!!

The rumbling sounds like an earthquake and the noise must've thundered through the whole fuckin' city. The whole building just fell apart and came crashing down to the streets. Mad smoke and dust fill the air again . . . we all stood watchin' it through the window from our cell.

"Oh shit . . . did ya see that? The fuckin' building fell . . . the whole fuckin' building . . . holy shit." The old heads yes man sits down and grabs his head shakin' it. "Mad dudes just got killed ova' there . . . in the thousands." Nobody could say anything. Everything is happening so quick, right in front of our eyes . . . no one can believe it.

I watch these nigga's faces, they scare, sad and I am too. I'm trapped in this fuckin' cage in the middle of probably one of the biggest events in history taking place, probably world war 3!

Like ten minutes pass and the other tower collapsed too . . . and it crushes our hearts in this cell. This shit is unbelievable . . . bombing buildings was one thing, but knockin' buildings down? The Twin Towers?! That's something nigga's don't see everyday! We all silent, especially the two loud mouths who was talkin' crazy shit a lil' while ago about America this and these white mothafuckas' that . . . now these nigga's got tears in they eyes.

Outside there's more screamin, smoke, crying, mayhem just plain ol' fuckin' mayhem. The Spanish C.O. returns to the cell with another C.O. and quickly cracks our gate open.

"Listen fellas . . . lets make this quick and fast as we can." They call out our names and slap cuffs on our wrist as fast as possible.

"C.O what the fuck is going on? I got family ova' there man . . . asks the quiet dude. Son looked like he was ready to breakdown.

"Listen Bro, it's a war zone out there . . . not a pretty sight, there's a lot of dead people out there." We get on the elevator downstairs to the intake area where every fuckin' cell's packed to the tee. There's T.V.'s in every cell that's designated by the facility you were going to. Every T.V. has news on and everyone's face is glued in front of one.

I was uncuffed and made my way to the T.V in our cell. The reporter says the World Trade Center was attacked at around 8:30 A.M. when a Commercial Airplane flew into the upper floors of tower one, then a second plane hit tower 2 about twenty minutes later. Then an hour Tower 1 collapses and then tower 2. Everyone's saying that it's the end of the world, world war 3, judgment day . . . nigga's is buggin'!

I don't know what to think but I know that I'ma lucky mothafucka'. Around last summer I had a Sgt. from the Army tried to recruit my lil' ass. Now wit' this ain't no question that nigga's is going to war! I even had a chic from Lehman name *Jackie* wit' green eyes trying to convince me to join up wit' her . . . damn Jackie was beautiful. Thugged Out introduced me to her one day when we signed up for Summer Youth. Jackie is a sweetheart, I hope she didn't sign up for no fuckin' army.

I watch the footage of the planes crashing into the building then the building fallin' . . . god please let Pedro be ok. I hold back the tears but I don't know how long I could remain calm. We finally get taken to our buses and taken away back to the island. Damn people everywhere! The streets is packed wit' tourists and New Yorkers, all watching the drama unfold. They evacuated the streets for our buses so now we lika' fuckin' parade ridin' through the streets. People is snappin' pictures' waving and screamin' at us . . . some girls even flashed us their titties! Nigga's on the bus go crazy too, shouting out their names and numbers. I can't lie it's kinda' excitin'.

When we got on that B.Q.E and see the aftermath of the shit we all stuck. There's smoke and dust everywhere. The shit is so thick that you can't even see the sun! Mad helicopters and planes flying in the sky . . . the city looks fucked up. The bus pulls into the island and there's military people wit' big ass fuckin' guns at the entrance of the bridge and in front of each facility.

They locked down the whole island but all I'm thinkin' about is Pay and hoppin' on that phone as soon as I step in the house. We get processed and searched then escorted back to our units. I see the phone by the door not being used and hurry to make the call. Just about the whole house is in the day room watching the news footage of the attacks. After three rings someone finally answers the phone.

"Hello." It's Momma' Luv.

"Ma? Biendicion . . ." I ask her if she's watchin' the news and she said yes. Then I ask if Pedro was there at home.

"Si . . . *sniff sniff* . . ." Moms start cryin' but I'm thanking god that Pay's ass is okay. I tell her to put him on and thank god too.

"Yo' Ant?"

"Pedro?! Nigga' you don't know how good it feels to hear your voice B'."

"Dogz is you seein' this shit on T.V.?! That shit is hectic down there mo' word . . . but don't worry I'm good kid I got my ass outta' there quick! As soon as the first plane hit the other building." I wipes a few tears from my eye realizin' that my brother is alive and safe . . . thank you god.

After speakin' to Pay I find Tye at his bed reading his bible wit' his earphones on.

"What's the dizzy clizzy my nizzy?" I give em' a pound and grab a New Yorker from an open pack that I had in my locker. I lit the shit up and shook my head at him.

"Yo' . . ." I took a long ass pull and managed to smile. "That shit down there is fuckin' mayhem B word . . ."

"They sent ya back right? They sent a whole bunch of people back." Tye closes his bible and sparks his own loosy up.

"Yea but we seen it son . . . through a window from our cell when we was waitin' for court." Tye looked at me confused, he must've thought that I didn't make it down to the court.

"Oh so ya' did make it down there? And ya' seen the shit blow up and crumble? Damn son . . . we've been watchin' that shit on the news all fuckin' morning. I got tired of seeing that shit, but every station on the radio is talkin' about it."

"So what was you listenin' to?" One of the Mexican dudes in the house walked by to give him dap ask me about the court trip. I told him the same thing that I just told Tye. He walks off and leaves us alone again.

"Noffin' son, I just kept them on to block out the noise and shit . . . Readin' a couple of verses . . . this is some crazy shit that's happenin'." Tye goes on to tell me about the other planes in Washington and the one in Pennsylvania too. The news was talkin' about some nigga' name Bin Laden and some other terrorists.

He believes that it was all prophesied in the bible. I watched the news with some of the guys and just prayed for the people who were killed and hurt. Thankin' god that my brother was alive and prayin' also to help delay this sentencing shit as long as possible.

CHAPTER 27

Judgment Day

"Diaz! Let's go!" So I guess this is it . . . not even the World Trade Center being attacked a few weeks ago could hold up these mothafuckas' from sendin' me up north for most of my life . . . fuckin' bastards! The stocky black C.O escorted me up those same stairs that led up to Part 62, where the beginning of my end is gonna' happen. He cracks the cell and I think about it all . . . Hakala, N.W.O. L.B. beatin' Thugged Out's ass, gettin' sucked off by Francine on 111th street . . . damn I am the man, but now it's a wrap!

I didn't bring my bible this time fuck that shit! God ain't tryin' to hear me right now, later maybe but not now. I love this nigga' Thugged Out tho'. He came to see me last week and even brought along Jasper's white ass wit' em'! The last time I seen Jasp' was probably around Halloween. He was hollerin' at

Desiree's friend *Shaquita* from 111th Street, a proper Morena chic word.

He couldn't believe when I told em' about the 12 years and neither could Kenny, but it is what it is. I wish I could've told nigga's that I was comin' out sooner . . . but I'm not. The door heading into the courtroom opens and this nigga' Hall steps out. He got on a light brown suit wit' that faggot lookin' earring on ha ha.

"How are you Anthony?" I don't say nuffin' back, I just get straight to the point.

"Did you receive a copy of the motions to withdraw my plea and Insufficient Counsel?" Hall sighs, like he don't like that I'm accusin' him of insufficient assistance, but fuck em'!

"Yes I did . . . now you do know that your motions will not hold up in her court right? Insufficient Counsel? Really?" Oh this nigga' got a lot of balls man!

"Listen Hall, this ain't your life that's facing twelve years in jail . . . you sound like if you wanna' see me get hanged and shit . . . I didn't want the twelve years, ya forced me to take it so I want it back and I don't want you for my lawyer no more! And if I can I wanna speak on my better half." Silky told me to come at this nigga' hard. I can't lie my fuckin' heart is beatin' like crazy and I'm scared to death but I gotta' go down swingin'. Hall rubs his eyes and don't say nuffin.

"See you inside . . ." He finally says and walks into the courtroom. I wish that I could escape this fuckin' cell yo . . . this motion shit ain't gonna' work. The court officer brings me inside and walked me ova' to the same wooden table. There was some people in the courtroom but I didn't see Pay', Big Tee, Momma Luv' nobody!

The court clerk opened up by announcing the indictment number and date. But instead of just me, now it was the people against L.J. and me! They joined our case. Hall introduces himself and then the A.D.A introduced himself as Mr. Cho, and Judge Judy sets it off.

"First I will put on record that your client filed a Pro Se motion to withdraw the plea . . . the motion is denied, and I'm hanging the defendant and the D.A. a copy of the decision. And at this time you will proceed to arraign the defendant for sentencing. You can have the defendant stand for sentencing."

I wanna' to cry hearin' the bitch shoot my shit down like that. I looked at Hall who didn't look my way. He just stared at the ground. I stood up and stared at the flags and woman wit' her eyes blind fold. She was holding a pair of scales in her hands. In the yard I asked Osiris who she was and he told me some shit called Maat, whoeva' that is.

My eyes get watery as the clerk started reading the charges and counts. These nigga's made me sound like John Gotti or the Son of Sam and shit. The Judge asked Cho if the same plea still stood and he said yes, then she asks Hall if he had anything to say.

"I rely on the promise as well but I wish to add that, although Mr. Diaz was involved in the incident, it was an unfortunate incident, it was really unfortunate due to the fact that so many lives have been affected by not only the complaint who was injured, but also Mr. Diaz who prior to this time had actually been attending school and was or at least seemed to be on the right track . . ."

This nigga' Hall . . . he knows how to sound lika' real lawyer. "It is my profound hope that Mr. Diaz, during the time in which he has to serve will be able to go beyond the tragedy of this incident and become a better person behind it." Hall finally finishes and I can't lie what he was sayin' hit me hard . . . fuck man it's ova' . . . it's really ova'.

I did my best to not look at anyone, I know if I look at any of these people I'ma cry and shit. So I just stare at that wall and thug it out. I don't want to speak anymore, I just want this nightmare to be ova'. I realized that I fucked up my life but if you ask me, my shit's been fucked up for a long time. Where the fuck was my pops at? Why don't nobody bring up that I was twisted that night? That I confessed and turned myself in? Don't any of that matter?!

Wright read through the report again and asked me if I understood why my motions got shot down. I told her that I didn't want the plea but she didn't giva' fuck.

She said some shit about how serious the case was and my mind just shut off after that. My mind started going back to the block, the L. B.s, school, Nicki, Annie, Sonia, all that was dead now . . . I'm dead.

She sentenced me and said that I could appeal and passed Hall some appeal papers. I was taken back to the cell and I was ready to spazz! This is bullshit! I yelled mad loud then sat my ass down while the tears started gushin' out. This nigga' Hall came out again, I don't know why, I don't have nuffin' to say to this faggot.

"Anthony . . . . I'm deeply sorry that I wasn't able to help . . ."

"Bullshit Hall! FUCK YOU and that old bitch!" I scream. My eyes start hurtin' from all the crying I'm doing. I don't remember the last time I cried this much. "You don't giva' fuck about me, don't none of ya do! Fuck ya! Sniff sniff . . . I can't do no twelve years . . . so it's gonna' be your fault when I go back and hang the fuck up! So I hope you'll be able to fuckin' sleep at night nigga'! I wish a fuckin' plane would've hit this building and kill all you mothafuckas'."

I'm sobbin' now but I don't giva' fuck I'm fuckin' tight B' and still can't believe that this is gonna' end like this.

"Anthony! Don't say that . . . I can understand your upset, but don't threaten to kill yourself or I'll have the judge place you on suicide watch." Does this nigga' really think I giva' fuck about that?

"Tell her I'ma hang up Hall! And haunt all you mothafuckas' watch!" Hall rushes back into the courtroom to tell the bitch I guess. Fuck em' . . . I'm still tearin' and sobbin' and shit. I can't stop. From the courtroom next door a stocky Spanish officer creeps out, I guess he heard me spazzin' out here. He walks toward me and asks if I'm okay.

I don't say noffin' at first I just stare at him and shit. I shake my head no and wipe the tears from my face. "I just got sentenced to twelve years in prison . . . it's my first time . . . how the fuck am I suppose to do Twelve Years?!!" I yelled at him. He walks closer towards me.

"How old are you?" He asks real calm and shit.

"19." I say through my sobbin'. I don't know why but this nigga's makin' me feel real relaxed now. He stands right in front of me, and stares right into my eyes.

"Look son your gonna' be alright . . . it might not look that way but believe me your gonna' make it . . . trust me." Is this nigga' drunk? I just told em' that I'm 19 and got sentenced to twelve fuckin' years! I look at this brolic mothafucka' confused.

"Are you serious?" I chuckle a lil'. "I have to do twelve years, Twelve years!" I get up and stand in front of him.

"You can do it . . . I know you can . . ." I listen to this police deep, sincere voice. This nigga' got me stuck, I don't know what to say! For some reason tho' I don't feel like if it's the end of my world anymore . . .

who the fuck is this guy?! Another officer comes up to the stairs to take me back and this dude eased away back to the door of the other Court Part.

I get cuffed and slowly walk down the spiral steps. I take my time walkin' down each step and look up at the Spanish police standin' by the stair rail. He smiles and nods his head at me . . . Is this nigga' my angel or somethin'??

I can't stop thinkin' bout' that Spanish C.O. he fucked me up for real. This ride back to the island is my last ride through the city so I pay attention to every street, building and person who's walkin' up and down the streets. It makes me think about the highs and lows of my life. My first kiss wit' Clari, Ruby my first love, losin' my virginity to Jessica's smutty ass, the squad, C.B. getting' twisted one night in front of 1760 wit' L.J. and some other people. I was so twisted that I was doing the Harlem shake in the middle of the street! I was bent!

All my lil' memories put a smile on my face but all that shit is a wrap now. We got to O.B.C.C and my fuckin' heart drops before the bus pulled up. They gonna' make me pack up as soon as I step into the house. These dudes is gonna' be tight that I'm gone and I'ma miss em'. I can't cry man no matter what I can't fuckin' cry cuz' I gotta' man up. I walk inside and everyone eyes is on me.

"Hurry up and pack up Diaz five minutes!" The black C.O. escortin' me yells out. I walk towards my bed and was met by Silky, the Spanish dudes, damn half of the fuckin' house! I peep Tye on the phone he threw his hands up in the air probably hopin' that the motions worked but my face told it all. Silky hoped the motions worked but my face told it all.

Silky was tight and just stood by my bed shaking his head while I dumped my property is my quilt. The Spanish dudes was tight too and screamed on me for coppin' out in the first place. I don't know what to say I just tied my quilt up and dragged the shit towards the door. Tye put the phone down and met me by the day room.

"Damn my nigga' they didn't give you back the plea?" I shook my head and felt the tears up in my eyes. But I'm holdin' these shits! "Damn son! You got my info right?"

"Yea, I'ma be aight Tye I'ma holla at you if you still here aight? Hold your head bro, thank you ya heard." I give him and couple of other dudes hugs and dap then drag my shit towards the door.

"Damn baby boy! We love you A-Class! Be good aight! I'll be here for a while so holla at me son! Tye's been on the island for like three years fightin' his case. He was down wit' the B.T.M Blue Top Mob crew from Lexington Ave. There's like fifty of these nigga's up in the island fightin' their cases. The door closed and I made my way to the Annex.

The C.O. takes me to 2-North, supposedly one of the blood houses. There are two tiers in the house and about a hundred cells. The cell is smaller than mothafucka' daamn! Mostly females worked in the Annex and I always heard stories about nigga's blazin' these chics so that people could play cards and shit.

But I don't giva' fuck about the T.V. or cards. I don't want nobody fuckin' wit' me. I'ma only be here for like two or three days the most.

Big Tee and Guidi come to see me the next day and they both promise to hold me down and not turn their backs on me. Guidi was a hard workin' guy who could neva' keep a car. Word, every other month he had a new car! We always teased him cuz' Kenny's momz like him and always flirt wit' him. But from what I was hearin' Guidi was talkin' to his momz! Okay Guidi!

Big Tee was still mad at me, but vowed to ride the bid out wit' me no matter what. Big Tee was breakin' my heart. He was showin' me crazy love in here, even tho' we wasn't that close when I was out. I let you down Big Tee but I love you B', always did always will.

After the visit I bump into some dude name **D-Nice** who I met in the Bronx, D-Nice is Pay's peoples. He was on the V.I. wit' his baby momz and recognized Guidi and Big Tee. I was handin' in my jumpsuit when he called me.

"Yo' you Pays' brother right?" I nod my head and sit down to put on my sneakers. "I know you remember me nigga'! I was at the barbecue when you barked on your shorty that day and she bounced!"

"Oh Hell yea! Damn son you remember that!? Wow, what up D-Nice!" Dee was short, chubby and trigeno. He had mad tattoos on his arms and looked Kinda' bugged out too. "Yo' Pedro know you here?"

"I don't know, but I'll tell abuela to call him tonight tell em' where you at?" He sat down next to me to throw on his kicks too. I told him about getting sentenced and that I'll be going up north in a day or two. "Damn my nigga' hold your head aight? I'ma see you I gotta' go up top too, we'll probably land in the same spot watch . . . yo I gotta' go tell your brother I love em' and to holla' at me when he gets the chance aight?" I give D-Nice a pound and he bounced.

I'm about to get up and leave and I see Derrick from the clean up crew holdin' his clothes gettin' ready to change outta' his jumpsuit. I call him ova' to the bench where I'm sittin' at.

"Hey Woodz how you been kid? I don't see you anymore." Derrick was short and stocky, brown skinned, and rocked a lil' fro, sometimes he had it braided.

"Same shit bro what's going on wit' the crew Dee?" He sighs and shakes his head.

"You don't even wanna' know Woodz. Camby's been actin' lika' real asshole, these guys been getting' caught passin' shit to the brothers in there and Camby's been comin' down on us hard . . . Biggs told me that you copped out what happened?"

I explain a lil' of what was going on and told him that I was sentenced already, so this might be the last time he would see me. "Ah don't tell me that Woodz damn . . . you was probably the only guy outta' the crew who I enjoyed vibin' with. I don't see a lot of young guys like you in here, the majority of these guys are idiots.

"Thank you Dee . . . I appreciate that, but I can't be that smart, look where I'm at?" Derrick gets up to return his jumpsuit then sits back down to put on his kicks.

"We all make mistakes Woodz, that doesn't mean you not a good kid." Dee always made me feel special and shit.

"Yo' Dee, being that I'm going up north for the first time, give me a couple of jewelz or something that I can take wit' me." Dee looked down towards the ground like if he was in deep thought. I remember him tellin' me that he had been up north before and from what I could tell from him he was into spiritual shit. We always had deep conversations at work, so I'm hoping that he could hit me wit' somethin' deep now.

"Well, Woodz . . . believe it or not I think your going to be alright . . . it's a lot of time but all you have to keep in mind is that if you just be you, you'll have nothing to worry about . . . just be you, like the way you are with me and the fellas at work. Your quiet, smooth, act mature and you listen . . . don't go up there trying to be something your not . . . just be yourself."

Okay . . . I was expectin' some real philosophical shit from Dee, some real spiritual shit that wasn't what I expected! But for some reason I like what he said, almost what that C.O. at court told me Hmm . . . be myself . . . just be myself. I give Dee dap, a hug then asked for his numbers and promise to holla at him from up top.

I unpack my shit in my cell and stay in here for the whole night. I stare at my reflection through a foggy ass mirror over the sink. All the mirrors in here are like circus mirrors so you can't really see yourself. But I don't wanna see my face, I hate myself. I thought about what Dee told me about being myself and I think he was keepin' it official, but what is myself? What he said was some philosophical shit. I should've asked this nigga' to explain it more to me.

I take a shower and snack on some cold cut Potato Bread sandwiches wit' some Doritos and Kool-Aid. The C.O. had called me down to the bubble a lil' while ago and the chic actually had mail for me, it was Foxy! My baby Foxy finally holla'd at a nigga'! It's a one page letter written in pencil sayin' that she had to hunt down Thugged Out for my address and finally got it from Pay and Big Tee when she saw em' on the block.

This nigga' Kenny's playin' fuckin' games again! I don't know what this mothafucka's tryin to do but he's gettin' me tight wit' this bullshit. First Chula then Foxy? Who else was this nigga' blockin' from hollarin' at me? The police let us keep our cells open or close until count time so I keep my shit open to avoid being trapped up in this mothafucka'.

From the top tier I could see the whole floor. Nigga's is on the phones, showers, in front of the T.V. and hollerin' at the C.O. brawd at her post. I lean on the railing and look down. It's a long way down if a mothafucka' fell from this shit. There's a stocky Spanish and a skinny black kid talkin' to each other like two cells away from me.

The Spanish kid looks Puertorican, and he's holding a book in his hand tellin' son somethin' about it. I'm not trying to be nosy but they're talkin' loud enough for me to hear em'.

"Yea son they got underground bases, U.F.O.S and bodies in their laboratories!" Is this nigga' talkin' about U.F.O.S? The skinny black kid keeps noddin' his head like he agrees wit' em'. Is they talkin' about aliens and shit? I like shit like that. I used to always watch *Unsolved Mysteries* on T.V late night, but then the shit gave me the creeps so I would change it.

I wonder what's the name of the book. The Spanish kid peeps me watchin' em' and gives me a look like if he wants me to hear him too. I ease my way ova' to where they at and the Spanish kid is showin' the skinny kid pictures from the book.

"What up son? I knew you was ova' there listenin' to us." I smile and nod my head.

"Yea ya' ova' here talkin' about my kinda' shit." The black kid looks at me and nods his head. He's a lil' taller than me wit' waves in his hair.

"My man got this same book, didn't this nigga' die or get killed?" He asked. I finally get to peep the cover of the book, it's blue wit' a drawing of a white horse and black horse wit' guys riding both horses.

"Behold . . . behold what?" I can't see the rest of the cover.

"A Pale Horse . . . *Behold A Pale Horse* . . ." Homie told me. "By *William Cooper* . . . he got into a shootout wit' the feds or some shit and they killed the nigga' . . . word, the nigga' went out like a gangsta' son and he said in his book that they was probably gonna' kill em'."

Count was called and I went to bed wit' William Cooper's book. Son's name is *Chino* and the other kids' name was *Broadway*. Chino let me check out the book for the night. Cooper had pictures of classified files from the government and wrote about secret bases, U.F.O.s and a real life New World Order! This shit's blowin' my head off!

I stayed up til' like four in the morn' just thinkin' about the book and this bitch who gave me twelve fuckin' years B'. I know this nigga' L.J. ain't going to trial if he do then he's a stronger motha' fucka' than me. Chino told me that they gonna' send me to C-74 before I get sent up north. Damn! I wasn't tryin' to go back to the four building . . . fuck!

CHAPTER 28

Downstate

Boom Boom Boom! "Diaz get up!" I hop outta' bed after the second time . . . ah man I hope this ain't no fuckin' search!

"Yea?" I wiped my face and strained to see the C.O. chic bangin' on the cell. Oh it was my lil' cutie pie chic wit' the big titties who nigga's be all ova' in the bubble.

"The psyche wanna' see you now! Get yo' butt up." The psyche? What the fuck . . . oh shit Hall, you mothafucka'! It took me like fifteen minutes to get to the clinic. The psyche is a tall weird lookin' white guy, askin' me a bunch of questions like if I wanna to hurt myself. Do I feel safe? Am I suicidal? This nigga' Hall wasn't jokin'.

I explain to him about why I'm placed on suicide watch and surprisingly he believes me and is gonna take me off. I get back to the house and cutie told me I had to pack up. Everyone is asleep except for me and an old white guy. I slid Chino's book under his cell door and packed up my shit. I hate fuckin' movin' around so much, carryin' all this shit be hurtin' my back!

Ms. M the C.O cutie, calls me ova' to her desk while we wait for our escort.

"Diaz why the psyche wanted to see you? You crazy Diaz?" Ms. M was steady in the Mornin'. She was a sweet heart and loved the attention that nigga's gave her in the house.

"Nah Ms. M, I told my lawyer that I was gonna' hang up when I got sentenced, fuckin' around wit' him and he put me on suicide watch." Ms. M sighed and started signing her book as the escort finally arrived.

"That's not funny Diaz, stay outta' trouble okay??" I grab my shit and wave bye to her. I probably could bag Ms. M if I wasn't so fucked up in the game

*   *   *

The in-take are of C-74 is quiet this time. They keep a couple of us in the cells for like an hour. I'm catchin' flashbacks of Kriss Kross, Penguin and all of those crazy mothafucka's from the Sprungs. I wonder if I'm gonna' see any of them? The C.O brings us to 6-lower on the other side of the building where commissary is. The hallway is kinda quiet, I don't see anybody I recognize and that's probably good! 6-Lower, was downstairs and next to 6-upper, both is adult houses and king houses too I think. A light skin C.O. chic told me to find a bed so I picked a joint by the wall like I did in 7-lower.

I lay in bed readin' Foxy's kite thinkin' about that last night at her party when I saw her. She must've been buggin' when she heard I was locked up. The house is quiet and empty. Most of the guys are at school or in the yard. Like around two o'clock everybody started comin' back and I'm buggin' out seein' a couple of nigga's I know, my lil' son Chino and *Face* from 7-lower! The house is mixed wit' old timers, young guys and a lot of kings like I already knew.

Both Chino and Face got sentenced to their cases and is waitin' to be sent north too. Damn . . . we all got slayed wit' mad time. Face got hit wit' a dime for robbery. This was his fourth bid, damn! Lil' Chino had manslaughter, for killin' a cab driver in the Bronx wit' his friends when they tried to rob em'. Chino fucked me up when he told me that he was from around Melrose projects where my aunt Lily lives.

The three of us became a trio and shit. We eat, smoked and chilled together. I found out that everybody up in this house is gettin' ready to be sent up north, so guys left just about everyday. My mail is still poppin' tho'. I got letters comin' from Melly still, Chula, and Foxy hit me back as soon as she got my kite. But the letter that really had me open was Ms. Coles . . . Ms. Coles finally holla'd yo'!

She apologized for takin' so long and asked me if I was ok. It's a one pager and in script . . . damn Ms. Coles got beautiful handwriting. She tells me about takin' her moms to a Janet Jackson concert in Long Island and how she loves her. I probably read her kite like a hundred times! I tell Face and Chino about her and they thought I was bullshittin'. Chinos lil' big head ass couldn't read, so I read the letter for him and I let Face read it himself.

"So what you gonna' do son'? What eva' you do, make sure you hook a nigga' up alright?" Me and Chino cracked up at Face. He a kinda' old Puertorican dude who still thinks he's young. Skinny like me, from Brooklyn and always ready to pop off. The nigga' got mad juice up in here too and it wasn't long before I found out that he was king and beef brewing wit' them and the bloods in the building.

I felt crazy vibes when we went to the Mess Hall, plus there were a couple of fights next door in 6-upper. I didn't ask about the war brewing or any of the fights it's none of my business fuck that! I write my letters to Melly, Chula and Foxy, lettin' them know that I'm about to get sent up top. So if they not gonna' stick around wit' me fuck it, but I need a chic to ride wit' and from how it looks Melly is gonna' be the one. A part of me believes it but then I don't know . . . Melly ain't the same Melly from when I was fuckin' wit' her.

I ask Face for advice, but this nigga' be on some *que se hoda shit* . . . he don't giva' fuck about any chic.

It takes me a few days to holla back at Ms. Coles, I didn't know if I should be up front wit' her or keep it simple and work from there. I ask this nigga' face again and surprisingly he gives me decent advice.

"If you lookin' for a bitch to ride wit' you tell her what it is . . . if you don't believe she gonna' ride, keep her as a pen pal cuz' nigga' wit' 12 fuckin' years you gonna' need all the pen pals you can get! Na' mean!" Face is a stupid mothafucka' but I decide to be straight up wit' her fuck it!

I'm scheduled to leave this last week of Sept. My lil' man Chino got packed up a few days ago so it's just me and Face. I gave em' my home base info so he could have a place to write. He told me that his people's full of shit. He's my lil' man na' mean the nigga' didn't have no food, soap, noffin'! So I made sure he had whateva'. I got crazy love for son, he ain't a lil' pussy and his lil' ass is tough . . . but sometimes I had to hem his ass up to keep em' in check! Now Face is probably leavin' a week after me.

It's Sunday and Big Tee and Pedro see me to pick up my clothes and shit that I can't take wit' me to some place called ***Downstate***. Face told me about that shit the other night and from what he told me Downstate is gonna' be ten times better than this fuckin' building. This last visit wit Tee and Pay got me feelin' shitty. I let everybody down and now my life in the town is no more . . . it's a wrap for everything.

Pay told me that he heard from Jakkes and them that L.J. finally copped out to 12 and that Mr. Perez is officially outta' the hospital and livin' back home. Then Big Tee told me housing is tryin' to kick him and my momz outta' 1738! Oh shit these mothafuckas' is foul . . .

*   *   *

The C.O wakes me up at around four in the mornin' and tells me it's time to leave. I sit up in bed and look around the dark quiet house. Face sleeps in the bed next to mine and woke up when he heard the C.O wake me up.

"Time to go my nigga'."

"Fuck you doin' up Face?" I whisper and grab my toothbrush and to wash up.

"You know I can't let you leave wit' out sayin' peace nigga' . . . even tho' I'ma meet you Downstate . . . go slay that dragon in your mouth ya heard." I throw my pillow at his silly ass and step to the bathroom to take a shit and wash my face. I look into the not so foggy mirror and stare into the light brown eyes staring back at me. You gonna' be aight Ant. Dee said to be yourself and that's what you going to do . . . I'ma be me and make it through this shit . . .

I throw on my Pelle Pelle shorts and white long sleeve Pelle Pelle shirt, grab my bible and give Face a hug.

"Hold your head my nigga', I'll see you up there aight?"

"Face be careful down here, don't get caught up in the bullshit that's going on wit' these nigga's." He sucked his teeth and smiled

"My nigga' I don't fuck wit' these nigga's like that, I'ma be right on my bed chillin' when these nigga's pop off anywhere." He gives me dap again and I walk ova' to the door where the C. Os at wit' like three other guys. He escorted us to the intake area. We eat breakfast in the Mes shall then get strip searched, put in a big cell in the back of the in-take area wit' two young dudes and a bunch of old timers.

I'm quiet as a motha' fucka', just thinkin' about the last eight months. What a fuckin' celebration . . . instead of ballin' wit' nigga's after graduation, probably havin' Nicki to myself, I'm in this mothafuckin' place stressed the fuck out! An old timer sittin' on the other bench caught my attention by mentioning the name Osiris.

The old timer is a tall black bald headed dude, sayin' somethin' about a cypher in the yard and that the god Osiris had snuffed another god in the yard in Oh Boy. My son Osiris had broke one of those nigga's jaws ova' there! Osiris got a lil' size on him too. Long ass dreads, wit' a tattoo of his brother's face on his arm.

I vibed wit' him durin' our break time at work, Osiris was a cool mothafucka'. Old T ova' there was sayin' the same thing about him too. The two young nigga's are barkin' on the porter who was actin' scared to come to the gate.

"That's my word nigga' you soft! You lucky I'm I'm this mothafuckin' cell! Bitch ass nigga'!" It was a short Puertorican kid and a stocky black kid barkin' on son! I heard dudes in the other cells call the black kid Breeze and the Spanish kid Rob-Lo. They had to be from Harlem too, cuz' they reppin' Mahanttanville and Grant Projects.

The C.O finally cuffed us and stuffed us in a bus. I got cuffed wit' old timer who was talkin' about Osiris and the two Harlem nigga's got cuffed together. Old T's name was Fu or some shit cuz' that's what the other old timers called him. The bus pulled off and drove outta' Riker's Island.

I got a window seat so I can see the streets, buildings and the bitches good one last time. We drive on the highway across the river where the Piers at. Ah man . . . I feel like cryin' lookin' at the pier again. You know how many memories I got at that pier?! Jefferson projects, 1199, Wagner?! I looks at all this shit while the bus drives outta' Manhattan and into the Bronx.

The old timer is kinda' quiet, just lookin' out the window like me. I don't wanna' talk to anybody but I feel like makin' conversation fuck it.

"Scuse me big bro, you was talkin' about Osiris wit' the dreads? In O.B.C.C?" The bus passes by Yankee Stadium and both breeze and Rob-Lo say somethin' about when they was at a game.

"Yea I know Osiris, I worked in the Bing too ya' heard." Old timer is lookin' at me strange now.

"Hold up you worked in the Bing too? I knew you looked familiar . . . yea? They called you . . . um, picky? Was it picky?" I laugh cuz' I know what he's tryin to say.

"Nah, Pikachu . . . it's a stupid cartoon character."

"Yea! That's it Pikachu ha ha . . . oh shit, guys is crazy . . . is that what they really call you or was that only In there?!" I peep a sign that says somethin' about the Tappanzee Bridge.

"Nah that's not my name . . ." I pause for a minute thinkin' about when I was in the group in the Sprungs. Should I tell em' my name is Woodz? Or Ant? Shit this is crazy . . . I'm actually confused about my fuckin' name! From what I've seen so far in here your name is mad important. Nigga's be having names like Murda' Berretta, Black, Shorty, Penguin! Your name is like your life in here . . . it says who you are. Oh shit . . . I almost forgot about A-Class! The name that crazy ass Harv' gave me. Why not? The shit duz' sound fly.

"A-Class . . . they call me A-Class . . . ya heard?" Old T turned his head at me like if he was blown away by the name.

"A-Class . . . A-Class . . . where did you get that name from? Did Osiris give you that name?" I shake my head no and look out at the water we was crossin' ova' on the bridge. Damn, I thought the bridge on the island was official this bridge is longer than a mothafucka'! It's my first time crossing that bridge. There's boats and speedboats in the water . . . damn that shit looks butter.

"Well peace A-Class, they call me **Fruquan** . . . wow I knew you looked familiar . . . yea man Osiris was a cool brother . . ." We kick it about Osiris, and about jail period. I tell em' a lil' about the case and he told me about being a stick up kid down in the L.E.S damn hearin' him say L.E.S got me thinkin' about Jerlyn', my baby flash! That was probably her who came to the crib that day Big Tee told me about. Ms. Coles should've got my kite already . . . all these Chics.

After like an hour of driving we get to Duchess Country and pull into the Downstate complex. Shit is mad big wit' mad gray buildings everywhere.

"Aight fellas! Sit tight cuz' we here!" Yells the fat black C.O. Him and his partner joke about how they hate the assholes in Downstate. I see a couple of white C.O.s walk toward the bus through the window.

"I hate these mothafuckin' devils . . ." Mumbles Fru'.

"Devils? That's what ya' call these red necks up here?" I ask em'. He smiles at me and nodded his head.

"Somethin' like that A. I've been through this shit a few times in my life, I'm not proud of it but just to put you on, these mothafuckas' is gonna' act real tough and talk all crazy . . . just do what they say cuz' if you don't they gonna' make an example out of you. Don't say shit A alright?"

A C.O. and a fat white Sgt. come on the bus and call our names out. We have to say our names and date of birth. They have two porters outside loadin' our property on a wagon to to it inside. There's C.O.'s everywhere. We line up outside of the bus and get led inside into a large empty room. They take off our cuffs then lock us inside.

A few of us sat in the narrow wooden bench. The kid Rob-Lo sucks his teeth and curses the C. O's out. He had on a long white t-shirt, blue shorts and a pair of half new black on white uptowns. Breeze had waves in his hair and was rockin' a white Iceberg shirt, black jeans and scuffed up construction Timbs.

I just watch everyone in the cell. Nigga's look calm but I know they nervous like me. Outside the room we hear the police talkin' mad loud and comin' closer to the door then the shit flies open. A short bald headed skinny C.O called for everybody's attention.

"ALRIGHT LISTEN UP!! PLACE YOUR HANDS ON THE WALL STARE AT THE WALL . . . I DON'T WANNA' HEAR A FUCKIN' SOUND OUTTA' ANYONE'S MOUTH . . . IF YOU FAIL TO COMPLY WITH THESE SIMPLE INSTRUCTIONS,

WE WILL MAKE SURE THAT YOUR STAY HERE IN DOWNSTATE IS A FUCKIN' NIGHTMARE FOR YOU!!!" This nigga' sounds lika' cold hearted mothafucka' damn! I stare at the wall wit' my hands on em' and hope that everybody else is too. "NOW BEGIN REMOVING EVERYTHING OUT OF YOUR POCKETS . . . ANY PERSONAL BELONGINGS WILL GO IN THE GARBAGE . . . YOU ARE NOT ALLOWED TO CARRY PERSONAL BELONGINGS . . . PICTURES, WALLETS, CIGARETTES, LIGHTERS . . . EVERYTHING GOES IN THE GARBAGE!" I see Rob-Lo from the corner of my eye turn his head around from the wall and two tall C. O's surround him yellin' for him to turn around.

"My daughters picture B' . . . I just got it before I left." Lo sucked his teeth and faced the wall again. My fuckin' heart is pumpin' lika' mothafucka'! Lo nigga' don't fuck wit' these crackers son . . .

"NOW!" Yelled the lil' C.O nigga' again.

"REMOVE YOUR FOOTWEAR ONE BY ONE." After the kicks we have to take off our clothes and hand it to a C.O. Standing behind each of us. I can't see where Fru's at or the kid Breeze but I hope none of them make a movie. Rob-Lo starts fussin' about his picture again and two police start yellin' at him again. They both yell in his ear and dare him to make a move. Fuck man this shit is crazy! These nigga's is buggin'! We butt naked and these nigga's is ready to beat a mothafucka's ass? God damn!

412

Just like on the island we gotta to raise our arms, open our mouths, lift our nuts, turn and lift our feet then bend ova' and spread our cheeks . . . I hate this shit . . . this is some real degrading homo shit . . . only homos like lookin' up nigga's asses.

"Man fuck that! Ya' wildin'! Ya' want nigga's to bend ova' for mad long." Ah man, I hear this nigga' Breeze and hope that he don't get washed up in here! All the C. O's rush him and order him to turn around and place his hands on his head. I'm scared to even turn my head . . . but I do and see Rob-Lo lookin' back to where they pressin' Breeze.

"Fuck these crackers Breeze you heard!" He holla'd and now two big incest lookin' mothafuckas' rushed Lo' and ordered him to place his hands ova' his head. Holy fuckin' shit . . . these nigga's is tryin' to get killed!

The short loud C.O ordered them to put on their draws then they both got escorted outta' the room wit' out their gear! The C.O locked the door while the rest of us started Putin' on our clothes.

"Fru' where they going?" I ask tryin' to calm down. My hands fuckin' shakin' like crazy!

"I don't know maybe into one of the other cell . . . all they gonna' do is scream and yell at em' more. Damn they didn't even send the porter in here to get they clothes."

Just when Fru' said that the door opens and a porter comes inside to pick up the clothes. An older

Spanish dude, he gives us a tired look than shook his head.

"Scuse me where did those two kids go who's clothes you gettin'?" Fru' asked him. I tie my black Reeboks and look up at Papi.

"I dunno' . . . I just come to get clothes yo no ser."

*   *   *

After like twenty minutes the C. O's takes us to a bigga' cell by the reception area. Nigga's is starvin' and gotta' use the bathroom word! The cell is big enough for us to walk around in so nigga's pace back or forth, or try to lie on the wooden benches. The C.O.'s walk back and forth tellin' nigga's not to lie on the benches and that chow is on it's way.

From the cell you hear mad people screamin' up and down the halls and every ten minutes lines of nigga's shackled from head to toe come by back and forth. Mad dudes got the State Green shirts, pants and black boots on . . . shit looks crazy.

Chow finally comes and we get to eat. The tray is plastic wit' lids on em'. We got chicken patties, mashed potatoes, greens and a cup of hot orange Kool-Aid . . . ah man this shit is horrible! But nigga's is starvin' so I'm bustin' this shit down! I sit dolo on a bench tryin' to stay awake . . . Tired than a mothafucka', what's this downstate shit gonna' be like? These big ass hillbillies look like they be beatin' the fuck outta' nigga's up in here.

One by one a bald headed white C.O. calls one of us and takes us to where the Sgt. is sittin'. I ask Fu' what was happenin' now and he tells me that the Sgt. is gonna' ask us mad question and make us throw out our clothes. I guess that means more strippin' in front of these faggots too . . . fuck! I'm one of the last people to get called.

I step outta' the cell and follow the C.O to where the fat white Sgt was at. This mothafucka' is smokin' a cigar wit' two incest lookin' C. O's standin' by his side. He stares at me and shuffles a bunch of paper work on his desk. He asks me mad questions . . . my name, age, religion, D.O.B. Do I have enemies? scars? Tattoos? False teeth . . . a whole bunch of shit.

I answer the questions they make me strip, lift my nuts, open my mouth, turn lift my feet then squat ova' so they could look up my ass. God please let this be the last time I gotta' do this shit! One of the C.O.'s hands me a tight ass green towel and walks me ova' to a shower area. He hands me a lil' plastic cup wit some gel shit in it.

"What's this? Shampoo?" This C.O. looks like Casper the ghost damn!

"Somethin' like that, just be grateful we don't spray yous with the pesticides no more . . . you got five minutes Diaz hurry up." I don't even know what to do wit this shampoo shit. Casper realizes it and catches a fuckin' attitude about it.

"Apply it only where you have hair on your body, it's for lice and shit . . . 4 minutes Diaz" I step in the shower and pull down on a lever for water. Oh shit this shit is colda' than a mothafucka!!

"Wooo!! Oh hell no!" I rinse my hair and nuts and get the fuck outta' there!

"Oh I forgot to tell you the water is cold grab your towel and follow me." The fuckin' dick head takes me to a bench that got mad boxers, green sheets, white bed sheets and socks next to a fuckin' barber shop. "Get dress, get a cut then wait for me to come back to take your picture." I throw on the draws, the green pants and white T-Shirt.

I look ova' to the barber shop and see Fru' in one chair and both Breeze and Rob-Lo!

"A-Class! Tell em' to give you a baldly like me!' Yells Fru'. The Spanish barber and us laugh. I'm happy to see these two nigga's aight. I sit down in a seat and get my wig cut. The barber gives everyone basic Cesar's, no shape ups, tape ups or fades that I always got in the town. Rob-Lo's tight cuz' he gotta' cut off his braids. Breeze doesn't care about his waves. This haircut shit is fucked up.

We done so the white ass police takes our pictures then gives us a card wit' our names and pictures on it. He tells us to go upstairs then to stop at the first door that's open. The three of us grab our new property and march up the steps followin' Breeze who leads the way up to the open door.

"Hey!" This nigga' smiles and looks back at us. Rob-Lo asks who's in there whisperin' and licks his lips when he see's who eva's in the office.

"Card guys . . ." Says a Spanish C.O. chic. Damn this bitch is beautiful! There's another chic wit' her too, a pretty chubby black chic. This nigga' Rob-Lo asks for her name.

"Just your cards guys that means you too old timer." Me and these nigga's start giggin' on Fru'. He's not laughing tho'! The pretty Spanish chic does some shit on the computer on her desk and hands us each a blue I.D. card with our pictures on it. Damn I look crazy on my shit!

After the four of us get our I.D. cards. We joke about fuckin' these bitches and walk into a big ass Lobby wit' colorful plastic chairs. We all sit down and see the C.O. walkin' up the steps behind us.

"Alright guys I'ma call your name, just give me your Din number." He calls Rob-Lo's' name first then mine and I give em' my Din number *01A5273*. Breeze is last and asks about usin' the bathroom. "We're on our way to the housing units now Jeffries, everybody ready? Grab your shit and follow me."

I trail the fellas walking through a long ass dark hallway or tunnel. There's light at the end of this tunnel . . . but I wonder what's waitin' for me at the end of the tunnel . . . I guess I'ma bout' to find out . . .